QUEER PRECARITIES IN AND OUT OF HIGHER EDUCATION

QUEER PRECARITIES IN AND OUT OF HIGHER EDUCATION

Challenging Institutional Structures

Edited by Yvette Taylor, Matt Brim, and Churnjeet Mahn

BLOOMSBURY ACADEMIC
LONDON • NEW YORK • OXFORD • NEW DELHI • SYDNEY

BLOOMSBURY ACADEMIC
Bloomsbury Publishing Plc
50 Bedford Square, London, WC1B 3DP, UK
1385 Broadway, New York, NY 10018, USA
29 Earlsfort Terrace, Dublin 2, Ireland

BLOOMSBURY, BLOOMSBURY ACADEMIC and the Diana logo are trademarks of
Bloomsbury Publishing Plc

First published in Great Britain 2023

Copyright © Yvette Taylor, Matt Brim and Churnjeet Mahn, 2023

Yvette Taylor, Matt Brim, Churnjeet Mahn have asserted their right under the Copyright, Designs and Patents Act, 1988, to be identified as Editors of this work.

Cover design by Charlotte Daniels

All rights reserved. No part of this publication may be reproduced or transmitted in any form or by any means, electronic or mechanical, including photocopying, recording, or any information storage or retrieval system, without prior permission in writing from the publishers.

Bloomsbury Publishing Plc does not have any control over, or responsibility for, any third-party websites referred to or in this book. All internet addresses given in this book were correct at the time of going to press. The author and publisher regret any inconvenience caused if addresses have changed or sites have ceased to exist, but can accept no responsibility for any such changes.

A catalogue record for this book is available from the British Library.

A catalog record for this book is available from the Library of Congress

ISBN: HB: 978-1-3502-7365-8
PB: 978-1-3502-7364-1
ePDF: 978-1-3502-7367-2
eBook: 978-1-3502-7366-5

Typeset by Deanta Global Publishing Services, Chennai, India
Printed and bound in Great Britain

To find out more about our authors and books visit www.bloomsbury.com and sign up for our newsletters.

CONTENTS

Table vii
Contributor Biographies viii

INTRODUCTION 1
    Yvette Taylor, Matt Brim, Churnjeet Mahn

PROLOGUE: SOUR GRAPES 11
    Anne Balay

Part I
THE WORK OF QUEER CARE AND MUTUAL AID

Chapter 1
QUEER CARE WORK AS POSSIBILITY: HOW CARE SUSTAINS QUEER
SURVIVAL IN THE ACADEMY 21
    Della J. Winters and Holly Ningard

Chapter 2
REDISTRIBUTING RESOURCES BEYOND THE ACADEMY: A
ROUNDTABLE DISCUSSION WITH THE DAVIDSON COMMUNITY FUND 35
    Sanzari Aranyak, Katie Horowitz, Ashley Ip, Myka Johnson, Zach
    Neville, Isabel Padalecki, Margo Parker, Yara Quezada Marino, Jaelyn
    Taylor, Rahrah Taylor, and Emily Troutman (Davidson Community Fund)

Chapter 3
QUEERING COMPLEX CONVERSATIONS: SHARING ACADEMIC
EXPERIENCES DURING THE PANDEMIC 49
    Fen Kennedy

Chapter 4
QUEER KINSHIP AS COUNTERNARRATIVE: A PARADIGM OF
PERSISTENCE FOR CROSS-DISCIPLINARY COLLABORATION 66
    Shereen Inayatulla and David P. Rivera

Part II
FAILURE AND RESISTANCE IN DIVERSITY WORK

Chapter 5
UNAFFILIATED: THE DELEGITIMIZATION OF SCHOLARS OF COLOR
OUTSIDE OF ACADEME   83
    Monalesia Earle

Chapter 6
BEYOND BOX TICKING AND BUZZWORDS: A QUEER, WORKING-
CLASS, ANTI-RACIST, ANTI-ABLEIST SHARING IN UK ACADEMIA   97
    Leanne Dawson

Chapter 7
THE PARADOX OF BEING SEEN: STORIES FROM TWO QUEER
EDUCATORS AT A NEW YORK CITY HIGH SCHOOL   117
    Tiffany Lenoi Jones and Elana Eisen-Markowitz

Part III
QUEER COMMUNITY PEDAGOGIES

Chapter 8
SHARING ACROSS GENERATIONS: THE LGBTQ+
INTERGENERATIONAL DIALOGUE PROJECT   131
    Adam J. Greteman, Nic M. Weststrate, and Karen Morris

Chapter 9
PERMEABLE SPACES: CREATING STRUCTURED YET FLUID CULTURAL
EXPERIENCES FOR LGBTI+ ELDERS   147
    Lou Brodie and Lewis Hetherington

Chapter 10
QUEER KINSHIP AND THE PRACTICE OF FAITH DURING COVID-19   161
    Sadie Counts

EPILOGUE: QUEER FAILURE AND THE FIGHT FOR PUBLIC
COLLEGE FOR ALL   173
    Jennifer Gaboury

Notes   181
Further Reading   183
Index   184

Table

5.1 Table of Privileges   90

CONTRIBUTOR BIOGRAPHIES

Sanzari Aranyak (they/them) is a rising senior at Davidson College (on occupied Catawba and Sugaree land) majoring in gender and sexuality studies. As a South Asian queer and trans person in the South, they are interested in diasporic identities and community building, intergenerational and coalitional organizing, and historical legacies of abolitionist work in their local communities. At Davidson, they helped to cofound the Asian American Initiative, a working group advocating for Asian American Studies on campus, and are a core organizer and graphics creator with the Davidson Community Fund. Branching off of an internship with the Smithsonian Asian Pacific American Center, they focus on centering care, community, and disability justice frameworks within the QTPOC organizing spaces they inhabit.

Anne Balay has a PhD in English (Chicago, 1994) and she has taught college since then whenever the opportunity presents itself. Her life and work explore class, labor, and sexuality as they intertwine deliciously, which doesn't fit comfortably anywhere in the academy. No matter. Balay has worked as often elsewhere, including as a car mechanic, a long haul truck driver, and a labor organizer. Balay has published numerous articles and two award-winning books. *Steel Closets: Voices of Gay, Lesbian, and Transgender Steelworkers* was published in 2014 and *Semi Queer: Inside the Lives of Gay, Trans, and Black Truck Drivers* in 2018. Each is based on oral histories Balay did of people presently doing these jobs. Currently, Balay organizes adjunct professors at a range of Higher Ed institutions in St. Louis, Missouri. How people think about, understand, and try to transform their work via classed embodiments of sexuality, gender, and race is what Balay seeks to honor, challenge, and learn from.

Matt Brim is Professor of Queer Studies at the College of Staten Island and the Graduate Center, City University of New York. He writes about queer literature, the field of queer studies, and class and race hierarchies in the queer academy. He is the author of *Poor Queer Studies: Confronting Elitism in the University* (2020) and *James Baldwin and the Queer Imagination* (2014) and coeditor of *Imagining Queer Methods* (2019). Other publications include the open access Study Guide for the HIV/AIDS activist documentary film *United in Anger: A History of ACT UP*.

Lou Brodie is an applied artist, programmer, and project manager based in Scotland. Through an artistic process rooted in social practice and conviviality, Lou produces idiosyncratic artworks and events in collaboration with communities, people, and places. Graduating from the Royal Conservatoire of Scotland with a BA(Hons) in Contemporary Theatre Practice, Lou has worked with a range of national and international companies and artists, including Tramway Glasgow, Lyra, Platform Glasgow, Imaginate and the Edinburgh International Children's Festival, Mammalian Diving Reflex, Nic Green, Southbank Centre, The WOW Foundation, Perth Theatre, and The Touring Network. Much of her portfolio of work is preoccupied with the creation of spaces and performative actions that rely on or question the responsibility and power of the spectator/participant.

Sadie Counts is a doctoral student in cultural anthropology at the University of Tennessee, Knoxville. She received her BA in Global Studies from the University of Nebraska, Lincoln, with minors in anthropology, Spanish, and women's and gender studies, and will complete her MA in Cultural Anthropology from the University of Tennessee, Knoxville, with a Certificate in Women's, Gender, and Sexuality studies in the Spring/Summer of 2021. Her research interests include queer and feminist theory, museum studies, human sexuality, and visual culture. She is currently the graduate assistant of Exhibitions and Curation at the McClung Museum of Natural History and Culture at the University of Tennessee, Knoxville, where she is actively working on curating an exhibition that will highlight the queer history of Knoxville. She currently lives in Knoxville, Tennessee, with her archeologist partner Matt and their two dogs, Kanuvi and Kahlua, and two cats, Keanu and Kiwi.

Leanne Dawson is Senior Lecturer in both Film Studies and German Studies at the University of Edinburgh, although as a theorist of gender, sexuality, and socioeconomic position and class. She currently holds a prestigious AHRC Research Leader Fellowship (Early Career, until 2022), for which she is writing a monograph theorizing the intersection of LGBTQI+ and working-class representation on British screens (film, television, online). She was the first chair of the Scottish Queer International Film Festival, cofounded the Queer Screens Network, curates film for independent cinemas, is an invited jury member for international film festivals, and is frequently asked to share her academic expertise in the media (from small independent publications and films to Harper's Bazaar and the BBC).

Monalesia Earle is an independent researcher based in Liverpool, England. Her book, *Writing Queer Women of Color: Representation and Misdirection in Contemporary Fiction and Graphic Narratives* (2019), received Honorable Mention for the Charles Hatfield Book Prize, and was also runner-up for the John Leo and Dana Heller Award for Best Single Work in LGBTQ Studies.

Elana "E.M." Eisen-Markowitz is an experienced educator, a public school worker, and an education organizer with a focus on solidarity pedagogy, and transformative justice in secondary schools in the United States. She is a queer, white, Jewish, gender nonconforming woman who worked in the New York City public schools from 2007 to 2020—as a social studies teacher, a union chapter delegate, a Gender and Sexuality Alliance facilitator, and a Restorative Justice Coordinator at an alternative transfer high school serving students ages 16–22. She is currently the facilitator of the Boston Network for School Improvement with Eskolta School Research and Design. For over a decade, E.M. organized educators in NYC with Teachers Unite to try to work alongside students and their families in campaigns for racial, social, and economic justice. In early 2020, E.M. was a Fulbright distinguished teacher at the University of Strathclyde in Glasgow, working on an independent research project about LGBTQI+ affirming cultural change in Scottish schools.

Jennifer Gaboury is a full-time Lecturer on an adjunct conversion line in the Department of Women and Gender Studies at Hunter College, CUNY. She's currently working on a book about public commitments and forms of segregation in and around public bathrooms. She has served on the boards of CLAGS and Alternatives to Marriage Project, and has been a member of the Advisory Committee for the LGBT Rights Division at Human Rights Watch, where, in another lifetime, she worked. Gaboury is active within her union, the PSC CUNY, serving as on its Executive Council and Legislative Committee, as well as Chapter Chair at Hunter College. She also does organizing work with CUNY Rising Alliance and community groups in Southern Brooklyn.

Adam J. Greteman, PhD, is Assistant Professor of Art Education and Director of the Master of Arts in Teaching program at the School of the Art Institute of Chicago (SAIC). His teaching and research interests lie at the intersections of feminist, queer, and transgender theories, philosophy of education, and teacher education. He is a cofounder (with Karen Morris and Todd Williams) of the Intergenerational LGBTQ+ Dialogue Project. His work has been published in *QED: A Journal of Queer Worldmaking*, *Sex Education*, *Journal of Homosexuality* and *Educational Theory*. He is the author of the award-winning *Sexualities and Genders in Education: Toward Queer Thriving* (Palgrave-Macmillan, 2018) and the co-author (with Kevin Burke) of *The Pedagogies and Politics of Liking* (Routledge, 2017). His current projects include a book assembling an alternative genealogy of queer pedagogues, including the Marquis de Sade, James Baldwin, Andrea Dworkin, and S.T.A.R., whose lessons challenge the manifest fear of queers prevalent in educational thought and practice.

Lewis Hetherington is an award-winning playwright and performance maker. He was the 2019 IASH Creative Fellow for the University of Edinburgh and the Traverse Theatre, exploring how we tell stories in the age of the Anthropocene. He is Creative Lead on *The Coming Back Out Ball* for the National Theatre of Scotland, and he is on the board of Creative Carbon Scotland and Playwrights' Studio, Scotland. Recent credits include *Rocket Post!* (National Theatre of Scotland) and *BOYS* (The Pappy Show). As an associate of Analogue, he won two Fringe Firsts and the Arches Brick Award for his work on Mile End, Beachy Head, and 2401 Objects (with Oldenburg Staatstheater). His work has toured extensively throughout Scotland and the rest of the world, including performances in Australia, Canada, China, Germany, Japan, Saudi Arabia, Singapore, and the United States.

Katie Horowitz (she/her) is Assistant Professor of Gender & Sexuality Studies and Writing at Davidson College and an abolitionist working to support recently incarcerated and houseless folks in Charlotte, North Carolina. She is the author of *Drag, Interperformance, and the Trouble with Queerness* (Routledge, 2020), and her research has appeared or is forthcoming in *Signs, Porn Studies, CrossCurrents*, and *The SAGE Encyclopedia of Trans Studies*. She is currently working on a collaborative study of transformative approaches to gender-based abuse between university faculty and a second monograph, *Love Under Capitalism*.

Shereen Inayatulla (she/her/hers) is Associate Professor of English and the Writing Across the Curriculum Coordinator at York College, CUNY. Her areas of research include composition/literacy studies, autoethnography, and queer theory. Her work has appeared in a variety of publications, including the *Journal of Basic Writing, Changing English* and the *Journal of Lesbian Studies*. Shereen has presented her research at national conferences and delivered workshops on writing pedagogy for faculty at institutions across the United States. She is currently working on an autoethnographic project that celebrates the complexities of queer, immigrant storytelling practices poised to rebuke linear narrative as a weapon of colonization.

Ashley Ip (she/her) is a rising senior at Davidson College, majoring in anthropology and physics. She is passionate about fighting the medical-industrial complex and using data visualization as a tool to better communicate societal issues. She worked on the Davidson Community Fund as the "financial god" by managing the organization's finances and bookkeeping. As a queer woman of color, she is thankful for all the Black and queer POC elders who have helped inform the Davidson Community Fund's work.

Myka Johnson (she/they) is a 28-year-old Black Trans Woman who currently resides on occupied Siouan and Catawba land. She is a healer, yoga teacher, writer, dancer, filmmaker, and radical abolitionist. In 2020 she completed her yoga teaching training, returned to film to co-direct *Letters from a Black Trans Femme*, and she is currently working on publishing an anthology of letter-styled entries on which her most recent film is based.

Tiffany Lenoi Jones (she/her/all pronouns intended and impacted with love) is an abolitionist educator, artist, and healer. She is committed to the practice of unconditional TLC (tender love and care) to contribute to communities that thrive through the interdependent practice of teaching, learning, changing, creating, and/or challenging TLC. She believes radical care, imagination, and creativity are both the pathway and conduit to our collective liberation. Currently she is a full-time tenured art educator in the New York City Public School system. During her career as an art educator, she has created curriculum and experiences rooted in a critical pedagogy of love, liberation, healing, and transformative justice. She is a proud Harriet's Apothecary Leadership Circle member and healer. She works collaboratively with the collective to foster spaces that encourage wellness, care, and liberation of Black people through the creation of healing spaces. She founded and is the first Educator in Residence for Art and Social Justice at the New Museum. During her residency she cofounded and organized the New Museum's *Convening for Contemporary Art, Social Justice, and Education*.

Fen Kennedy is Assistant Professor of Dance at the University of Alabama. Their research—theoretical and physical—explores the articulation of social and cultural values, and how those values can be challenged and changed. Kennedy is a passionate advocate for equity in Higher Education, and their writing on this subject can be read in *The Journal of Dance Education*, on their popular dance blog *The Headtail Connection*, and is forthcoming in *So You Don't "Look Like" a Professor*. Kennedy also serves on the editorial board of *The Activist History Review*, recently producing the special issue "New and Old Normals" on strategies for growth and resilience during a global pandemic. Kennedy is an organizer for The Landingspace Project, which invites dancers to reimagine their socially distanced creative practices and build a global community for social justice. In non-pandemic times she also travels around the United States teaching and organizing social partner dances.

Churnjeet Mahn is Professor of English at the University of Strathclyde and a fellow of the Young Academy of Scotland (Royal Society of Edinburgh). Her research investigates the history and practice of travel with special reference to race, sexuality, and nationalism. Her first book, *Journeys in the Palimpsest: British Women's Travel in Greece 1840–1914* (2012), investigated competing discourses of Orientalism and Hellenism in Victorian popular culture. She has worked on queer and anti-racist heritage projects with migrant organizations in India and the UK. Churnjeet is currently working on queer and postcolonial contemporary travel writing.

Karen Morris, PhD, is a lesbian mother and cultural anthropologist. She is Associate Professor and Chair of the Department of Visual and Critical Studies at the School of the Art Institute of Chicago. As a graduate student and early career scholar, Karen conducted ethnographic research on gender, politics, and popular media consumption among transnational families living between Côte d'Ivoire, West Africa, and the United States. She was invited to speak about her research in a number of venues, including the Smithsonian Institution's National Museum of African Art and the Library of Congress' African and Middle East Division, and published pieces in an edited volume and *City & Society*. Karen's focus shifted to care work during her second year on the tenure track when she became the primary caregiver for her terminally ill mother. She spent the following eight years in this role, and also took on a new role as a parent to two children. As her children have grown, Karen's research focus has turned to sexuality, family, and care work among LGBTQ+ folks in the United States. She cofounded The LGBTQ+ Intergenerational Dialogue Project with Adam Greteman and Todd Williams in 2019.

Zach Neville (he/him) is a rising junior at Davidson College who is incredibly grateful to be in community with, and learning from, those around him. He is interested in a range of topics including the roles of individualism and free speech in oppressive political structures, the evolution of radical theory, and histories and impacts of racialization. Though constantly trying to orient himself in the context of radical politics, he sees transformative justice, direct action, and a self-critiquing approach as key to imagining a better world.

Holly Ningard is Assistant Professor of Lectureship in the Department of Sociology and Anthropology at Ohio University. Dr. Ningard's research interests focus on narrative criminology, green criminology, and state and corporate crime. Using qualitative data collection methods, she has recently examined the intersections of storytelling and law, and how stories shape our understanding of corporate environmental harm.

Isabel Padalecki (she/they) is studying history and gender and sexuality studies as a rising senior at Davidson College. In an academic context, she is primarily interested in studying histories of queer embodiment that destabilize the moral imperatives of the state and the medical-industrial complex. She is also a core organizer with the Davidson Community Fund. Outside of school, Isabel finds fulfillment and joy in creating (and appreciating) music, taking long walks around Lake Norman, and making frequent hair-color changes.

Margo Parker (they/them) is a postal worker on occupied Catawba and Sugaree land, as well as a member of the Davidson College class of 2021. During their undergraduate career, they have researched the connections between the carceral state and social thought in the US South, while interning at Critical Resistance and the Mecklenburg County Public Defender's office. They believe in the power of mutual aid and direct action to build a world without prisons or policing, and they are grateful, always, for the intergenerational radical queer and trans community.

Yara Quezada (she/her) is a soon-to-be Davidson College grad and avid DIY-er. She is rooted deeply in her belief that everyone is divinely created and worthy of dignity and respect. She is interested in the connections between faith and social justice, especially the biblical call for prison abolition and liberation. Through being part of the Davidson Community Fund, she has learned what it truly means to build community and work toward creating a new and more just world. Outside of her responsibilities, Yara can be found diffusing her essential oils, doing yoga on her back deck, or listening to Kacey Musgraves.

David P. Rivera, PhD, is Associate Professor of Counselor Education at Queens College-City University of New York (CUNY) and Founding Director of CUNY's LGBTQI+ Student Leadership Program. Dr. Rivera's research focuses on cultural competency development and issues impacting the marginalization and well-being of people of color and oppressed sexual orientation and gender identity groups, with a focus on microaggressions. His coedited book, *Microaggression Theory: Influence and Implications*, was released in 2019. Dr. Rivera is an adviser to The Steve Fund, faculty with the Council for Opportunity in Education, and holds leadership roles in the American Psychological Association. He has received recognition for his work from the American Psychological Association, the American College Counseling Association, and the American College Personnel Association.

Jaelyn Taylor (she/they) is a soon-to-be senior at Davidson College. Their work includes working as a core organizer on the Davidson Community Fund, co-organizing a five-week radical political education series called Imagining Davidson in fall 2020, and cofounding a community care space for Black femmes at Davidson College. She is immensely grateful for the numerous Black and queer POC folks in her life that have helped foster this growth and keep her in check.

Rahrah Taylor (she/her) is a Black trans femme mutual aid organizer living in Charlotte, North Carolina. At nineteen, she opened up her apartment to other Black trans girls and has been on the frontlines of the fight for Black trans liberation ever since. Currently, she works with Charlotte Uprising, where she is excited to put her body on the line to help people in need.

Yvette Taylor is Professor of Education, University of Strathclyde, and Fellow of the Academy of Social Sciences. Yvette has obtained a wide variety of funding, including the British Academy mid-career fellowship "Critical Terrain: Dividing Lines and Lives" (2013–14) and has published a range of books including Working-Class Queers. *Time, Place and Politics* (2023), *Working-Class Lesbian Life* (2007), *Lesbian and Gay Parenting* (2009), *Fitting into Place? Class and Gender Geographies and Temporalities* (2012), and *Making Space for Queer Identifying Religious Youth* (2015) and coauthored *Feminist Repetitions in Higher Education: Interrupting Career Categories* (2020).

Emily Troutman (she/her) is a rising junior at Davidson College intending to major in biology and Arab studies. She is from outside of Washington, DC, and was motivated to seek out community-based politics that prioritize direct action after growing up surrounded by the shortcomings of electoral politics. Her work through the Davidson Community Fund has taught her so much, and she is so grateful for the opportunity to collaborate with people who care so deeply for those around them.

Nic M. Weststrate's research orientation is informed by life span developmental, personality, narrative, and cultural psychology. He incorporates diverse quantitative and qualitative methodologies in his work, with an emphasis on narrative methods that capture the diversity, complexity, and cultural embeddedness of human development. His research program investigates optimal psychosocial development across the adult life span. His research examines human development at the intersection of personal, social, cultural, and historical forces. He is primarily interested in Eriksonian developmental constructs, including personal and collective identity, generativity, ego integrity, and, especially, the development, manifestation, and transmission of wisdom. In recent research, Nic has been exploring the influence of intergenerational storytelling on psychosocial development. He is currently examining this within the context of families and the LGBTQ+ community.

Della J. Winters is Assistant Professor of Sociology with a concentration in Criminology in the Department of Criminology, Sociology, and Geography at Arkansas State University in Jonesboro, Arkansas. Dr. Winters's research examines the consequences of the expansions of the carceral state and mass surveillance, particularly within the lives of women. Using qualitative data collection methods, she explores the intersections of privilege and disadvantage (i.e., race, gender, sexuality, and disability) within carceral mechanisms. Dr. Winters most recent research traces the emergence of long-acting reversible contraceptives as the primary mechanisms of reproductive healthcare and social policy in Tennessee.

INTRODUCTION

Yvette Taylor, Matt Brim, Churnjeet Mahn

Queers have been failed in institutional life, including via *un*employment, *im*permanence, and *mis*recognition, and their experiences of precarity are plural and intersectional, extending in and out of the university. "Precarity" alludes to states of flux, insecurity, and uncertainty, and in pluralizing this term, the collection recognizes patterns within these states. Patterns of precarity include: the successful Queer and Gender Studies degree, only ever available to certain queers, shut down by conservative right-wing backlash; the funding for the LGBTQ+ outreach program cut in the wake of hetero-activism; the queer student "Dreamers" caught in shifting anti-immigrant winds; the temporary premises for the community workshop closed as part of a continued austerity drive; and the not-for-profit venue regenerated and made into exclusive apartments. There is a long history of queers not getting into and getting pushed out of social and educational institutions (Bérubé 2011; Haritaworn 2011; Taylor 2013). In and beyond these examples, queer spaces are precarious, ever subject to financial, political, and emotional (dis)investment. This collection comes at a time when queer studies and (some) queer lives are incorporated into the university, while other queer lives are subject to threats from conservative, queerphobic backlash queerphobic backlash (Mahn, Brim, and Taylor 2022). In the context of sharp divides between us/them, precarity/privilege, inside/outside, academic-activist accounts are deliberately hyphenated as crossing over, bridged and (un)done repeatedly. Here, we are concerned with "success" beyond measured attainment, instrumentalized curricula, income accumulation, and (inflated) credentialism; our "inputs and outputs" surpass sanction or appraisal in normative institutional spaces and extend to questions of what constitutes living with, through, and beyond precarity.

The cases in this collection primarily focus on the UK and the US. "Precarity" has become a key term in European politics, especially since the 2008 financial crisis, which in the UK heralded the normalization of casualized labor, stricter legislation around union organization, and large-scale government austerity programs. What happens when the logic of the gig economy structures the social and economic experience of education? What do short-term contracts and short-term resources do to our sense of academic community or the possibility for working-class staff and students to believe they can continue beyond the semester or the academic year? In this collection, we bring together queer scholars, educators, and practitioners who have used precarity to critique elitist structures that celebrate individual success (often for white, cishet, middle-class men), and propose alternative communities of action, scholarship, and practice. Queer scholars have used precarity in a variety of senses to address how the experience of contingency, insecurity, and impermanence, belong to queer times. From the experience of perpetual "crisis" after 9/11 and the potential to forge new solidarities to address injustice (Butler 2006), to work in the wake of the 2008 financial crisis (Berlant 2011), the study of "precarity" has produced a field of inquiry which asks what justice can mean and look like amid the differential effects of structural inequality and insecurity. A roundtable convened by Jasbir K. Puar for *The Drama Review* (*TDR*) in 2012, brought together UK and US scholars in the backdrop of mass protests in Britain, Greece, and Spain against the effects of government programs of austerity. In the *TDR* discussions, Isabell Lorey offers a useful general definition for precarity: "I use the term 'precarity' (*Prekarität*) as a category of order that denotes social positionings of insecurity and hierarchization, which accompanies processes of Othering" (Lorey qtd. in Puar 2012: 165). We stretch this term to think about *queer precarities* within the overlapping and intersecting processes of othering that have become a mainstay of institutional life in the university. We use the university as a site of inquiry in this collection because it combines so many hopes and refusals. Higher education is inseparable from social imperatives around "betterment" and promises of enhanced economic prospects. But with larger loans, higher fees, and lowering working conditions (especially in non-elite institutions), who gets to benefit from the sunny economic forecasts of a life with a degree?

Judith Butler points out that "more and more laborers within the academy are subjected to new forms of precaritization. In a way, the situation of nontenured academic workers (I believe they hold *basura* positions in Spain: 'trash' or 'garbage' positions) forms a bridge between the institutional crisis of knowledge within the university and the production of disposable populations of workers" (Butler qtd. in Puar et al. 2012: 167). If more and more people are rendered precarious, then there is arguably a broader base of politicization and collectivization. And yet some "bridges" are crossed, pulled up, and re-made: middle-class workers may find their lifelong educational success or career entitlement *suddenly* challenged; others may find this to be a familiar bridge—or border—with the usual exacting tolls. Does "precarity" suddenly capture our attention when it circulates and becomes more recognizable in the Global North while being a perpetual presence within the Global South? If so, does "precarity" reinforce a North/South binary and miss the chance to forge solidarity? Such questions suggest that our academic attentions and imaginations circulate with and through constrained vocabularies and concepts (and as "ours" and "theirs"). This collection attends to the kind of subjects and bodies that find themselves holding increasingly "trash" positions through the "adjunctification," or casualization, of higher education.

The chapters in this collection speak across disciplines and debates in the arts and humanities, including critiques of "equality, diversity, and inclusion" (EDI) initiatives (Ahmed 2009; Mahn 2019; Puwar 2004), queer working-class studies

(Brim 2020; Taylor 2007, 2022), and Black radical traditions (Harney and Moten 2013). While the majority of the chapters focus on the university, we aim to consider the academy as a community of practice. We want to be critical of some of the barriers around who gets to count as a "scholar," recognizing how the idea and site of the university filter into queer life and practice in and outside institutional walls. We value Stefano Harney and Fred Moten's definition of what being a scholar can be as an inevitably social commitment: "It's talking and walking around with other people, working, dancing, suffering, some irreducible convergence of all three, held under the name of speculative practice" (Harney and Moten 2013: 110). As a speculation, we bring together queer theory and queer practice to articulate some of the everyday struggles in making a life in the midst of structures that continue to render our presences out of place, and our futures uncertain.

We use "precarity" mindful of the scholars whose intellectual labor has been turned into hourly paid short-term contracts with no benefits or security. But we also point to a broader range of educators, whose experience of structural discrimination on the basis of race, class, gender, disability, and/or sexuality increasingly makes "successful" futures in the university harder to imagine. The intention is not to draw equivalences between different kinds of precarity or to erase the usefulness of thinking about *class* specifically. Rather, it is to create a space to disrupt definitions and begin creating solidarity through queer(ed) practices of care, inclusion, and kinship. The chapters in his collection use "queer" not only to speak to the lived experience of people outside heteronormative structures but also to point to how queer practices can challenge and resist structural exclusion through critiques of classism, capitalist exploitation, and racism. The chapters draw on the transformative potential of queer pedagogies to resist structural inequalities in our educational communities and challenge the logic of free market capitalism in our educational institutions (hooks 2003).

We think through the possibilities of other educational spaces in and beyond the university. We think of (inter)disciplinary dialogues, and of stretching the meaning of *doing* education, and *becoming* educated. Contemporary educational spaces confound the limits and possibilities of the bounded hierarchical classroom, existing in and as community education, as responsive online forums, and as do-it-yourself activities. This doing is in some ways an un-doing—of working in and against the (un)professional places and positions we uneasily occupy. Here, contributors speak of being precariously employed in the third sector, as cultural or even voluntary workers; they speak as part of an ever-growing temporary academic workforce, and in some cases, they speak as permanent academic workers, yet at times feeling their own potential impermanence in conditions such as annual performance reviews, in excessive monitoring and metric scoring, and in massive pension loss.

In this collection, we push back and against contemporary educational precarity, mobilizing collectivized queer insight and insistence; we push back against the confinement of education and locate the past-present-future of educational and learning divides. Together, these accounts reactivate our stories, struggles, and successes: while queer "failure" interrupts (Edelman 2004; Halberstam 2005, 2011) less has been said about a queer pragmatism, a participative practicality that we locate here in terms of "getting by." Often, queer pushback is exhausting (Breeze and Taylor 2020). This "bridgework" takes a toll, even if it leads to another place—and as Gloria Anzaldúa notes being present as the bridge might mean being "walked on" and being "used" (Anzaldúa 1990: 223). Often institutions, colleagues, peers, and students use each other up, pushing labor back onto certain individuals, communities, and groups. Minoritized staff point to the flip side of the meritocracy myth: not only are white faculty helped by meritocratic norms but non-white faculty are punished for being exceptional, "sticky" subjects (Ahmed 2012).

The pragmatism—of recognizing moments of goodness and hope in, through, and beyond educational institutions—is also located in intersectional class-race-gender frames which understand racialized and classed communities and actors as *having* to get by. The cumulative promise of "getting on" revolves around achieving accreditation from the "right" university, becoming a promoted member of staff who accrues publications and income, and accumulating community impact as individual acquisition. Reimagining ways to get by, through, and beyond our classrooms may offer some pushback. The "here and now" of the (post-)COVID-19 locked-down university is situated alongside the long histories of feminist interventions into the academy, particularly the labors of working-class women (Mahony and Zmroczek 1997), Black Feminists (Gabriel and Tate 2017; Sobande 2021), and queer feminists (Taylor and Addison 2013). Attending to the histories and presences of pushing out, in, and through education allows us to also think through possible futures, as a positive pushback. Fractures, cracks, and glitches in thinking back-forward open up spaces of possibility (Butler 1990; Halberstam 2011; Taylor and Lahad 2018; Breeze and Taylor 2020). Our prologue to the collection, "Sour Grapes" by Anne Balay, explores the "adjunctification" of higher education. As short-term precarious labor becomes increasingly normalized, Balay asks what this does to the experience of labor, of belonging, of place in higher education. Her work outlines some of the themes and questions that run throughout the collection: How, in the exhaustion and anger of working in the university, do we find the hope that can forge different ways of being, doing, and knowing?

The authors in Part I speak to how structures of class privilege and racism conspire to hoard the social, intellectual, and economic capital that life in the academy might promise, and how forms of queer care and mutual aid can offer more hopeful bases of intellectual community making. This section demonstrates a form of queer pragmatism that is more than a response to everyday necessity; in its practice, it sows the seeds of what more equitable futures might look like (and how they are in our reach in more immediate and intimate connections). In "Queer Care Work as Possibility: How Care Sustains Queer Survival in the Academy," Della J. Winters and Holly Ningard consider how queer kinships become vital in an academy. The value of queer research can be recognized (if it brings recognition to an institution) as can the value of queer academics (when it can be used to demonstrate diversity), but this often fails to address the lived experience of structural inequalities related to class, race, and sexuality. Winters and Ningard navigate the contradiction of the university as a site of "refuge" and as a space of violence for queers and offer imperatives for more inclusive approaches to distributing resources.

The Davidson Community Fund is a queer student-led mutual aid project founded in 2020 at Davidson College, a small liberal arts college in North Carolina (US). In this chapter the Davidson Community Fund discusses the tension between the role of queer studies in elite institutions versus the lived reality and experience of BIPOC queer students struggling with food insecurity, housing, and employment. This chapter details the disproportionate impact of COVID-19 on BIPOC and working-class queers and offers a consideration of the practical, emotional, and political challenges involved in redistributing wealth.

In "How Do We Go Forward? How Do We Go Back? Conversations Across Classes," Fen Kennedy describes the active doing of bringing the community together through dialogue in response to the global pandemic. In a time of crisis, or even an "end point," Kennedy is concerned with talking as a collective way backward and forward and as a repeated engagement that actively constitutes community. This chapter queers space-making done through the university yet not adhering to its go-to structures or hierarchical spaces, instead prioritizing shared vulnerabilities and shared strengths. Where universities have "dealt with" COVID-19 by issuing health and well-being statements and instructions to "take care," this chapter eschews vacuous messages and aims to actively do something. The potential of DIY is highlighted as with many chapters in this collection, but with this comes labor—even if a "labor of love" done in, for, and by queers. Part of a queer pedagogy might be to celebrate the margins, to come out against getting (back to) normal, and to do this over time as an ongoing dialogue or a live "question and answers" session. And yet this chapter also raises questions about the limits of voice, of being heard, and the potential of silence. Can silence be a queer pushback or does it always represent a queer push-out?

In "Queer Kinship as Counternarrative: A Paradigm of Persistence for Cross-disciplinary Collaboration," Shereen Inayatulla and David P. Rivera contribute a dialogue between academics who cultivate and celebrate queer kinship, a relation that "blurs personal and academic spheres of influence." Inayatulla's and Rivera's queer kinship is grounded in a sense of the different colonized rural and urban lands on which they were raised and now live, and it is elaborated in their current shared institutional setting, the City University of New York (CUNY). As their queer kinship challenges normative familial and academic structures, it also experiments formally by interspersing conversation with critical reflection. The authors thereby enact a dialogic of "curtain lifting" that challenges norms of knowledge production in order to share the queer care work of "friendlove" with readers.

Part II addresses how initiatives around equality, diversity, and inclusion fail to address and resist the everyday mechanics of racialized, gendered, and classed exclusions. How has the instrumentalization of "EDI" as an equality practice helped to consolidate particular vectors of exclusion? Who gets to be "included" and on whose terms? In "Unaffiliated: The Delegitimization of Scholars of Color

Outside of Academe," Monalesia Earle explores how institutional whiteness works to delegitimize scholars of color. From interview screening to citational practices, Earle demonstrates how and why academia is a type of hostile environment for scholars of color, who, as a consequence, are more likely to feel precarious (in terms of employment and in terms of imagining a secure future). Devalued, and overrepresented in the "bottom tiers" and "margins" of academia, Earle's chapter raises questions about who the university is really for.

In "Beyond Box ticking and Buzzwords: A Queer, Working-Class, Anti-racist, Anti-ableist Sharing in UK academia," Leanne Dawson proposes "straight sharing" as the term for the normative ways the university distributes resources, even as it professes its commitment to equality, diversity, and inclusion (EDI). Dawson argues that an embrace of metrics and buzzwords (e.g., "Knowledge Exchange," "Widening Participation," "Impact," and "Decolonizing the Curriculum") stands in for meaningful supports for people long excluded from higher education's institutional spaces, funding streams, and positions of power. Grounded in case studies and the author's personal experiences of queer-class marginalization in academe, this chapter is a call to action to share more queerly in the university, connecting students and scholars who are queer, working-class, BIPOC, and disabled.

In "The Paradox of Being Seen: Stories from Two Queer Educators," Tiffany Lenoi Jones and Elana Eisen-Markowitz (a Fulbright scholar at a UK university) explore creative engagements with their students and coworkers at a publicly funded secondary school in New York City. Their ongoing conversation—captured in the chapter through extracts—as collaborative practice highlights the intimate connection between thinking, feeling, and doing as "queer educators." They reflect on their status as "queer educators" beyond declarative identity statements, where to be out with students is to inhabit the city and the classroom differently. As with many working in the context of EDI directives, they sometimes find themselves surprised and confused, feeling awkwardly "included," yet still exhausted. They grapple with *being seen* in the context of a school and consider what structural pains and privileges are still unseen.

Part III turns to research, practice, and collaborations outside the structures of the university. This section of the collection thinks more expansively about the site of the university; here we evoke the cross-over between academics, students, and organizations, who form communities of queer practice which have asked what we need to survive, or get by. In "Sharing Across Queer Generations: The LGBTQ+ Intergenerational Dialogue Project," Adam J. Greteman, Nic M. Weststrate, and Karen Morris highlight the possibilities of cross-generational contact as an embodied queer pedagogy, pushing against ideas of generational divides of being in or out of time and overburdened with history or futurity. Cross-generational conversations also extend across classes, where participants do not access or go to queer theory to deconstruct queer lives. Instead, they draw on a wealth of lived experience which they themselves render complex, changing, and contested, rather than simply known or always authentic. Categories of knowledge become undone through acts of collective storytelling that are interrupted, questioned, and recirculated. This is a different form of (not)reading rather than rote-reading queer(s).

In "Permeable Spaces: Creating Structured Yet Fluid Cultural Experiences for LGBTI+ Elders," Lou Brodie and Lewis Hetherington dwell on their participatory project with older community members, reflecting on how it adapted through different funding pressures and timelines and as interrupted by COVID-19. When final showcase events are canceled we are forced to think beyond project deadlines and to interrogate what success—or ending a project with marginalized groups—looks like in practice. Do our projects and practices ever end? Brodie and Hetherington explore the difficulties and pleasures of moving activities online and among geographically remote LGBTI+ Elders. Describing theater practices as potentially "breaking down walls," this chapter also considers how participants themselves become (digitally) equipped to challenge, break down, and reconstitute queer spaces on their own terms. Some of this breaking down and pushing back also involves letting go—but letting go of funding and contracts produces a precarity which doesn't always sit well with pleasure, creativity, and play.

In "Queer Kinship and the Practice of Faith During COVID-19," Sadie Counts explores the Metropolitan Community Church of Knoxville (MCCK) as it adapts to the pandemic. As a church "in, by, for" queer community, responding to queer crisis might be thought of as its default rather than new way of being. Counts relates this to the AIDS crisis of the late 1980s and early 1990s, connecting with studies on families of choice and faith communities as long buffering social inequalities. Often dismissed as clashing with or contradicting sexuality, religion is located as a queer practice, confounding nuclear family models and countering shared experiences of marginalization. As a queer-religious space, MCC invites in a wider community, including those without faith. Yet there are limits to these practical extensions, including individual withdrawal from intimate embodiments, from touching others, as distance is maintained. "Risk sharing" plays a part in the daily lives of queer individuals whose sociality is created in, through, and beyond religiosity, including in repeated crisis periods.

As institutions move further toward transactional thinking and practice, this collection asks what we might need if we are to imagine more equitable educational futures. The epilogue by Jennifer Gaboury renews the call for a broad-based commitment to public higher education, taking the City University of New York as a case study of one institution's struggle with state disinvestment and encroaching elitism. Gaboury traces the logic of uplift by which students and their families view public college as a fallback choice for students who can "do better." University structures such as "honors colleges" create privatized spaces within public ones in order to attract "the best" students. But Gaboury argues that shared educational spaces are better than isolated, cordoned-off, private ones. She names proximity, difference, exposure, and vulnerability as educational values that can decouple achievement from elitism, and she traces the efforts of one campaign to shift resources and opinions toward the institutions that can best embody these public goods.

The impact of producing this collection during COVID-19 is felt on these pages, especially in the chapters by the Davidson Community Fund, Kennedy, Brodie and

Hetherington, and Counts. As editors, we have felt our distance from one another. The last time we met was in March 2020, on the cusp of the first COVID-19 lockdown in the UK. Matt had come to Scotland to give a workshop about working-class queers. We were also in the midst of large-scale industrial action against proposed cuts to the UK's national pension scheme for many higher and further education workers, which was part of a larger Universities and Colleges Union campaign called the "Four Fights" (tackling issues related to pay, casualization, workloads, and equality). As we get ready to submit this collection, a number of UK universities are getting ready to go on strike again. At a time when there's a lot to be pessimistic about, where can we find hope (Duggan and Muñoz 2009)? The condition of precarity is one of fundamental insecurity (Mahn, Brim and Taylor, 2022). Yet, authors variously show how queer precarities might, in the margins, offer hopeful counternarratives of life and possibility in and out of financialized educational structures.

References

Ahmed, S. (2009), "Embodying Diversity: Problems and Paradoxes for Black Feminists," *Race Ethnicity and Education*, 12 (1): 41–52.
Ahmed, S. (2012), *On Being Included: Racism and Diversity in Institutional Life*, Durham, NC: Duke University Press.
Anzaldúa, G. (1990), "Bridge, Drawbridge, Sandbar or Island: Lesbians-of-Color Hacienda Alianzas," in L. Albrecht and R.M. Brewer (eds.), *Bridges of Power: Women's Multicultural Alliances*, 216–33, Philadelphia: New Society.
Berlant, L. (2011), *Cruel Optimism*, Durham, NC: Duke University Press.
Bérubé, A. (2011), *My Desire for History*: Essays in *Gay, Community*, and *Labor History*, ed. John d'Emilio and Estelle B. Freeman, Chapel Hill: University of North Carolina Press.
Breeze, M. and Taylor, Y. (2020), *Feminist Repetitions in Higher Education: Interrupting Career Categories*, London: Palgrave Macmillan.
Brim, M. (2020), *Poor Queer Studies*: Confronting Elitism in the University, Durham, NC: Duke University Press.
Butler, J. (1990), *Gender Trouble: Feminism and the Subversion of Identity*, New York: Routledge.
Butler, J. (2006), *Precarious Life: The Powers of Mourning and Violence*, London: Verso.
Duggan, L. and J.E. Muñoz (2009), "Hope and Hopelessness: A Dialogue," *Women & Performance: A Journal of Feminist Theory*, 19 (2): 275–83.
Edelman, L. (2004), *No Future: Queer Theory and the Death Drive*, Durham, NC: Duke University Press.
Gabriel, D. and S. Tate (2017), *Inside the Ivory Tower: Narratives of Women of Colour Surviving and Thriving in British Academia*, London: Trentham Books.
Halberstam, J. (2005), *In a Queer Time and Place*, New York: New York University Press.
Halberstam, J. (2011), *The Queer Art of Failure*, Durham, NC: Duke University Press.
Haritaworn, J. (2011), "Perverse Reproductions: Notes from the Wrong Side of the Classroom," *Journal of Curriculum and Pedagogy*, 8 (1): 25–8.
Harney, S. and F. Moten (2013), *The Undercommons: Fugitive Planning and Black Study*, Wivenhoe: Minor Compositions.

hooks, B. (2003), *Teaching Community: A Pedagogy of Hope*, New York: Routledge.
Mahn, C. (2019), "Black Scottish Writing and the Fiction of Diversity," in M. Breeze, Y. Taylor, and C. Costa, (eds.), *Time and Space in the Neoliberal University*, 119–42, London: Palgrave Macmillan.
Mahn, C., M. Brim, and Y. Taylor (2023), *Queer Sharing in the Marketized University*, London: Routledge.
Mahony, P. and C. Zmroczek (1997), *Class Matters. Working Class Women's Perspectives On Social Class*, London: Taylor and Francis.
Puar, J. (2012), "Precarity Talk: A Virtual Roundtable with Lauren Berlant, Judith Butler, Bojana Cvejić, Isabell Lorey, Jasbir Puar, and Ana Vujanović," *TDR*, 56 (4): 163–77.
Puwar, N. (2004), *Space Invaders: Race, Gender and Bodies Out of Place*, Oxford: Berg.
Sobande, F. (2021), "By Us, for Us? The Narratives of Black Women in Past and Present British Feminist Publishing," *Women: A Cultural Review*, 3–4: 395–409.
Taylor, Y. (2007), *Working-Class Lesbian Life: Classed Outsiders*, London: Palgrave Macmillan.
Taylor, Y. (2013), "Queer Encounters of Sexuality and Class: Navigating Emotional Landscapes of Academia," *Emotion, Space and Society*, 8: 51–9.
Taylor, Y. (2022), "Queer-Class Repetitions and Interruptions," *Gender, Place and Culture*, doi:10.1080/0966369X.2022.2056147.
Taylor, Y. and M. Addison (eds.) (2013), *Queer Presences and Absences*, London: Palgrave Macmillan.
Taylor, Y. and K. Lahad (eds.) (2018), *Feeling Academic in the Neoliberal University: Feminist Fights, Flights and Failures*, London: Palgrave Macmillan.

PROLOGUE: SOUR GRAPES

Anne Balay

I have been an adjunct on and off for thirty years; I have signed single-class contracts, single-semester contracts, and single-year contracts at twelve different institutions in the United States. At my thirteenth, I was on the tenure track and worked for eight years. I left academia for extended stints as a car mechanic, and then a truck driver, and for shorter gigs doing editing or other office work. Currently, I work for a union, organizing casualized, contingent faculty at four institutions in St. Louis, Missouri. When I describe the adjunct experience, I am drawing on my own background and on conversations I have had with other part-time faculty. I have detailed notes on organizing conversations I've had with 444 adjuncts since January 2020. This data set covers a wide range of institutions from community colleges to selective liberal arts colleges to R1 universities.

"Sour grapes" is an idiomatic expression used by an adjunct I organize to describe how adjuncts are viewed by full timers. Is this a dated idiom? Maybe, but it's a lively one that does much to explain the skilled labor that is college teaching and the queer practice of camp-inflected storytelling that can undermine its narrative hegemony.

If someone gets married, finds love, or gets laid and you don't, you must respond by celebrating with them. Any deviation from this response, especially any critical or sarcastic message about romance, can be called sour grapes, an act of disparaging something desired but out of reach. As far as I know, this particular shamey name-calling was always only directed at women. And like most stigma, it doesn't actually need to be spoken—people self-censor their words and their reactions to dodge it. That it has faded from use does not then mean it has lost rhetorical or psychological power.

Full-time faculty, whether tenure track or not, cause adjuncts to fear being accused of sour grapes. Adjuncts and full timers do the same job under drastically different conditions, so why are adjuncts are the ones pictured with puckered faces: old, bitter women resenting the success of others? That's hardly fair. Full-time faculty don't need to admit to doing this for it to be true—for it to have coercive power.

How does it feel to work under these conditions? Is change possible, and how? Adjuncts stories and experiences can begin to answer these questions. (Readers might wonder why I don't listen to the voices and stories of full timers as well, for a balanced view. I would respond that I don't need to seek out these accounts. Full-time faculty are the mediocre white men of academia: they both talk and get an audience without invitation. Wait and see.)

"Rachel" had a good job that she left to come to St. Louis chasing an opportunity her husband had here. Though she found work, it was complicated by childcare which was expensive enough in the 1990s to consume almost all of her starting salary. When her husband left, her kid was still not school-age, and adjuncting seemed like a lifesaver. Classroom hours were few, breaks were long, and the prep work could be done with her kid present. Almost thirty years later, what seemed like a solution has become a trap. Though "Rachel" has left adjuncting several times for temp gigs in corporate America, these contracts never become permanent and she wound up adjuncting again. Nearing retirement age she has no pension, no savings, no house... retirement is impossible.

And that's not the worst of it. Twice this past year "Rachel" has taken out payday loans—short-term, high-cost loans—knowing full well that they're financial suicide. Fall semester of 2021 she is scheduled to teach five classes at two institutions, and she taught two classes over the summer. But two of the fall classes are on a delayed calendar and two are at a school that waits six weeks to dispense the first paycheck. August had no paydays. For a renter who buys health insurance on the marketplace, has a car note, and services no small amount of credit card debt, this pay schedule is untenable. To avoid late fees she will take out a payday loan in September, if she can even wait that long.

"Rachel" is a passionate and committed teacher. When I call her for updates or on union business she is as likely to share a challenging classroom exchange that she's thinking through how to address effectively as she is to describe financial pressures. This many years in, she cares so much and works on her pedagogy and on building community with other adjuncts.

I became a labor organizer because I believe unions are our best hope for improving the lives of adjuncts and other precarious workers and because I learned while doing oral histories that I love talking to strangers. People inspire me so much. Organizing overlaps with oral history: my first goal is to build relationships with workers and learn what their issues are; what they like about their work, and what they would prefer to see changed. And I agitate. I ask them to think about why their work is so disrespected and if it has to be like this. I want them to imagine that change is possible—that there's a better way to staff higher education—and to think through why their institutions (and the United States) choose this instead.

If I can successfully light a fire under someone and switch them from fatalist apathy to a sense that oppression, if shared, can be overcome then I ask them to contact others and try to get that spark to become a wildfire. One adjunct can't change anything because one adjunct can be dismissed faster than I can write down their name, with no notice or reason given. It's at-will employment and I never tell anyone they're safe from termination. However, they can't fire *all* the adjuncts tomorrow.

"Jeff" is an adjunct with another perspective. He began grad school in philosophy decades ago and made it to the dissertation stage but then floundered.

Needing to eat every day, he saw that the tech industry was flourishing and got a corporate job in IT. He worked decades there until they pushed him to early retirement. Unbeknownst to "Jeff," the adjunctification of higher education snowballed during those years, and now his master's degree was enough to get him steady and plentiful work at two or more area schools. He knows that pay and working conditions are appalling and he's working hard to improve them, but still. . . every new semester and every teaching day is a thrill. A dream he thought he lost has been returned to him.

How do I get these two very different people to join together in solidarity? They need to find what they have in common so they will want to support each other, risking their jobs and their autonomy. To do so, I weave together organizing strategies for moving from personal trauma to collective action with queer theories that destabilize binaries in order to shift between embodied experience and a fluid, unfixed imagining of what's possible.

Union organizing is uphill work, and organizing adjuncts is no exception. The people I call are overworked, underpaid, and desperate. I encourage them to join with other adjuncts, contributing some of their money and lots of their time to the goal of improving the lot of all adjuncts collectively. With temp contracts, anyone can be fired if they call attention to themselves, and they know that.

This is twenty-first-century America, and Missouri is a conservative state. Building a union involves trusting strangers and understanding that the collective good outweighs any individual striving. Like everyone else, adjuncts are greedy and competitive: they're humans at the bottom of the food chain fighting for scraps. I have two options: I can argue that the only power available to them is the power of collective action and if they want to improve their job they need to take the risk of organizing. That is, argue that unionizing is actually the greedy option.

Or I can make moral arguments about justice and need.

One of the schools I organize just bargained a new contract and my members have been spreading the word through the unit. It's a publicly funded school so the labor laws governing organizing are less than ideal. Therefore, in spite of my best efforts, our density falls a bit short of 30 percent and we have about fifty active members. Don't laugh; I'm proud of these figures.

Nevertheless, they don't give us the worker power we needed to win progress like health insurance or a seat on faculty governance. But we did win raises and compensation for anyone who completes a long list of required trainings. Adjuncts could argue that even at Wal-Mart associates are paid for any training time their jobs require, and enough adjuncts were angry enough about the time required to complete online trainings to teach remotely that the college was scared.

I collected letters from adjuncts that described the time these trainings took, and explained how wrong it felt to be required to compete them the summer *after* they had moved their classes online on short notice with virtually no support. Retroactively, they were deemed unqualified to do what they had already done well, in the panicked weeks of March 2020. Because they're contingent faculty, they had to supply their own laptops, internet, and (usually) technical support. But they did it well, with flexibility and tact, and they resented being required the following summer to complete long and flatfooted trainings in the systems they had already navigated. There was no pay for these trainings, and they were told that unless they completed them, they would get no classes in the future. However, completing them guaranteed nothing.

Quantity: I sent a bushel of these narratives to the admins. Quality: I chose four detailed accounts and had them read into the record at an online Board of Trustees meeting. These accounts were personal, intimate, professional, and very raw. I can't (even today) read them without tears. When they were read out loud by a staff member on a public YouTube channel, the College Chancellor and the former President of the Board of Trustees visibly stopped listening and turned their bodies toward other screens, which they started scrolling through. They were the suited white men shown on screen. The others (women and POC) at least pretended to attend, and some allowed their faces to register an emotional response.

It's a truism in organizing that if you set things up well, the boss will do your organizing for you, and this incident proved that rule. The blatant rudeness with which these comfortable men tuned out when adjuncts' lives became the focus that angered adjuncts who had previously felt that the school was doing its best under difficult circumstances. And this groundswell of anger increased activist energy on campus, which encouraged the bargaining team. They went from feeling fatalistic but committed to being passionately driven to defend the common good. They almost wanted to avenge the four stories their chancellor had disrespected. This drove them to hold out for pay for future trainings.

This powerful storytelling didn't change the fact that both our union density and our public sector bargaining position were weak, so the win was qualified. As an adjunct told me in a phone call the day she learned when training pay would be dispersed and what limits constrained it. She was appalled that she would have to wait till June 2022 for this year's pay. Further, she said the college had designed a mechanism for keeping track of who did what trainings that placed the burden of proof on the adjuncts and, my informant opined, made it likely that some adjuncts wouldn't even get this compensation in June. "It almost feels like they don't want us to get paid."

Rather than telling her that she had discovered the obvious, I used her conclusions as a starting point. I often tussle with adjuncts who believe that admins and tenure-track faculty are their allies, while the union and the adjuncts who align with it are alien, self-serving outsiders. In this case, "Alexis" had done some of this job for me so I could reinforce her own conclusions with stories and evidence: nope, the college doesn't want to pay out the training honorariums and will fight it every step of the way, but because of her colleagues' efforts, they'll have to. Further, getting there can be made less daunting if more people join the union, adding their strength to the bargaining efforts.

"Alexis" was unconvinced. Paying dues offends her—she says she would happily protest or strike, but she can't afford 2.5 percent. That one year's raise will more than cover this does not change her claim. She says she's from a union family, and she appreciates the work I do (which she understands is funded by the dues of other workers) but she will not pay into the union voluntarily—ever.

Her response is not rare; I hear it in my dreams and struggle to find effective responses. How people think about dues, and about unions, links to how we think about class. Though adjuncts frequently live below the poverty line, qualify for food stamps, and take on absurd numbers of classes simply to survive, many resist understanding themselves as working class or poor.

Fear is the defining condition of adjunct life. Typical contracts are by the semester, and management has no obligation to renew them. Unions do not materially change that fact. I wish profoundly that this wasn't true; the best I can do is be honest with adjuncts, telling them that I can't protect them, and adding that the only way to fight fear is to acknowledge it. Queer theory helps here— outsider status, if embraced and celebrated, enables a critique of the structures that generate it. Still, it's hard to own that you're scared all the time about everything. We build confidence through collective action, which begins with stories.

For adjuncts, this fear (which is hard to acknowledge, in any setting) is counteracted by a commitment to the job, which complicates class identification. "Betty," who has adjuncted since the 1980s initially to supplement her main job and now as retirement income, says that the college treats adjuncts "like missionaries or something. They think we're so passionate about teaching that any pay is just incidental." She calls bullshit on this way of thinking and tries to find ways to convince other adjuncts that loving their work, being good at it, and believing in the mission of higher education can coexist with being respected and paid accordingly. Full timers who invoke the missionary zeal of the classroom are paid a living wage, after all.

Confused class identification complicates organizing at many workplaces. When I ask blue-collar workers (steelworkers, truckers, and car mechanics are my main data set here) how they are perceived by the general population, one word recurs: dumb. Dirty, physical work that requires a uniform and limited education or training before employment is stigmatized as brainless and boring. Everyone who works these jobs knows that's inaccurate, and meant to perpetuate income inequality, racism, and the imaginary meritocracy that we call late capitalism (or, alternately, "America") yet the perception remains because of the work that it does.

Some of that work is to keep adjuncts and other members of the expanding professional precarious classes from identifying as workers.

Historically, the project of encouraging workers to imagine themselves apart— to prevent identification with other workers and other struggling people—has relied on racism, sexism, and elitism. Because the adjunct pool is overflowing with women, queer folks, immigrants, disabled people, and people of color, many find that identifying as educated professionals is what saves them from drowning. Disrespected by their employers and humiliated by their pay, adjuncts have to fight the urge to shed the taint of associating themselves with other adjuncts, and with other low-wage workers.

Sharing stories helps adjuncts see that identifying "up" with the professors they are supposed to pretend to be (without any of the supports that enable that role) serves the goals of management. The temptation to conceal or deny their shame is part and parcel of working-class life, and community is its antidote.

At one college's zoom session, an art adjunct I'll call "Marie" described her day to her colleagues. She has two school-aged kids doing remote school and another side job in addition to adjuncting at two colleges.

"Marie" teaches studio classes which run for two hours and forty minutes, with only a ten-minute break between them. This break used to be longer, but during COVID-19 the college shortened it to limit the time students mill around the halls engaging in dangerous viral behavior. Fine, but during that break, "Marie" does this routine: she uses the bathroom, walks to her car in the parking lot, sanitizes her hands, removes her mask, eats lunch and gulps water, replaces her mask, and returns to the classroom. After she runs through this routine, camping it up but also almost crying, another adjunct on the zoom fills in the punch line: "if you complain and ask for accommodation, like to be let into one of the now-empty faculty offices in your class building, next semester you'll find you have no classes, and they'll make up some excuse."

It's not an easy story to tell, and "Marie" manages the sting of that through humor. Both she and her listeners know the chilling fear that her self-mocking slapstick conceals, and our initial response is silence. If it were experienced alone, that silence would equal death. Shared in a collective, it can lead to power.

Both the professoriate and the adjunct pool have experienced demographic fluctuations. Joe Berry argues that adjunctification happened (in part) to prevent the tenure-track professoriate from changing. POC, women, and queers held an increasing proportion of the PhDs starting in the 1990s as a result of social changes incubating during the long 1960s. While academia might have struggled to confine straight, cis, white PhDs to a permanent underclass, it was easier to permit for these new workers. While it is true that tenured faculty are disproportionately male and adjuncts are disproportionately female, Berry's is a more historical argument: everyone in academe allowed adjunctification to occur because it enabled them to exclude the upstarts; people with PhDs could teach college, but their work was contingent, paid little, and gave them no power to shape the institutions in which they labored. Now that the labor pattern is established, its profitability is the sole justification it needs to spread.

A parallel shift occurred in organized labor. We hear that unions began to languish in the 1970s as neoliberal individualist rhetoric gained traction and bloated union hierarchies self-destructed. Lane Wyndham adds another ingredient to this mix: the working class began, in the 1970s, to include more women, immigrants, and people of color. It's in response to that shift that the government hamstrung unions, and that we let it. And unions were not quick to recognize these new workers and job types; they proceeded as though their old organizing model still pertains, thus losing at least thirty years of opportunity.

Therefore, the tools of the labor movement are weak and the task of organizing adjuncts pressing. "Carole" is a single mother who taught ten online classes in the spring semester of 2021. Ten. While her children were home attending online school. COVID-19 made this possible because scheduling ten sections in-person on five campuses would have required a miracle. But COVID-19 also made it scary, and by any definition, it's just brutal. If "Carole" can repeat this pattern in the fall semester, she will gross 48,000 dollars. She has no health insurance, no pension, and no job security.

"Tessa" is a retired school teacher whose pension does not cover the costs of supporting herself and her disabled mother. So she adjuncts. Most of her students are adults with jobs in patient care. They are taking a required course for the degree they hope will move them from the bottom rungs of health care work to something less dangerous and better paid. Their COVID-19 exposure is high. To minimize risk, the college put one cohort of these students in three consecutive classes, all in the same room with the same instructor. They are in a room together for three and a half hours, without breaks. This contains viral spread outside the circle of their class but increases it within. Students try to mask, but that's too long to go without water or a snickers bar.

But "Tessa" was told this was the only class available to her, and that she would be paid for nine credit hours if she agreed to do it. She's both grateful for the work and angry because her life is devalued by her own employer. Full-time faculty are teaching from home, which is why this class series is available to her, but which increases her isolation on campus.

I don't tell these stories just for shock or sympathy. Sharing them within and outside the adjunct collective is the first step in generating change. Before I started organizing I assumed it would mostly be about bargaining for better contracts and filing grievances—it would be fighting the boss. Almost two years in, I now know that was wrong; these tasks aren't even in my job description—other union employees handle them. My fight isn't with the boss, but with the adjuncts. I need them to believe that they deserve better and that they won't get that without a fight. Since they can't win that fight alone, they need to admit to other adjuncts, to their students, to me, to themselves the fear they live with and the pain they share.

Sour grapes doesn't mean that you secretly want someone else's beaux. It means that you recognize your powerlessness and you refuse to be blamed for it. Instead, you wear it proudly, share stories about what it means for you and use these stories to challenge received, often invisible, structures and norms. To change the world.

Part I

THE WORK OF QUEER CARE AND MUTUAL AID

Chapter 1

QUEER CARE WORK AS POSSIBILITY: HOW CARE SUSTAINS QUEER SURVIVAL IN THE ACADEMY

Della J. Winters and Holly Ningard

Universities in the United States are commonly assumed to be welcoming spaces for queer students, faculty, and staff. Such an assumption arises, in part, due to the perceived representation of queer folks and ideas on campus: through course offerings, programs/departments devoted to queer studies, and the existence of LGBTQ extracurricular clubs and centers. Historically, universities have served as sites of political and social organizing. A majority of Americans view campuses as politically progressive, further strengthening this assumption (Parker 2019). However, decades of dwindling public funds through austerity-based policies have resulted in the corporatization of higher education which challenges the existence of these departments, clubs, organizations, and centers (Smeltzer and Hearn 2015). Further, queer faculty members are rendered precarious in the context of the lack of job security and stagnant wages which follow the adjunctification of positions previously held by tenure-track faculty members. The systemic implementation of neoliberal policies not only impacts budgets, resources, and available job positions but for those who remain in the academy, their time—both at work and at home—also becomes a site of crisis (Meyerhoff, Johnson, and Braun 2011). Ongoing "scarcity" within the academy, then, amplifies the structural violence at the complex intersections of privilege and disadvantage (Crenshaw 1989), disproportionately harming queer scholars who are also poor, trans, disabled, Black, or brown (Harris and Nicolazzo 2017; Settles et al. 2022; Nadal 2019; Settles, Buchanan, and Dotson 2019; Johnson et al. 2018). We remain when we are unwelcome, unreadable, unseen. We remain.

Sites of education are essential to the state's biopolitical power of control wherein educators are expected to take on structural issues—poverty, unemployment, illness—as failures of personal responsibility rather than failures of the state (Puar 2017; Spade 2015; Morgensen 2010; Foucault 1982). The expansion of the carceral state explains the shift beyond the integration of neoliberal logics to the replication of surveillance and disciplinary techniques from punitive penal management within the academy (Beckett and Murakawa 2012; Gottschalk 2015; Wacquant 2010; Caputo-Levine 2022). The carceral logics at work in the academy require more than reform or redress, but rather, transformation. Speaking on the hurdles faced in academia by marginalized groups, we—as members of the undercommons—build upon the demands of Halberstam (2013):

> what black people, indigenous peoples, queers and poor people want, what we (the "we" who cohabit in the space of the undercommons) want, it is this— we cannot be satisfied with the recognition and acknowledgement generated by the very system that denies a) that anything was ever broken and b) that we deserved to be the broken part; so we refuse to ask for recognition and instead we want to take apart, dismantle, tear down the structure that, right now, limits our ability to find each other, to see beyond it and to access the places that we know lie outside its walls. (Halberstam 2013: 6)

Insight gained from Halbertstam is important for understanding that it is not enough to just add queer faculty to a department's ranks without meaningfully addressing the structural barriers which prevent them from succeeding in the academy. The limitations of visibility or inclusion alone do not address these barriers, which include persistent homophobia, epistemic exclusion, and research being disregarded as "mesearch," and journals which favor publishing mainstream scholarship that often excludes queer voices and perspectives. For now, we—those who are not welcomed or embedded in the academy and occupy the undercommons—remain in pursuit of a world where we do not need refuge, where finding those who are like us, is neither difficult nor dangerous.

We utilize and amplify care work, a praxis developed by and for sick and disabled queer, trans, Black, and brown people as world-building strategies to facilitate support and inclusion within the ableist world, as a framework from which the care work of queer kinship in the academy is explored. At the very foundation, the continued existence and visibility of queer people in the academy are important. Dalton (2016) and Ball (2016) argue the inclusion of queer scholars produces a disruption that, while not sufficient, is necessary for our continued survival. In this chapter, we discuss the promise and failure of the academy as a site of refuge for queer scholars and, as a consequence of the systemic violence in higher education, the integral role of queer studies and queer care work as mechanisms which enable the survival of queer scholars in the university. In an institution which continues to be hostile toward queer faculty and research, we set forth strategies for individuals to form community and connections which serve as resistance and resiliency.

The Academy: Site of Violence, Site of Refuge

To be a queer scholar in the US higher education system is to live within the contradictions of the academy as both a space of refuge and a space of violence. Universities are often discussed as safe havens for the creation and spread of ideas, particularly those which challenge common sense assumptions about the way our social worlds are structured and organized. The work done in universities is often coded as progressive. It is also assumed to be a place where queer faculty and students can be free to be themselves without prejudice, as supported by the existence of queer studies departments, LGBTQ centers, and more (Harney and Moten 2013).

In day-to-day life, universities contradict these assumptions both materially and epistemologically. Regarding the former, social policies regarding higher education in the 1980s reduced financial resources from many public institutions within the academy. The problem was exacerbated by the Great Recession (2007–9), following which state funding for public colleges and universities dropped significantly, and has yet to recover. Schools have raised tuition to compensate for the lack of state funding, but tuition raises have not alone been sufficient, resulting in a reduction of both quality and quantity of opportunities for students and faculty alike (Mitchell, Leachmen, and Masterson 2017). When cuts need to be made, resources for marginalized groups are often the first to be cut.

Queer faculty are also shaped by epistemic exclusion. In the transformative work *Poor Queer Studies*, Brim (2020a, 2020b) notes that scholars are trained and socialized to research mainstream topics in order to publish successfully in high-ranking journals. These journals, which carry the farthest reach, often do not include queer scholarship in favor of more mainstream topics. As such, faculty engaged with queer studies may see less recognition for their research work. Further, readers will be less likely to encounter their ideas unless they look to smaller, less often circulated niche journals. The erasure, marginalization, and oppression of particular knowledges and particular people serve to further exclude queer scholars. For scholars who are subject to this erasure and marginalization of the knowledges they possess, the mechanisms of this process are clear—top-ranked journals with high impact factors publish mainstream scholarship which often does not include queer identities or experiences. Access to journals is dependent upon university budgets, where scholars at underresourced institutions are systematically denied support for their scholarship and teaching. Finally, participation in professional conferences is often out of reach for precarious scholars, where underresourced universities provide no funding or insufficient funding to support registration and travel costs. Each of these serves to center mainstream scholarship which privileges straight, cisgender ways of knowing the world at the expense of the vantages and viewpoints offered by marginalized scholars.

Limited funding often results in faculty and departmental cuts, often to smaller programs such as African American Studies, Diversity Studies, and Gender and Sexuality Studies. Further changes have led to the adjunctification of higher education, where universities higher fewer tenure-track faculty in favor of contractual instructors. As the protections of tenure-track positions diminish, queer scholars experience tremendous precarity within a hierarchical system which has always been a site of contention with the state (Jaffe 2021). In spite of this tension between the university and the state, universities are always already sites which reproduce the settler-colonial, capitalist, and heteropatriarchal carceral state. The university thus renders its queer members what Farahani and Suruchi (2018) identify as the "(un)comfortable subject . . . [who] becomes more (un) comfortable by being (dis)acknowledged as one who does (not) fit and one who is (not) at home" (Farahani and Suruchi 2018: 93). The resulting sense of exclusion is felt in multiple ways: first, by a lack of representation among faculty ranks, and second, by epistemic exclusion whereby their research is underfunded and undervalued. Despite the presence of queer scholars, queer theorists, and queer studies, the contestations of queerness preclude queer people from becoming embedded and integrated within the university. Compounding the experience of the uncomfortable subject are the other interlocking, systemic oppressions within the academy, particularly white supremacy, ableism, and poverty.

With such barriers for scholars who are not embraced or embedded in the academy, Harney and Moten (2013) advocate for scholars to "steal" from the university when they argue

> [t]his is the only possible relationship to the American university today. This may be true of universities everywhere. It may have to be true for the university in general. But certainly, this much is true in the United States: it cannot be denied that the university is a place of refuge, and it cannot be accepted that the university is a place of enlightenment. In the face of these conditions one can only sneak into the university and steal what one can. (Harney and Moten 2013: 26)

The promise of the university is exemplified in this paradox: the university is simultaneously a site of violence and a site of refuge. For queer scholars, remaining in the academy is to be in desperate pursuit of refuge. We remain in the university as the knowledges we have are what is necessary for transformation, for refuge to be realized.

In this way, queerness serves as both epistemology and praxis. Queer experience transformed into queerness as a way of knowing enables the development and utilization of theories and methodologies which elucidate and embed queerness into bodies of knowledge which have excluded and derided queer knowledges. In rethinking praxis through the lens of queerness and queer epistemologies, queer praxis moves within, against, and beyond the hostile and marginalizing practices within universities and disciplines by demanding more than visibility and surface-level inclusions in pursuit of systems and knowledges built by and centering experiences and knowledges of the oppressed. By embracing, using, and transforming the knowledges which become the foundations and canons of disciplines, queer knowledges are essential for the creation of a new academic world.

What does it mean to survive in an academy that was not built for you? One way to conceptualize survival is "to live beyond. Beyond what? Beyond disasters, systemic and interpersonal. Beyond the halted breathing of our ancestors. Beyond yesterday. And five minutes ago. Beyond that" (Gumbs 2021: 3). Survival does not imply the violence many queer scholars experience is not brutal nor does survival imply naiveté—some of us will not survive the academy, literally and metaphorically. Instead, we are writing about survival as one way we, as queer scholars, have engaged in active harm reduction to continue to survive in the academy during this time. To move beyond individualistic, neoliberal solutions to systemic harms. To push for the academy to be transformed, for the university as a site of refuge to be actualized.

Queerness: Transformative Power of the Contested

Before discussing queer care work, we must define our use of "queer" as a concept, acknowledging the inability to provide a complete history of queer scholarship and queer theory and acknowledging the inherent contestations of the meaning of "queerness." Within the academy, queer scholars and queer theorists have used "queer" in nuanced and dynamic ways. Ball (2016) highlights the usage of "queer to signify people, groups, communities, attitudes, behaviors, practices, social phenomena, activism, scholarship, cultural artefacts and critiques, which are considered out of the ordinary, abnormal, or in some way unfamiliar" (Ball 2016: 23). Reclaiming "queer" from a pejorative homophobic and transphobic slur, the intentionally confounding, contested, and fluid nature of "queer" is embraced as it is precisely this inability to contain or confine "queer" that enables queerness to be a site of disruption and transformation.

"Queer" is often limited to a presumed "inclusive" term for the shifting acronym LGBTQIA+, which represents lesbian, gay, bisexual, trans, queer, intersex, and asexual people (Sedgewick 2011). The use of "queer" as a stand-in for same-sex sexualities, sexual minoritized people, or trans or nonbinary gender identities neglects the political history and nature of queer identity. As Ball (2016) argues, confining "queerness" to an extension of lesbian and gay scholarship and politics ignores queer scholarship and politics as *"reactions to* the limitations" of previous lesbian and gay movements, particularly limitations of political and intellectual work (Ball 2016: 26).

Queer life is, inevitably, political and, thus, connected and indebted to the work of queer activists and organizers. Much of the political work has focused on legal recognition and protection, particularly around desires to conform through same-sex marriage, state-recognized parenthood statuses, military enlistment, and religious inclusions (Sedgwick 2011). This pursuit of legibility and acceptance within mainstream legal and political systems has largely been devoid of nuance or inclusion. Trans people continue to be excluded within many lesbian, gay, bisexual, and queer frameworks, significantly limiting the power to dismantle current constructions of gender and sexuality. Trans scholars have focused on the experiences of trans people in medical systems (Joynt and Harsin Drager 2019), within specific academic disciplines (Walker, Valcore, Evans, and Stephens 2021), on college campuses (Beemyn 2019), and within the criminal legal system (Spade 2015).

Additionally, white people continue to be centered within the mainstream lesbian and gay political movements, ignoring the systemic oppression and discrimination of people of color (Duran 2019; Snorton 2017; Vaid 2012). As we discussed earlier, poor queer people have been marginalized within the queer community, while middle-class and wealthy queer people have maintained and promoted queer problems and solutions from their social positions. Duggan's (2003) concept of homonormativity is based on the adherence to and pursuit of white, middle-class values. Queerness as a practice critiques the limitations of homonormativity as the predominant framework of lesbian and gay political work, where the focus has been on visibility and inclusion by pursuing legal cases in the United States. Although LGBTQ+ people have achieved cultural visibility, rights to marriage equality, and limited legal protections, these victories have never centered the experiences of the most precarious LGBTQ+ people. As one example, in *Bostock v. Clayton County* (2020), the Supreme Court of the United States affirmed the protection of employees who are gay or trans against discrimination. This decision was celebrated as a significant victory, while, seemingly, ignoring that 2020 and 2021 have been the deadliest years for trans people in the United States.

In spite of the limitations of identity as an organizing concept, queer scholars and theorists recognize the real impact being queer has on the lived experience which becomes necessary in the pursuit of political work (Jagose 1996; Butler 1993). The use of queer here validates the existence of queer scholars and their work in the academy as having inherent worth and value, rather than being seen as subjects of study by others. The tensions within the concessions of using "queer" as a categorizing concept remain—"queer" as simply another category of identity limits the power of queerness as a site of contestation and deconstruction.

As queer studies emerged challenging the limiting binaries of gender (male/female), sexuality (heterosexuality/homosexuality), and static identity or experience, "queerness" became a generative space where new possibilities are created and identities and subjectivities could be questioned and deconstructed. For queer scholars and theorists, utilizing queerness in this way is often characterized as "queer work" or "queering"—defined as a "diverse, often conflicting set of interdisciplinary approaches to desire, subjectivity, identity, rationality, ethics, and norms" (Giffney 2009: 2). Thus, queer work enables queer scholars and theorists to move beyond the limitations of theory to utilize queerness as analysis and praxis. With the nature of "queer" being a space of contestation, "queer work is constantly troubling what we take for granted, and constantly refusing what is taken as solid" as the necessary requirements for queerness as a site of transformation (Ball 2016: 35). For us, queer work as practice allows us to challenge hegemonic power structures at the root, in hopes of creating new spaces not formed on the basis of exclusion.

The possibilities of transformation through the queer work of scholars and theorists do not mean this queer scholarship is without critique. As discussed earlier, the contentions and contestations of queerness are inevitable and necessary. The refusals of queer work challenge the canonical principles on which many scholars and theorists rely. Given "critical scholarship still remains, in many cases, quite marginalized, and activism is seen as outside the scope of proper academic work" (Ball 2016: 474), the challenges and rejections of queer work have been severe and swift. These reactionary responses from mainstream scholars and theorists obfuscate legitimate, concerning critiques, particularly for queer work which does not utilize an intersectional lens to analyze the interlocking experiences of oppression beyond gender and sexuality. Some queer work does not integrate the ways in which race, class, and disability interact with gender and sexuality, thus, prohibiting queer work from realizing the promise of deep transformation of our ways of thinking, knowing, and acting (Jagose 1996; Sullivan 2003; Duggan 2003).

With socioeconomic status inextricably woven into higher education in the United States through the selection of schools and fields of study, we argue Brim's (2020a) "prestige pipeline"—the systematic enshrinement of wealth, whiteness, and gender normativity at prestigious institutions—becomes an essential framework to move beyond queer representation as sufficient to combat queer precarity within the academy. Addressing queer precarity demands analysis of the material conditions from which we learn and build our scholarship. In a higher education system where a small number of scholars at elite institutions generate the works which become the celebrated and widely reproduced versions of queer studies, marginalized knowledges become systematically erased and silenced. In this way, we argue precarity emerges from the material conditions and disciplinary dominations of the elite within the university.

We integrate Berlant's (2007) conceptualization of slow death as a consequence of living in liminal, precarious, and unpredictable conditions. The current political moment exemplifies the structural violence for the queer precariat, who find themselves at the margins—economically and theoretically—in the United States. In the ongoing, systemic destruction of stable, sustaining occupational positions in the academy through decreasing of tenure-track jobs, increasing adjunctification of instruction and stifling wages, material conditions structure who and where the precariat can remain. Waves of state laws banning instruction on race, gender, and sexuality designed to silence marginalized voices further exacerbate the precariat through the lacking embeddedness of critical and intersectional perspectives. We argue, then, remaining in the academy for the precariat is made possible through networks of queer care work.

Queer Care Work: Contestation in Practice

In scholarship, care work is often discussed through gendered and neoliberal perspectives—specifically, the ways in which paid and unpaid care-based labor, such as child, elder, or kinship care, disproportionately impacts women and the ways in which care work develops and supports "good" neoliberal subjects whose work generates capital for the state (England 2005; Pavalko and Henderson 2006). We are, however, troubling this narrow definition of care work to a conceptualization of care work which enables us to survive the violence of the settler-colonial, capitalist, heteropatriarchal carceral state and to build new worlds based on care, pleasure, and liberation.

Queer care work relies upon a framework of mutual aid. Using Spade's (2020) description of mutual aid, we argue for a radical transformation of our communities by providing help, resources, and care for one another. Although subtle, understanding oneself as part of a collective requires us to move beyond care as a transactional practice—I care for you so you will care for me—but rather as a collaborative, radical practice of social solidarity. In other words, care work is a form of mutual aid, not charity work, which implies people with financial resources and/or state actors providing some form of support to poor people. As a result, charity limits who can receive help, the types of help available, and the constraints under which help can be received. Thus, charity work is a temporary fix not designed to disrupt or dismantle systems of violence. Queer care work, then, requires us to begin the process of reimagining and creating a new world—a world where we take care of one another—by embedding the knowledges of the most marginalized as our guiding frameworks.

Dean Spade (2020) defines mutual aid as "collective coordination to meet each other's needs, usually from an awareness that the systems we have in place are not going to meet them" (Spade 2020: 13). Not only will our current systems not meet our needs but far too often, these systems create and reproduce the forms of violence from which we are seeking reprieve. Although mutual aid is not a new concept, the effects of the COVID-19 pandemic brought mutual aid into the mainstream. Spade (2020) identifies three key elements of mutual aid: (1) mutual aid projects work to meet survival needs and build shared understanding about why people do not have what they need; (2) mutual aid projects mobilize people, expand solidarity, and build movements; and (3) mutual aid projects are participatory, solving problems through collective action rather than waiting for saviors. For us, queer care work utilizes the practices of mutual aid in the pursuit of social solidarity and liberation, not a transactional practice designed to produce and support queer scholars as academic "workers."

Throughout this chapter, we draw from and amplify the abolitionist scholarly and organizing work of Black, Indigenous, and women of color as the practices of care and collectivity are central to abolition: "Care: because 'care is the antidote to violence' (Saidiya Hartman). Collectivity: because 'everything worthwhile is done with others' (Moussa Kaba)" (Murakawa in Kaba 2021: 2). Although Kaba and Murakawa focus primarily on the abolition of the prison industrial complex, the principles of abolition provide a useful framework in our critical examination of what refusal, care, and collectivity might look like in the academy as abolitionist work is designed to build new worlds based on cooperation and mutual aid. Central to the work of abolitionists is building social solidarity within the community and engaging in chronic experimentation as the mechanism to build the worlds in which we want to live. Thus, we amplify through citation and teaching the disability justice work, developed by and for sick and disabled queer, trans, Black, and brown people as world-building strategies to facilitate support and inclusion within the ableist world, as one way to support and sustain those who are marginalized within the academy by integrating the transformative and liberatory possibilities of queerness and mutual aid into queer care work. Such possibilities include supporting each other emotionally, establishing writing groups, coauthoring publications, and sharing and collaborating on teaching materials. In helping others achieve teaching, research, and service goals, the community-building exercises mentioned previously lessen burnout and keep queer scholars in the field.

Leah Lakshmi Piepzna-Samarasinha, a queer disabled nonbinary femme writer, educator, and disability/transformative justice worker, started writing *Care Work: Dreaming of Disability Justice* (2018) "right after [they] quit the job at a giant corporate university that [they] had hoped would be an accessible way of making a living but ended up giving [them] pneumonia for three months" (Piepzna-Samarasinha 2018: 20). The irony of the significant influence of Piepzna-Samarasinha's work on this chapter about queer survival in the academy when the failure of the academy to provide refuge while subjecting them to systemic violence is not lost on us. However, it is precisely this disability justice work which is necessary for the transformation of the ablest structures of the academy. The commitment of disability justice to intersectional, anti-capitalist, collective, sustainability which centers the most impacted has a deep resonance with the transformative possibilities of queer work and mutual aid.

As an exemplar text by and for queer, disabled, people of color, Piepzna-Samarasinha's *Care Work* (2018) situates the experiences and knowledge so often silenced in queer studies as the foundational knowledge needed to move beyond survival into sustainable networks of care and refusal. Beginning with an overview of the principles of disability justice, Piepzna-Samarasinha integrates reflections, interviews, practical tips, and stories demonstrating a convergence of queer knowledges and queer praxis. We argue that if we want to transform our world through care work, we must follow those who have come before us and survived in systems designed to silence and exploit.

Conceptualizing of queer care work through care webs is designed to shift care work from an individual chore into collective care work. Emerging from the work of disability justice activists, organizers, and scholars, care webs challenge notions of families and focus on sustainable community practices. Care webs have often been a critical component of queer care work, particularly during times of crisis. Stories of queer care work through care webs during the height of the AIDS epidemic are of particular historical significance (Hawkeswood 1996). Despite historical celebrations of, and empirical support for, the power of queer care work, violence and suicide remain leading causes of death within the queer community, with isolation and homophobia cited as contributing factors (Cochran and Mays 2007; Hayes, Turner, and Coates 1992). Queer care work and care webs, then, are essential to survival within our current academy and to transformation of the knowledges and practices as we build new worlds together.

It is from this position we outline the ways in which institutional and personal resources can be shared through queer care work as a critical strategy for supporting queer survival. Many of the strategies here are designed to disrupt the embedded assumptions and practices which create and maintain capitalism and colonialism. Anti-capitalist and anti-colonial strategies are radically different than the way we are socialized to think and act, and therefore, many of us are not familiar with how to interact with others in this way. At the core of this queer care work are strong, collective social structures, which take a considerable amount of time to cultivate, do not resemble our structures, and likely, do not reflect the goals of the university as a hostile system. The work of supporting one another—with emotional support, childcare, help with day-to-day tasks, and academic support—is often not counted by end-of-year evaluations but is nonetheless important for survival. We will now turn our attention to several specific ideas and resources which can be utilized by queer folks in the academy to resist the hostile environment of the university. While these strategies are deeply rooted in long histories of mutual aid (Spade 2020), they represent both what has worked and what can possibly work to establish community in spaces which seek to isolate and alienate.

The work of care work is, indeed, work. We must resist the concepts we have learned from the dominant culture as the frameworks we default to out of habit. We must build the worlds which enable us to do more than just survive. We recognize and acknowledge the difficulties of being in "a capitalist, patriarchal, white supremacist culture that encourages us to compete, distrust, hoard, hide, [and] disconnect" (Spade 2020: 77). However, this is precisely what we must refuse to build a world that is liberatory for all. Establishing a strong, nonhierarchical structure with clear, intentional processes for making decisions, distributing care work, solving problems through collective action, and addressing harms and conflict which will arise within our care webs is essential. We argue queer care work can sustain the precariat in the academy through the development of care webs which challenge the hierarchical, competitive structures of academe to enable us to remain, resist, and reimagine.

Institutional Resources

Scholars at well-resourced research institutions often have access to resources that scholars at underresourced universities do not. The following examples are ways in which resources can be redistributed as a form of queer care work.

Downloading and sharing paywalled articles for activists, organizers, practitioners, and scholars who have been denied access. Peer-reviewed scholarships—particularly articles and academic books—are inaccessible and/or cost-prohibitive for anyone who is not at a well-resourced university. As one example, queer care work might include developing a system for requesting, finding, and distributing research to people who would not otherwise have access.

Sharing university resources for grant writing, teaching, research/scholarship. Activists, organizers, practitioners, and scholars at underresourced universities lack access and/or structural support to tacit information within the academy. Sharing resources provided by well-resourced universities to those outside of the academy and/or scholars at underresourced universities can help to support scholarly and political work.

Advocating for policies and practices which center the directly impacted. For less precarious members of the care web, it is essential to advocate for policies and practices which disproportionately harm the most marginalized. Challenging established, violent systems and advocating for policies and practices are critical harm reduction strategies which can provide some immediate relief for the most precarious.

Reviewing materials—job applications, grant proposals, manuscripts—before submission. Essential to the survival of the precariat in the academy is being given and utilizing the tacit knowledge of the university. One form of tacit knowledge is related to publishing and applying for jobs and grants. Those who have experience successfully obtaining grants, jobs, and publications can review materials as a way to redistribute their labor and experience while supporting the work of more precarious scholars.

Volunteering your expertise and labor to freedom schools, community organizers/ activists, or colleagues at underresourced institutions. Data and institutional prestige can be useful when developing and advocating for harm reduction strategies. Those at well-resourced institutions can use the cultural capital and resources of their institutions as a way to provide legitimacy and support for those who might not have access or legibility.

Personal Resources

Reconfiguring family and collectives queers the narrow frameworks and constructions of family and community. Working in pursuit of collective building through mutual aid can produce forms of queer care work which surpass the limitations of queerness as identity.

Building social solidarity within your community to identify needs and goals. Essential to determining issues which need to be addressed and developing solidarity to address identified needs is foundational to care work. Reconceptualizing our personal relationships as interdependent care webs requires a shift away from the highly individualistic US culture. It is through the creation of interdependent forms of social solidarity that we can distribute care work throughout the group.

Developing nonhierarchical social structures to address community needs and goals. In order to reject the structures which produce harm and violence, we must build solidarity through nonhierarchical care work. Developing care work which exists outside of hierarchical structures requires clear, established practices and structures within the community to ensure needs and goals are recognized and addressed.

Learning and sharing collective responses for conflict resolution. All collectives experience tension and conflict. Care webs can establish practices which normalize conflict and address tensions without resorting to carceral logics of policing, punishment, or retribution.

Providing transportation, physical care, childcare, or food. Establishing a care web which can address tangible needs while refusing an individualized model of care can distribute caretaking within the conditions established by the group. This provides members of the group with the support of care work with the agency of determining the ways in which this care work is given, distributed, and received.

Establishing a mutual aid fund. Developing methods of collecting and distributing economic resources through mutual aid is an excellent strategy to address financial needs which arise within the group. Not only does mutual aid address an immediate need but a financial support can alleviate the stress associated with financial needs.

The suggestions outlined earlier represent a glimpse into the possibilities of queer care work. Queerness, queer people, and queer knowledges survive in spite of systematic oppressions designed to erase, silence, and remove us from universities and systems that have never welcomed us. Queerness as a site of contention and contestation situates queer scholars, particularly queer scholars who are also poor, trans, disabled, Black, or brown, as visionaries who build worlds where we do not need refuge (Kaba and Murakawa 2021; Spade 2020; Harris and Nicolazzo 2017).

References

Ball, M. (2016), *Criminology and Queer Theory: Dangerous Bedfellows?*, London: Palgrave Macmillan.
Beckett, K. and N. Murakawa (2012), "Mapping the Shadow Carceral State: Toward an Institutionally Capacious Approach to Punishment," *Theoretical Criminology*, 16 (2): 221–44.
Beemyn, G. (2019), "Get over the Binary The Experiences of Nonbinary," in G. Beemyn (ed.), *Trans People in Higher Education*, 159–83, New York: State University of New York Press.
Brim, M. (2020a), "Poor Queer Studies: Class, Race, and the Field," *Journal of Homosexuality*, 67 (3): 398–416.
Brim, M. (2020b), *Poor Queer Studies*, Durham, NC: Duke University Press.
Butler, J. (1993), "Critically Queer," *GLQ: A Journal of Lesbian and Gay Studies*, 1 (1): 17–32.
Caputo-Levine, D. (2022), "Deconstructing the Hustle: Investigating the Meanings of Hustling Within the Carceral State," *Critical Criminology*, 30: 267–84.
Cochran, S. and V. Mays (2007), "Prevalence of Primary Mental Health Morbidity and Suicide Symptoms among Gay and Bisexual Men," in R Wolitski, et al. (eds.), *In Unequal Opportunity: Health Disparities Affecting Gay and Bisexual Men in the United States*, 97–120, Oxford: Oxford University Press.
Crenshaw, K. (1989), "Demarginalizing the Intersection of Race and Sex: A Black Feminist Critique of Antidiscrimination Doctrine, Feminist Theory and Antiracist Politics," *University of Chicago Legal Forum*, 1 (8): 139–67.
Dalton, D. (2016), "Reflections on the Emergence, Efficacy, and Value of Queer Criminology," in A Dwyer, et al. (eds.), *Queering Criminology*, 15–35, London: Palgrave Macmillan.
de Oliveira Andreotti, V., S. Stein, C. Ahenakew, and D. Hunt (2015), "Mapping Interpretations of Decolonization in the Context of Higher Education," *Decolonization: Indigeneity, Education and Society*, 4 (1): 21–40.

Duggan, L. (2003), *The Twilight of Equality? Neoliberalism, Cultural Politics, and the Attack on Democracy*, Boston: Beacon Press.
Duran, A. (2019), "Queer and of Color: A Systematic Literature Review on Queer Students of Color in Higher Education Scholarship," *Journal of Diversity in Higher Education*, 12 (4): 390–400.
England, P. (2005), "Emerging Theories of Care Work," *Annual Review of Sociology*, 31: 381–99.
Farahani, F. and S. Thapar-Björkert (2018), "The Racialised Knowledge Economy," in S. Khadka, et al. (eds.), *Narratives of Marginalized Identities in Higher Education*, 86–99, London: Routledge.
Foucault, M. (1982), "The Subject and Power," *Critical Inquiry*, 8 (Summer): 777–95.
Giffney, N. (2009), "Introduction: The 'q' Word," in N. Giffney and M. O'Rourke (eds.), *The Ashgate Research Companion to Queer Theory*, 1–13, Burlington: Ashgate Publishing.
Gottschalk, M. (2015), "Razing the Carceral State," *Social Justice*, 42 (2): 31–51.
Gumbs, A. (2021), "Forward," in E. Dixon and L. Piepzna-Samarasinha (eds.), *Beyond Survival: Strategies and Stories from the Transformative Justice Movement*, Chico, CA: AK Press.
Halberstam, J. (2013), "Forward," in S. Harney and F Moten (eds.), *The Undercommons: Fugitive Planning and Black Study*, London: Minor Compositions.
Harney, S. and F. Moten (2013), *The Undercommons: Fugitive Planning and Black Study*, London: Minor Compositions.
Harris, J.C. and Z. Nicolazzo (2017), "Navigating the Academic Borderlands as Multiracial and Trans* Faculty Members," *Critical Studies in Education*, 61 (2): 229–44.
Hawkeswood, W.G. (1996), *One of the Children*, Oakland: University of California Press.
Hays, R.B., H. Turner, and T.J. Coates (1992), "Social Support, AIDS-Related Symptoms, and Depression Among Gay Men," *Journal of Clinical Psychology*, 60 (3): 463–9.
Jaffe, S. (2021), *Work Won't Love You Back: How Devotion to Our Jobs Keeps Us Exploited, Exhausted, and Alone*, London: Hachette UK.
Jagose, A. (1996), *Queer Theory: An Introduction*, New York: New York University Press.
Johnson, J.M., G. Boss, C.G. Mwangi, and G.A. Garcia (2018), "Resisting, Rejecting, and Redefining Normative Pathways to the Professoriate: Faculty of Color in Higher Education," *The Urban Review*, 50: 630–47.
Joynt, C. and E. Harsin Drager (2019), "Condition Verified: On Photography, Trans Visibility, and Legacies of the Clinic," *Arts*, 8 (4): 150.
Kaba, M. and N. Murakawa (2021), *We Do this' til We Free Us: Abolitionist Organizing and Transforming Justice*, Chicago: Haymarket Books.
Meyerhoff, E., E. Johnson, and B. Braun (2011), "Time and the University," *ACME: An International Journal for Critical Geographies*, 10 (3): 483–507.
Mitchell, M., M. Leachman, and K. Masterson (2017), *A Lost Decade in Higher Education Funding: State Cuts Have Driven Up Tuition and Reduced Quality*. Center on Budget and Policy Priorities, Washington, D.C. Retrieved from https://www.cbpp.org/research/state-budget-and-tax/a-lost-decade-in-higher-education-funding
Morgensen, S.L. (2010), "Settler Homonationalism: Theorizing Settler Colonialism within Queer Modernities," *GLQ*, 16 (1–2): 105–31.
Nadal, K. (2019), "Queering and Browning the Pipeline for LGBTQ Faculty of Color in the Academy: The Formation of the LGBTQ Scholars of Color National Network," *Journal of Critical Thought and Praxis*, 8 (20): 1–19.

Parker, K. (2019), "The Growing Partisan Divide in Views of Higher Education," *Pew Research Center*. Available online: https://www.pewresearch.org/social-trends/2019/08/19/the-growing-partisan-divide-in-views-of-higher-education-2/ (accessed March 7, 2022).

Pavalko, E.K. and K.A. Henderson (2006), "Combining Care Work and Paid Work: Do Workplace Policies Make a Difference?," *Research on Aging*, 28 (3): 359–74.

Piepzna-Samarasinha, L.L. (2018), *Care Work: Dreaming Disability Justice*, Vancouver, BC: Arsenal Pulp Press.

Puar, J. (2017), *The Right to Maim*, Durham, NC: Duke University Press.

Rose, S. (2021), *Our Work is Everywhere: An Illustrated Oral History of Queer and Trans Resistance*, Vancouver, BC: Arsenal Pulp Press.

Sedgwick, E.K. (2011), *The Weather in Proust*, Durham, NC: Duke University Press.

Settles, I.H., N.T. Buchanan, and K. Dotson. (2019), "Scrutinized But Not Recognized: (In)visibility and Hypervisibility Experiences of Faculty of Color," *Journal of Vocational Behavior*, 113: 62–74.

Settles, I.H., M.K. Jones, N.T. Buchanan, and S.T. Brassel (2022), "Epistemic Exclusion of Women Faculty and Faculty of Color: Understanding Scholar(ly) Devaluation as a Predictor of Turnover Intentions," *Journal of Higher Education*, 93 (1): 31–55.

Smeltzer, S. and A. Hearn (2015), "Student Rights in an Age of Austerity? 'Security,' Freedom of Expression and the Neoliberal University," *Social Movement Studies*, 14 (3): 352–8.

Snorton, C.R. (2017), *Black on Both Sides: A Racial History of Trans Identity*, Minneapolis: University of Minnesota Press.

Spade, D. (2015), *Normal Life: Administrative Violence, Critical Trans Politics, and the Limits of Law*, Durham, NC: Duke University Press.

Spade, D. (2020), *Mutual Aid: Building Solidarity During This Crisis (and the Next)*, New York and London: Verso Books.

Sullivan, N. (2003), *A Critical Introduction to Queer Theory*, New York: New York University Press.

Vaid, U. (2012), *Irresistible Revolution: Confronting Race, Class and the Assumptions of Lesbian, Gay, Bisexual, and Transgender Politics*, New York: Magnus Books.

Wacquant, L. (2010), "Class, Race and Hyperincarceration in Revanchist America," *Daedalus*, 139 (3): 74–90.

Walker, A., J. Valcore, B. Evans, and A. Stephens (2021), "Experiences of Trans Scholars in Criminology and Criminal Justice," *Critical Criminology*, 29 (1): 37–56.

Chapter 2

REDISTRIBUTING RESOURCES BEYOND THE ACADEMY: A ROUNDTABLE DISCUSSION WITH THE DAVIDSON COMMUNITY FUND

Sanzari Aranyak, Katie Horowitz, Ashley Ip, Myka Johnson, Zach Neville, Isabel Padalecki, Margo Parker, Yara Quezada Marino, Jaelyn Taylor, Rahrah Taylor, and Emily Troutman (Davidson Community Fund)

Introduction

The Davidson Community Fund (DCF) was founded in June 2020 by a group of students at Davidson College, a small liberal arts institution near Charlotte, North Carolina. Davidson is consistently ranked in the nation's top fifteen liberal arts colleges as determined by *US News & World Report* and is arguably the premier liberal arts college in the Southeast (*The 10 Best Liberal Arts Colleges in America*, 2021). It serves roughly 2,000 undergraduates, 27 percent of whom are domestic students of color. As of 2021, Davidson had an endowment of $1.3 billion, a figure typical among elite liberal arts institutions in the United States (*Fast Facts*, 2021). In recent years, the college has begun to reckon with its historical origins in enslavement, including the domestic slave trade. Not only were the campus' first buildings constructed by enslaved people, but enslaved men, women, and children performed much of the domestic and manual labor on campus and in the homes of college administrators and trustees. The wealth of Davidson's founders and early trustees, which enabled the establishment of the school and allowed young white men to pursue higher education, was produced by enslaved people (Foxx et al. 2020).

DCF was conceived in response to emergencies resulting from houselessness, resource scarcity, and state violence during national uprisings for racial justice and the COVID-19 pandemic. It began as a project to encourage Davidson students to reflect on and redistribute their wealth to marginalized community members and quickly became a sustainable model for supporting Black trans femmes in the Charlotte area. DCF educates and crowdfunds primarily through Instagram and in coalition with well-funded student organizations and experienced community organizers. By extracting and redistributing the college community's wealth, DCF aims to support those in its network while also engaging students, alumni, and Davidson locals in direct action and radical systems of support.

In March 2021, college and community members of DCF assembled virtually to discuss the collective's past, present, and future. In the following we reflect on sustainable activism, shifting the crisis economy of mutual aid, transforming white guilt into redistribution of resources, building relationships across and beyond the academy, and resisting both the nonprofit industrial complex and the neoliberal university.

> KATIE: How did DCF get started? What inspired you to get involved with mutual aid and wealth extraction and redistribution? And how did you go about building trust with folks in the Charlotte community?
>
> ISABEL: When we started, we didn't know any of this was going to happen. It began as one very chaotic Instagram post, a wealth redistribution bingo, that targeted Davidson students and asked them to assess certain things they had access to because of wealth. For example, if you could pay full tuition, then you had to pay a certain amount of money, which we would distribute to marginalized people we were already in community with. We got thousands of dollars. So then other people joined, and that's when it became a group project.
>
> MARGO: When the COVID-19 crisis in the United States entered the spotlight and Davidson's campus closed, the Black Student Coalition began collecting canned goods and other food that people had in their dorm rooms. We connected with Ash Williams, an organizer in Charlotte, to find ways to redistribute food that was going to be wasted by people evacuating the campus. That's how I met Rahrah, who was doing mutual aid work in Charlotte.
>
> RAHRAH: When they reached out to me, a group of us were trapped in a hotel during the stay-at-home order at the beginning of the pandemic. I had not seen any of these people a day in my life. I didn't even know them. So for them to reach out and say, "Hey we can help. We're here to be by your side and stand with you and starve with you, be out here in the cold or be trapped in this hotel with you," that's what made us stick together and check in with each other as community.
>
> SANZARI: There were already strong mutual aid networks in Charlotte, which a couple of us Davidson students had got to know through events that Katie and other professors put on. When I was a freshman there was a symposium where Rah and Myka [Johnson] and a bunch of other organizers came to Davidson to give presentations on abolition and mutual aid, and that radicalized me and, I think, a lot of other people at this roundtable. It made us rethink our relationship to the institution as one of wealth extraction. We started to think of events we held as opportunities to get money to marginalized people in Charlotte. When almost all of us moved off campus due to COVID-19, it forced us to think about different modes of organizing and redistributing resources and building networks

virtually. That is why we made the bingo card post on June 2, 2020, which eventually led to us raising $40,000.

ASHLEY: The original team was Margo, Sanzari, and Isabel. They posted on Instagram asking anyone interested in joining the work to text them, and we held a meeting to find a long-term solution for all this money coming in.

YARA: Because of the pandemic, there were a lot of requests for emergency funding, and we had a lot of conversations about how to respect and not police the people we were redistributing funds to. For me this was really important faith work in terms of understanding how to build community and be there for people.

MYKA: I originally got involved with Davidson College through Katie and a former student, HD Mellin, who knew about our work from the Charlotte Uprising in 2016. We were organizing around people who got locked up after the police shootings of Keith Lamont Scott and Justin Carr.[1] We crowdsourced hundreds of thousands of dollars to fly people out to their court dates and get people rides and temporary shelter. So that was my introduction to mutual aid work and to the idea that when we talk about abolition, it's not just about getting people out of jail; it's about creating solutions to make sure jail is not an option—to make sure that the consequence of not having housing, food, and all the things we need to survive isn't jail.

We started doing a lot of abolition talks at Davidson about redistributing access and wealth and understanding your privilege. We were talking about raising money for bail and the crisis of Black trans people all over the world, specifically Black trans women, getting murdered and how hypervisible our deaths have become while the support for our lives is not.

From there, Sanzari reached out to me to talk about DCF. They needed help with navigating boundaries and how to tell people there's not enough money or that we need to cycle in another person because we've been supporting you for these months. These are really hard conversations to have because it's people we're talking to who are struggling or dealing with multiple crises throughout their life. It's very difficult to tell people no, and as someone who comes from a Black trans background, a very people-pleasing background, it took a long time for me to learn to set boundaries and say no because I was afraid of hurting someone's feelings. They may not respond well to me setting boundaries and telling the truth; however, that's not my responsibility, and it sets a standard of honesty that people will come to expect from me. I relayed that to Sanzari, and that's how I got connected with DCF.

KATIE: *What is DCF's model? How do you operate, and how did you go from having a Venmo full of money that you didn't know what to do with to where you are now?*

ASHLEY: Emily [Troutman] and I have a very elaborate spreadsheet in case the feds come for us! But originally through Rahrah and other organizers we connected with Black trans femmes in the Charlotte area and identified needs. We knew that a lot of money was coming in through the COVID-19 crisis, and we had a lot of access to Davidson alums at that point, because they really wanted to help current students.

Over the summer we did a lot of emergency fundraising. Sanzari would make these incredible graphics that listed the CashApp and Venmo, we would post them on our personal Instagrams, and once we had met the need I would send the community member the money through whichever platform was most accessible to them. But with that emergency fundraising came a lot of burnout and stress. We had a lot of talks about what counted as an emergency, whose emergency we post, and how much money we give each person. That summer we redistributed $20,000 or $30,000 just trying to get folks housed, food, and transportation. We were starting to gain a lot of traction on Instagram, and this is around the time that the George Floyd protests erupted, and all the white people were like, "I'm not racist! Here's my $20!" But at the end of summer we had come to this point where the semester was starting and we had to rethink things. So we took a break and restructured.

EMILY: We picked up a very different pace when we came back from our break. We did a lot of restructuring of our processes and organization, as well as some of our values and ideology. During that time we shifted to our new method of fundraising, which is a monthly recurring donation. We have people signed up to give amounts ranging from $5–50 a month. That's where we get 80–90 percent of our funding, and we distribute around $300–400 a month to each of our recipients.

ASHLEY: Our monthly sustainers are mostly Davidson students and alums. We're definitely trying to expand that, especially as we've seen such a decrease in one-time donations. But right now we do monthly distributions on the Sunday of the second-to-last full weekend of the month so that there's enough time for beginning-of-the-month expenses. We have eight people in our community that evenly distribute all the money to. We still post emergency graphics, but this allows for something stable for our community members. Since we switched to monthly distribution about six months ago, we've raised $16,500, which averages out to about $350 per person per month.

MARGO: Relationship building is really important to us. The eight community members are people who we were and are regularly in contact with. And then there were some folks who we were also regularly in contact with who, when we explained the new model, let us know that they did not want to be monthly recipients so that someone else could.

EMILY: This shift was instigated by the need for us to step back as school was starting. We couldn't continue with the breakneck pace we were going at over the summer. So we talked to some other people who had been doing work like this for a lot longer than us, and we realized we had to make it sustainable so that we didn't all burn out.

At the same time, we were having conversations about how we're not the arbiters of need. We can't make that decision because we don't have that shared experience. We're not in people's shoes, so it's not for us to decide whose need is more valid. And this was so hard because you want to fix every problem. You want to make sure everybody has money for rent and everything, but you can't. We had to acknowledge this, and then we had to take a step back and say, "Okay, how do we make it fair? How do we not give ourselves this power that we just don't deserve?" And that's how we landed on the monthly sustainers and monthly distribution system. It's a lot easier, and it takes the decision of whose need is more "deserving" out of our hands. Everybody gets equal funding, and though we're not meeting needs in the same way that we did over the summer, we are still confident that we're making an impact and keeping our values at the center of the work.

MARGO: Before this we weren't able to make any stable commitment to folks because the money was completely out of our hands. However much people sent us on an emergency basis was what we were able to redistribute. So even if we were able to make someone's entire rent in one day, then someone else would have an emergency that just needed a couple of hundred dollars and we wouldn't be able to make any dent at all. We've also recently seen an intense drop-off in individual one-time donations, which underscores the importance of the sustainer model.

SANZARI: A large part of how we figured out structures over the summer was through Tiz Giordano and Sharon Holland, two organizers in the Triangle Area who run the QTIPOC Survival Fund. Sharon is a professor at UNC, and both of them have been organizing for decades. They were the ones who told us about the monthly distribution system and about different ways of being in a community with people.

At the beginning of June, there were several crises that happened for DCF community members, and we had lots of conversations about boundaries, and I remember reaching out to Tiz for advice. So they were the ones who were like, "Y'all need to consolidate. You need to figure out what your role is here." Both Tiz and Sharon emphasized sustainable activism, so we decided to follow their monthly distribution structure. But the monthly sustainer model is something that we started doing in August 2020 and they have now started doing in January 2021. So there's this element of intergenerational organizing across North Carolina.

MARGO: And these conversations weren't just one-time things. They were continual. I think of everything I learned about flyers and fundraising on social media from Rahrah and Jayla [another DCF community member] and Myka. This idea of raising funds on Instagram wasn't something that we came up with. It was something that y'all had been doing long, long, long before we had even met. At the beginning this was just a way of amplifying the audience of people who would see these kinds of posts.

SANZARI: Yeah, it was really about making graphics that would appeal to white people so that they would see these posts that were already going around.

KATIE: *So Sanzari is in charge of graphics. Ashley and Emily do finances. I'm interested to know what everyone else's role is within DCF.*

ISABEL: We came up with these roles during our restructuring break. We were trying to find a balance between avoiding hierarchy but still having a structure that empowered each of us to use our own skill sets. Jaelyn [Taylor] and I are "Admin Bros" [laughs], so we schedule meetings, set agendas, take notes, and keep things on track. But in addition to individual roles, we also have committees with several people each, including Fratergy, which is our campus outreach/frat wealth extraction strategy group. And then I was also recently part of the Onboarding committee because in the last week we brought on four new members to alleviate the workload and make DCF more sustainable long-term.

JAELYN: As Isabel mentioned, I'm an Admin Bro, and I'm also on Fratergy, mostly because I have quite a few connections on campus. I serve on the executive boards of several student organizations, so I have this in. And that's what this committee is about: getting the in, getting the money, period. And then the last committee is Direct Communications, which is the heart of it all. They're the folks who stay in contact with our community members and update us on what graphics need to get pushed out, who's in need, and what we need to be staying up to date on.

ZACH: I'm on a couple committees, but I focus mainly on Direct Communications. I talk with our community members, generally over our Google Voice number and sometimes over Facebook Messenger, depending on what's easiest for them. I'm also on Fratergy, and I was involved in the Onboarding committee too.

MARGO: Zach is on every committee. Basically everything that we just said about burnout and specialization of roles does not apply to him.

SANZARI: [laughing] We love Zach! Our token white man! He takes on so much labor, and we are so grateful.

MARGO: I'm also on Direct Communications. Like Zach said, we get to talk to our community members all the time, and we also answer Instagram DMs. It's a lot of fun.

YARA: "Frat Bro" is the title that I have been given because I'm the one in the group with both frat connections and a lot of patience for talking to white men, especially those in white fraternities on campus. My role is to use those relationships to build connections. Over the summer, a bunch of Fiji [Phi Gamma Delta] guys were getting their dues refunded due to the pandemic, and we were able to get them to donate a bunch of that money to us. And we've been planning events with other Greek organizations and building these connections with people on campus who we know have power and money.

RAHRAH: My role is if y'all need to reach out to any Black trans girls, you reach out to me first because they would trust me more. Sometimes people don't feel comfortable with giving a white person their address, so I'm another Black femme who looks like them and can use my body to protect them. Or money gets donated, but some of the girls don't even have a CashApp card because they get robbed or they lose their purses. So I use my credit card to help support the girls. Y'all send me the coin and all the girls get hotel rooms and food to eat.

SANZARI: Emily and I are the "Canva Gods,"[2] and I also do Fratergy and Onboarding. When the George Floyd protests started in May 2020, there was this huge transition from on-campus student organizing to organizing in larger communities. One of the areas where I had expertise was making flyers for campus groups. Canva has been such an important tool for fundraising because it allows for very easy graphic design. There's been a lot of thought put into fundraising through the Instagram square and slideshow. We learned most of what we know about online fundraising from Myka and Rahrah and other Black trans femmes who've been doing this stuff in Charlotte for ages. I just brought some Canva expertise to the table.

EMILY: Something that's really important to acknowledge in social media fundraising is the anti-Blackness of people being way more willing to trust a graphic with DCF's Venmo on it than one with a community member's personal CashApp or Venmo. Racism is inherent in how people process Instagram fundraisers. You have to recognize the prejudice that people have and how that's made its way into who people are willing to trust, which is so messed up. But recognizing that has allowed us to cater posts to our audience so we can raise as much money as possible.

MARGO: Rahrah, would you mind talking about what it's like fundraising on Facebook? You have a lot more expertise doing that because DCF doesn't fundraise on Facebook.

RAHRAH: I make posts for the Black trans femmes that are homeless or need food or need protection, because a lot of them are getting attacked nowadays. Some of them don't even have access to credit cards, because you have to get CashApp connected to a card to access the money, and some of them don't have that. So when I come across some of the girls, I want to have at least a couple of hundreds on me so I can bless them.

Before I even started fundraising, I've always been viral on Facebook for posting funny statuses. The way I used to do that was I would make groups and add everybody on my friends' list to that group. Since I'm not friends with most of y'all's friends on Facebook, starting a group would be good, because I can make you guys an admin of that group, and then you can add your friends and we can start sharing donation flyers and fundraisers.

SANZARI: Something DCF does very specifically is fundraising on Instagram to a slightly different audience, and I think that's what was helpful for us in raising so much money: catering to a white student audience and taking graphics from Facebook and putting them on Instagram for people to share in very different circles.

KATIE: I'm interested in this theme of making people feel like they're part of something special, either through forming groups on Facebook or making them part of this sustainers club or framing an ask around what will appeal to them rhetorically. It seems like that's also the motivation behind Fratergy. How do you convince folks who wouldn't necessarily be the most obvious allies to get on board?

ZACH: We had a conversation recently that was very helpful in framing this. We listed organizations that we work with in any capacity on campus and thought of them in one of two ways. One was an extractive way: these are not people we are in coalition with, but they have a lot of social and financial capital, and the purpose of the Davidson Community Fund is to extract and redistribute that wealth. And then there were some affinity groups that we wanted to be more in coalition with, and though that still involves wealth extraction, I think that that differentiation helps because all the Greek organizations fell under the extractive category.

During summer 2020, there was a lot of pressure on these white, wealthy organizations to prove themselves, usually in a pretty superficial way, but we wanted to capitalize on that and offer ourselves up like, "Hey, we can give a presentation on community care and mutual aid, and with relatively little labor you can give us money and we'll talk to you about this stuff that you want to look interested in." So that is how we've understood our relationship to Greek life.

JAELYN: It took a lot of humbling and a lot of self-reflection to realize that talking to frats is a necessary evil. We've had so many conversations about this as a group, which is why I love the dynamic we have between us. We check each other in a lot of different ways when it comes to capacity or ego and making sure that we are not centering ourselves in this work.

ISABEL: And it hasn't worked out for every group we've tried to work with. There are some groups who aren't down to let us take their money and redistribute it, and I think there's necessarily a process of trial and error to figure out who you can and can't trust. We see ourselves as starting a process of figuring out where we can make inroads on campus so that people who do this work in the future can use the knowledge we've accrued.

KATIE: I think that's a part of all organizing. Sometimes you just have to take the risk and hope that it works out, and then if it doesn't you regroup and you try something different. Are there any other specific challenges that you've faced in your work as a collective, and how have you navigated them?

ASHLEY: We had a member who worked with us over the summer, and there were roles defined and expectations that we had decided as a group that we would all meet. This person didn't meet them, and there was some harm done. We had to have a very honest conversation, and it was challenging because we have this trust between all of us as students. We put full trust in each other to make sure that these roles are executed, and after that meeting, I was proud of how honest everyone was in naming the hurt that this person had caused and acknowledging how truth is so important in the work we do.

SANZARI: This person was one of the people who started DCF, and what happened with them exemplifies a lot of conversations and struggles that we have had to work through: burnout and thinking that we can solve every problem, figuring out how to deal with ego in organizing, talking about privilege, talking about where exactly we fit into the Charlotte community and where we don't. What does it mean to work with people that you're friends with, and what does it mean to become friends with people that you work with? How can we hold each other accountable, and what does being in a community with each other mean? And that's what that conversation ended up being, and that person ended up leaving.

JAELYN: I'll also throw in that it's been a challenge that I haven't seen y'all. Since I'm taking classes remotely rather than on campus, I have yet to meet Zach and Emily in person, and I have never met any of our community members in person. This is the first I've seen Rah and Myka face to face! For me, as someone who's pretty extroverted, that hurts. I don't want to get all emotional, but we're talking about our growth, and something we've had to navigate through is keeping ourselves sane in the midst of it. The Admin Bros try to schedule a fun night every now and then where we just mess around and remember the fact that we are college students. We're nineteen, twenty, twenty-one years old, doing some pretty hardcore shit. And we have to remind ourselves that it's okay to be that age and not have to shoulder it all.

KATIE: *I really appreciate the emotional depth of this conversation. It's easy to intellectualize this stuff, but it's also your life, and it's emotional work. I don't know if this was a challenging step in your development as an organization, but how did you decide not to become formally chartered as a student organization? And how might this relate to conversations community organizations in Charlotte have had about resisting incorporation as nonprofits?*

ISABEL: In the beginning, we were using the Davidson Young Democratic Socialists of America Instagram account to post fundraisers. And even before we formally decided to move away from that, it caused us problems. I got angry emails about using school money to buy a loaf of bread for someone who didn't go to Davidson. There are many strict rules and hyper-surveillance of how student organizations use funds, so ultimately it's just logical not to be chartered and instead use connections to those who are.

ASHLEY: I'm grateful for the student organizations who have been willing to partner with us. Especially in the time of COVID-19 where in-person events can't be held as normal, a lot of these student organizations have money, and they've gotten in touch with us and been like, "Who in the Charlotte area can we ask to present on Zoom so we can funnel money to them?"

But the college does this thing where they don't actually help certain organizations yet will publicize the hell out of them just to flex. And I'm sure once we graduate, they'll say, "Look what our students did!" And that's another reason why we strictly say we're not affiliated with Davidson College because they haven't done anything for us really.

MARGO: When we were making these decisions, a lot of our thinking came from what we learned from Myka and Rah and glo [merriweather, a Charlotte community organizer] about their experiences with the nonprofit industrial complex. We were thinking about the way that Davidson positions itself as an institution of social progress but is built entirely on stolen land and stolen wealth that it continues to hoard to this day.

EMILY: Eventually we got to this point where a lot of money had been passing through our Venmo, and we wondered, "Is the government going to do something about this?" So we looked into 501c3 status to protect us because we could get audited and our financial aid could be affected. We know many wonderful organizations that do have this status, and they use it to protect and support their activity. But any time you're "nonprofit-izing," you're moving toward the nonprofit industrial complex, which has this very high barrier to access. It forces you to look at people and ask, "Are you deserving of our help?" And we wanted to stay away from that because, again, we're not the arbiters of need.

For a long time I was lobbying pretty heavily for becoming a 501c3 because of our position in the community. We're at a school that has access to a lot of people who are looking for those tax write-offs on their donations. So it could potentially get wealthy alumni and parents to donate larger sums of money if it's tax deductible. We did our due diligence on the idea. We met with a lawyer and talked about what that would look like, what are the benefits. But at the end of the day we decided that the structure that works best is doing this all through Venmo. No government documentation, just spreadsheets. At the end of the day, our priority is keeping our support low barrier, keeping it easy for community members to access. You don't need an address to get support from us—how messed up is it that so many places require that? So many organizations that are trying to help people who are disadvantaged have absurdly high expectations. That's why we're glad that we've gone the route of having no school affiliation, no government status because it allows us to keep our help accessible.

2. Redistributing Resources Beyond the Academy

MYKA: I think nonprofits can play a specific role in housing funding without tax restrictions, not having to worry about people getting singled out like with Venmo or CashApp. Unfortunately, the restriction of nonprofits is that they work in the same capitalistic anti-Black model that extracts from communities and moves performatively, saying they're doing all these things to get more funding but then not actually redistributing the money. Now there are nonprofits that actually are invested in redistribution.
But it's few and far between. It's not the standard model. And even when nonprofits are anti-white supremacist, they can't move quickly. If you need funds now, you're gonna have to wait. You have to fill out a form and wait three to five business days to get approved. But in terms of sustainability, nonprofits can always hit up grants [which non-501c3 mutual aid orgs are usually excluded from]. So I think nonprofits have a role to play until we can phase them out. Because we won't get saved through nonprofits. We will get saved through the work that DCF is doing, and the work that many communities are doing around mutual aid. Not through institutions, but through relationship building and through community.

KATIE: I really appreciate this emerging description of the nimbleness and agility of nonincorporated collectives that can move outside of and in between systems. You can still partner with organizations that are formally chartered or have 501c3 status, but you can get people's needs met quicker. I also want to acknowledge that DCF has moved away from calling itself a mutual aid organization to using the term wealth extraction. What was behind that shift in language?

ZACH: We conceive of mutual aid as a radical community-oriented and operated care program. We got to having conversations about our positionality as college students who are geographically and positionally distanced from a lot of our community members and whether it was fair to call what we were doing mutual aid. Did that imply that we were part of a community that we couldn't really claim? When we looked at our work, which was focused around taking money out of Davidson and redistributing it, wealth extraction was not only a more accurate term but a fairer and more honest term. Mutual aid has a meaning, and we didn't want to claim a political practice that we weren't really engaging in.

JAELYN: Margo sent us readings on mutual aid, and we did our homework on this one. We wanted to be as accurate as we could in defining ourselves, and at that point in time, we were barely even in community with each other. We had only been working together for a couple of months. We were still forming friendships among ourselves, so how could we say we were in community with the folks we just redistributed money to? As we mature as a collective, that definition could change. We could become more of a mutual aid organization that is truly in community with its members. And if that day comes it'll be so beautiful to see it come full circle.

YARA: We've also been intentional about navigating the tension between what will appeal to people and the integrity of our organization. In the summer of 2020, the term mutual aid was being thrown around everywhere, and people didn't know what the hell it meant, but we were like, "Okay, if we can capitalize on this and get people housed and get people fed, we'll do it." But then we came to the point where we decided to push people to not just feel good about giving money but to actually think critically about why they are giving this money and their role in this broader system of capitalism.

KATIE: Since part of what the volume we're contributing to is about is queering sharing, why is it important for students and scholars of queer studies specifically to actively redistribute wealth to multiply marginalized LGBTQ+ folks outside of the university?

ISABEL: Part of what has challenged us is that we're only here for four years. So it's important for students to take charge of this work during those four years because we're never going to have access to this kind of institutional wealth again. But I also think we are creating a network of sharing that will continue after we leave. That's why we've focused so much on onboarding new members: to create larger pipelines through which money is leaving Davidson even after we graduate.

JAELYN: I also want to acknowledge that we came together as a collective because a lot of us share queer or BIPOC identities, and sharing is just ingrained within those communities. It's intrinsic. I'm not a scholar of queer studies, but I certainly engage in the praxis in my everyday life, and a lot of this just feels natural. It's hard. It's taxing. But I don't ever really question why I'm doing what I'm doing. There is a historical practice of sharing within queer and BIPOC communities, and we are simply an extension of that. We're an iteration of a story so long told. So as we learn from Myka and Rah and Ash and glo about their sharing practices, we're also making our own.

MYKA: I want to offer that it's important to acknowledge when taking queer studies or even naming yourself as queer that there are a lot of queer and trans people who are still very much aligned with anti-Black sentiments. Something that another Black trans femme I'm in community with said is, "I don't just need you to be queer in your expression and your identity. I need you to be queer politically." Your praxis needs to align with the things that you say. Because if you're queer, you'll understand why police, prisons, and detention centers don't serve us. You'll understand why borders don't serve us. You'll begin to connect all the different ways that white supremacy has systematically and socially and intrinsically shown up in how we talk to each other, how we relate to each other, how we are in community with each other. It's more than just the knowledge. It's a question of what you do with it. A queer politic lies in actions and self-reflection and critical thought and collectivity.

ASHLEY: I think about how often Davidson students can be so radical in the classroom, but when it comes down to it, they're really not. I think about how a lot of people in Charlotte like Myka and Rahrah and Ash and glo have been doing this work for years, and it's taken this long for Davidson to really tap in. We have millions of dollars at Davidson, and it makes no sense that it's taken so long for this money to be redistributed to folks in Charlotte.

ZACH: I want to add that that bingo graphic was the beginning of my political radicalization. Before that, it was still very abstract. There was no introspection about how I practiced the cool ideas I was being exposed to. And I have DCF to thank for being very explicit that you need to have a politic of praxis and not just intellectualized classroom discussions, which are helpful sometimes but don't do the work of redistribution.

SANZARI: Something that's come up in a lot of conversations we've had is this idea from Stefano Harney and Fred Moten that "the only possible relationship to the university today is a criminal one" (2013: 26). The only relationship you should have to the institution is stealing from it. Otherwise, what the fuck are you doing?

MARGO: We're trying to think of ways in which our relationship to Davidson can destroy it piece by piece.

KATIE: What suggestions do you have for students at other colleges and universities who might want to start a wealth extraction network of their own?

SANZARI: Find out what people are already doing in the community that you're in and find out what your niche is. Our niche is wealth extraction. We do a very specific thing. So don't have an ego about it. Find out who your organizing elders are, who have been doing the work and laying the foundation, and build on that.

MARGO: And part of that is understanding the history of your institution. Your college or university didn't just appear one day. All of these institutions are built on stolen wealth and histories of extraction, and Davidson's relationship to the greater Charlotte community and to Black and Indigenous people in Charlotte is still extractive. You have to hold that knowledge in everything you do.

EMILY: Something I've wrestled with is making sure you're participating from a place of care and love for community rather than hate and anger. You hear about all the awful stuff that your university has done and that our institutions have done in this country, and the knee jerk is sometimes anger. And I'm not saying that anger against the institution is invalid. But especially for people like me who come from privileged backgrounds, focusing on care is so critical because care is what keeps us going. You have to do this because you love your community and not just because you hate your institution.

JAELYN: Whatever you're gonna do, it does not have to look like what we've done. We don't call ourselves the model or the rule book. We did what felt natural to us with the tools we had at our disposal to best serve the folks that we are committed to. But on your campus it can look like being a more vocal supporter of the affinity groups and the leaders on campus who are already doing the work. And if you are that leader, know that you don't have to do everything. Make sure you know what you're getting yourself into because it's work. It's emotional labor, it's mental labor, it's sometimes physical labor. Know the stakes and be honest with those that you're in community with about what you can and can't handle.

ASHLEY: Know that no one's going to protect you. The government doesn't care about you. The only people that care about you are your community. And you can't go in there with an ego because you're one person. If it could've been fixed by one person, it already would have been.

YARA: Decenter yourself. Even with the best of intentions, we found ourselves thinking we could pay everyone's rent or make sure everyone was fed, and there was a lot of gentle confrontation that had to happen within our group to realize we cannot fix everything. Homing in on our gifts was a game changer for us. Sanzari is a Canva god and so they make these beautiful graphics that people respond to. If I made the graphics, no one would donate money. But Sanzari probably is not going to talk to these white men, so I'll talk to the white men. And whoever's trying to start a chapter might have completely different gifts, and that's okay. That's the beauty of it.

MYKA: There's no one way to do things. When I first got into organizing, I was just putting on hats and roles because they needed to get done instead of figuring out what was my niche, what were my passions. Those are the things that sustain you because it's not hard to come back to the things you're drawn to. But when you're continuously doing things that are not aligned with who you are, it's going to get extractive. You're going to burn out. Go back to things that fill your cup. What are you passionate about? I promise the movement has a place for it.

References

Fast Facts (2021), Davidson. Available online: https://www.davidson.edu/about/fast-facts (accessed March 24, 2022).

Foxx, A.R., B. Andrews, M. Arellano, J. Blodgett, L. Bowles, R. Boyce, M. Brandon, B.P. McCrae, S. Rahman, T. Saintsing, J. Shepherd-Smith, J. Stovall, and R. Stremlau (2020), *Report from the Commission on Race and Slavery*, Davidson, August 19. Available online: https://www.davidson.edu/about/commission-race-and-slavery (accessed March 24, 2022).

Harney, S. and F. Moten (2013), *The Undercommons: Fugitive Planning and Black Study*, New York: Minor Compositions.

The 10 Best Liberal Arts Colleges in America. (2021), US News & World Report, September 12. Available online: https://www.usnews.com/best-colleges/rankings/national-liberal-arts-colleges (accessed March 24, 2022).

Chapter 3

QUEERING COMPLEX CONVERSATIONS: SHARING
ACADEMIC EXPERIENCES DURING THE PANDEMIC

Fen Kennedy

In the summer of 2020 educators around the world grappled with how they could return to teaching in the middle of a global pandemic and civil rights crisis. As a nonbinary academic teaching at a US institution, I wanted to queer the conversations around the pandemic and so I curated a weekly conversation series *How Do We Go Forward? How Do We Go Back?*[1] held in real-time and later uploaded online. The title of this series was inspired by the contradictory needs I witnessed in my academic community: How could we go back to in-person teaching while keeping ourselves and our students safe? How could we go forward together in the face of the civil rights violations being enacted on marginalized peoples? How could we go back differently, navigating and even casting off normative processes and structural oppression? How could we go forward as leaders, even as we dealt with isolation, grief, and burnout? Each week I brought together two guests from various areas of academia, including graduate and undergraduate students, department chairs, administrators, adjuncts, academic celebrities, and those who'd abandoned academia altogether. After a moderated conversation we opened to a discussion with the audience.

Facilitating a productive conversation under these circumstances—virtually, publicly, and across large differentials of power and privilege—is the challenge that forms the heart of this chapter. In curating the conversations, setting up the space, moderating discussions etc., I was guided by explicitly queer principles of access and equity. As you will see, following these principles resulted in a "queer sharing" of vulnerability and honesty, allowing for a complex conversation around the intersections of individual and institutionalized experiences and needs. Guests were encouraged to speak freely to each other while aware of extant power differentials and external authority, to value the honesty of complexity and individual need over the push for an easy or unifying solution, to accept their own vulnerability, and that of those around them, into our calculations of what going forward or backward might look like, and to remember that any backward or forward action must also entail a conscious movement away from the inequities of past methods and systems. Guided by these principles, this chapter shares major takeaways from the conversation series, centered on questions that remain central to academic life today: How can we go forward? How can we go back?

To Speak Freely

Academia is a world of hierarchies, and of power-based behaviors that can stifle the free expression of social and political opinion and that can also stop students and staff from speaking up or intervening in oppressive situations. As an out, transgender, nonbinary teacher I am no stranger to speaking out. Every time I introduce myself with they/them pronouns, for example, I challenge the cisgender normativity of my audience, or whoever I am speaking with, and I challenge them to confront their ideas about the reality of my gender identity. For generations queer people have been silenced in the expression of their identities: to keep their lives behind bedroom doors, to don't ask don't tell, and to pass. It was, therefore, critically important to me to make space for disempowered voices in this conversation series, and in particular to give undergraduates the same space and attention that I gave to administrators, professors, and department leaders.

To facilitate a conversation in which speaking freely was possibly, I had to somewhat counter-intuitively remain alert to, and be transparent about, silencing factors in the space. My guests knew they were being recorded, and that their interviews would be published. To support them, I allowed them to set boundaries on the space, and on me: were there questions they did not want to be asked, or topics they wanted to avoid? Did they want me to give them prompt questions? How should I signal the need to wrap up? As I grew more experienced as a moderator, I also adopted an explicit anti-harassment announcement at the beginning of my talks, stating that due to limited time I would adopt a policy of ejection first and restorative discussion later, rather than allowing the conversation to be derailed by harmful behaviors, or forcing guests to defend themselves. Rather than stifling disagreement, I believe that this policy—which I never had to resort to—created a container for people to hold and express conflicting opinions while being clear about the kinds of safety marginalized voices were entitled to in the space.

The success of this principle is best illustrated by two conversations from the series: "Undergraduate Students," and "Writers and Publishers." The speakers in each of these conversations brought up many common themes and advocated for the need to speak freely. Undergraduates need to be heard by their professors, and by each other. Writers need their work to be valued outside of the traditional structures of tenure. On a more personal level, open and honest discussions of what life is really like for individuals can help people overcome their sensations of selfishness, guilt, and shame at feeling bad, or able to do less. When we can speak freely to those in power, and our communities, it is vital that we are honest, and that we respect the richness and complexity of individual situations if we truly want to invest in social justice and change.

As a commitment to speaking freely I draw on Chandler and Emilia's accounts: Chandler Davis and Emilia Stuart were, at the time of their conversation, both undergraduate dance students at the University of Alabama. They spoke to a large audience that included freelance dancers, academics, and their own faculty, about their experiences over the summer and their perspectives on returning to their program. Both students spoke openly about the need for those in power over them to shift in their attitudes and behavior, even as some of those individuals were in the room as guests. Chandler, who was a rising Junior at the time of our conversation, remarked how even the decision about whether or not to go back to school involved claiming her own opinions and authority, as adults around her left gaps in how she was supported:

> It's challenging when the guidance isn't coming from above . . . I feel like I'm not being told what to do with my time and choices, I'm in a family where I'm an adult person, so my opinions and beliefs are weighed into the conversation . . . If I were a little kid right now I could follow what my dad said and trust that they were adults and they knew what they were doing. Chandler wished there was a clear "right answer"—should she return to campus or take classes online? How should she talk to roommates who went out to socialize? What would she do if a travel ban left her stuck on campus and unable to return home? Emilia added: Even if we make all the right choices, the people in the bigger picture might not . . . I don't necessarily trust that the Dean, who's thinking of football, can make the right choices in terms of supporting the arts.[2]

Perhaps because of the additional responsibilities placed on these students, a strong theme that came out in the conversation was the idea of selfishness: feeling selfish for staying safe rather than socializing, feeling selfish for wanting to go out, feeling selfish for grieving over lost opportunities. Just as so many queer children describe their first experiences of Tumblr or other queer spaces as a sense of liberation from shame—"There are people out there who are like me!"—Emilia and Chandler's realization that another person shared their feelings helped reduce this sense of shame: "I didn't know that someone was feeling the same way until I came into this dialogue where I could talk about just my concerns." As Emilia described elements of the senior experience she would miss, and the guilt she felt for valuing those experiences during a pandemic, Chandler stepped in to reassure her: "You don't have to feel bad for valuing and wanting something, that is significant, even if it's insignificant to everybody else." If students are being asked to make life or death decisions about their own well-being, and community well-being, then it is important that we also validate their own assessments of what is valuable and what they need to grieve over. Educators and adults must break down those cultural currents that shame others into hiding their feelings and desires.

One benefit of the increased accountability placed on students was an increased sense of authority in their own opinions, especially around issues of social justice. Chandler, a young Black woman anticipating future conversations about Black Lives Matter and the Civil Rights Movement said: "I'm going to tell you what's right. I'm going to have an open dialogue with you. I'm going to make you uncomfortable." This newfound confidence is a vital counter to a contemporary political environment where censorship around race is being actively mandated by our Alabamian state government, as well as debated on the national stage. A year-long survey involving around 2,500 students at UNC Chapel Hill, another major Southern university, found that in classes where politics came up, nearly half the student body engaged in some form of self-censorship in the classroom (Larson, McNeilly, and Ryan 2020: 27). Avoiding contentious subjects, including issues of race and racism, provides a stifling and harmful environment to students marginalized by those issues (Castagno 2008: 318). The burden of starting and holding these conversations must not be placed solely on marginalized students. Emilia, who is white, said that she also felt the responsibility to talk to her white friends about issues of race, even if it meant being wrong and messing up and saying things imperfectly because she would rather move toward something better than stay silent. Both Emilia and Chandler were excited about being invited to the table and allowed to speak, as well as to hold people around them, even those in authority, accountable for change.

Students are not the only ones facing shame-based barriers to talking about their needs and circumstances. Zane McNeill and Dr. William Horne, both writers and editors, spoke about the additional burdens placed on them during the pandemic and how these burdens affected their writing practices, often perpetuating cycles of shame. As the primary caregiver for three children, William struggled with finding time for writing and activism, and the resultant stressors of having to work less: "I think a lot of us were used to our productivity being integral to who we are, right?" Zane experienced health issues that forestalled his own writing, but also noted that remaining politically engaged, going to civil rights demonstrations, many of which faced violent retaliation from the Police, took an additional emotional toll: "It's very hard to write when your Facebook is full of your friends' images of their wounds from being hit by rubber bullets and tear gas canisters . . . seeing that every day makes it very difficult for me to concentrate." How could they manage their own needs, speak for themselves, and give others a platform to share their own voices also?

In addition to their own writing, Zane and William also produce edited collections and journals, facilitating others in their own expression. They saw first-hand that writers everywhere were experiencing a vastly increased struggle to produce work: prior to the pandemic, William noted that usually an issue of his journal, *The Activist History Review*, would see about 5 percent of authors drop out between acceptance and publication. At the time of the interviews, this rate of attrition had risen to 50 percent. He dealt with this by putting out smaller issues, by accepting more articles, by offering a lot of first-time writers a chance to publish with increased editorial support from an expanded board, and by accepting articles in alternative formats, such as films, or photo essays. Zane was frustrated at seeing so many authors lose publishing contracts and funding, including several grants he had secured for activist organizations that were canceled due to COVID-19. He wound up creating sustainable working partnerships with spaces that supported activist goals, notably Sanctuary Publishers, whose profits go to queer and trans people of color.

Overshadowing the conversation was the subject of tenure, and the "publish or perish" mindset of many academic institutions. How can we write freely, and respect our own human needs, when our professional reputations, jobs, our financial security, and our access to healthcare rely on producing "enough" of the "right kind" of writing? The US tenure system is a multiyear path to a permanent academic contract, dependent on excellence in teaching, research, and service. Progress toward tenure is reviewed regularly, often annually, and failure to meet institutional criteria during these evaluations usually results in job loss. Access to tenure is deeply affected by structural privilege, but individual political choices can also have a tremendous impact. For example, Nikole Hannah-Jones, author of the Pulitzer Prize–winning, anti-racist, 1619 project, was initially denied tenure at UNC Chapel Hill after donors expressed concerns about her political activism to the tenure board (Jaschick 2021), only to have the decision reversed after a national protest on her behalf. William described his approach to tenure as: "Burning down the house that you're trying to get tenure in," or rather, making sure to write and publish works that actively resist the systemic injustices of the tenure system. Zane encouraged professors to build a new writing culture: to publish with students in order to give those students a jump-start on their own writing careers, to share resources and sources with each other, and to realize that even something as small as access to a printer can be a huge hurdle in someone's ability to work.

While writing is often romanticized as a solitary pursuit, Zane and William's most powerful message was that writing is a communal, activist project. William estimated that he gives about twenty hours of free labor each week to archiving, editing, and publishing so that the people traditionally erased from history can have a voice in this moment. This of course is deeply complicated when the labor of editing and publishing becomes another demand for free labor from marginalized populations, and further investment in establishing sustainable publishing structures is necessary in this moment. Zane addressed this labor slightly differently, saying that when he brings together authors for a book or even a chapter, it's: "a gift of friendship, a form of organizing and community building—that's why I do this work . . . " Whether it was reforming academia from the inside or using the freedom of independence to send stronger political messages, Zane and William saw writing as a versatile, communal form of activism that had the potential to respond urgently and create long-term positive impacts in a moment of historical crisis.

Creating a climate where individuals from all across academia can address vulnerability without shame would also help those who desperately require additional structural support, a group which includes those in authority, as well as our students. Students, professors, administrators, writers, and leaders, many of us are caring for dying family members, have been abused, are suffering from extremes of mental and physical illness. University systems currently create hefty financial and administrative barriers to anyone trying to access that support. For example, during the 2015–16 application cycle of the Free Application for Federal Student Aid (FAFSA) of the 150,000 students who self-identified as homeless, only 32,000 were officially deemed homeless for the purposes of financial aid

(Goldrick-Rab 2017). The costs of meeting university criteria for disability accommodations are also higher than some students can afford, ranging from hundreds to thousands of dollars for evaluation alone, without which, students are not legally entitled to support. For faculty, systems for recognizing disability and receiving accommodations may be present theoretically, but nonexistent in practice, and also involve major stigma-based barriers to disclosure. As one professor struggling with disability and the tenure process put it: "There's nothing they can do, they can't take my work from me, they can't give me any less work, they can't do my work for me, they can give me the career progression that I want . . . there's no such thing as a mitigating circumstances form" (Quoted in Brown 2020: 63). If, within academia, we can create a climate where everyone can speak freely about their circumstances and needs without shame, new communal and institutional forms of support and change become available.

Major Takeaways

- People feel "selfish" for having needs, strong feelings, or discomfort, and this shame is often reinforced by institutional or other systemic barriers.
- Shame is reduced when other people express the same feelings.
- Workloads need to change, and be more communal, during times of stress.

To Value Honesty and Complexity

To be queer is to value complexity, and to move beyond identity-driven categorizations of experience and validity. The term "queer" itself resists the normative social insistence on taxonomic classification and categorization, instead embracing blurring intersections of multiple identities and fluidity of the self (Meek 2021: 191). If the first principle of *How Do We Go Forward? How Do We Go Back?* was that people from many different levels of power should be able to speak to each other freely, the second principle was to remember that one's categorical position in the structure of academia—student, professor, administrator—was at best a hazy and inaccurate guide to someone's lived experience within that structure. For this reason the talks were framed as a series of conversations, eventually developing to the point where guests were explicitly told to talk to each other as individuals, rather than following any impulse to present to or teach to the audience. Framed this way, the conversations focused on intimate knowledge of context-dependent best practices, rather than broad-scale solutions. Administrators Trina Phillips and Amy Schmidt were exemplary in this regard, speaking passionately about the need to see the individual student, and to think flexibly about the demands placed on people, especially during the pandemic. Professor Molly Faulkner and independent artist Julia Gleich, however, added that there are some aspects of institutional experience that do not always need to be communicated. Exploring their theory of "Burden Sharing," they illustrated how some kinds of pressures—

passed down in the name of transparency and community building—added to a sense of powerlessness and frustration.

Trina Phillips is the program coordinator for the city cohort of Columbus in the Office of Diversity and Inclusion Young Scholars Program, and Amy Schmidt is the academic program coordinator at the Department of Dance at Ohio State University, serving as BFA and minor student adviser, course/curriculum manager, and undergraduate and graduate studies committee support. As administrators, Trina and Amy described their lives as a balance between constant movement—different recommendations, changing policies, incessant accumulation of needs and concerns—and stuck stillness—waiting for the next decision, the next piece of data, the next consideration to be added to the list before anything can start to happen. Trina, whose work serves students in eight different Ohio cities, including city-based and suburban students, had to juggle wildly conflicting policies about who could meet where, which sometimes, in turn, clashed with individual building regulations and her own work schedule. On top of this, as Amy pointed out, students often weren't able to abide by the policies because of their own resources: "They're like, 'we have one device to share in our household for all of the things that everyone in that household has to do—learning, meetings, work—everything,' and then others that are like, 'I have five different devices but out internet bandwidth isn't strong enough to handle it all.'" Even when the technology worked, some students were in other countries trying to join the program but were unable to get to their embassy or acquire the right visa.

Trina and Amy were in an ideal position to note the different ways that the pandemic impacted individual students as they tried to provide equitable experiences. Trina notes:

> Their parents are essential workers. So now they're at home and they're a babysitter and they're the cook and they're the teacher and they're doing all of those things. Some of them are college students that were in the program when we found that when COVID-19 hit and they had to leave campus. Some of our students didn't have anywhere else to go. Their home was their residence hall or their home was on campus, their food supply was off-campus or their meal plan was on campus. The program had to really dig for resources and things like that to make sure that our students did not feel the program failed them, or that they felt like a failure themselves . . . my colleagues were on the phone: "Do you have someplace to go? Do you have food? Do you have groceries"? Do *you* know all of these things that many of us take for granted?

Trina and Amy found themselves in a constant flow of new information and policies, rapidly flexible and mobile, and often perceived as "all-knowing" because of their administrative roles. They would watch a live news broadcast on television, and then turn to their phones to find emails asking for the institution's response! But they themselves were rarely in a position to make the decisions. Stuck waiting for answers, they instead acted as mediators and translators between students and institutional leadership, none of whom—as I will explore later—had necessarily a better sense of the correct way forward.

Speaking honestly, however, allowed guests with radical differences of opinion to come up with innovative perspectives on the pandemic and suggestions for creating structural change. Julia Gleich and Molly Faulkner are long-term collaborators whose projects are driven as often by their disagreements as by what they have in common. Julia holds degrees in mathematics and arts administration as well as her MFA in dance and left academia after a very successful career to focus on her own work and in rejection of institutional fatigue. Molly holds a doctorate, was entering her nineteenth year of teaching at the time of her interview, and fully intends to stay within higher education until her retirement. Their talk focused on sources of institutional fatigue and ways to handle it, including why an individual might stay with the system and why it might be more productive for someone else to walk away. In academia, where faculty are frequently encouraged to push for the next milestone, and the next, and leaving is often couched as an intellectual, creative, or personal failure, an honest discussion of how another path might be necessary and joyful was a much-needed addition to the conversation, especially given the additional stresses and dangers of the pandemic.

Together, Molly and Julia centered on "Burden Sharing" as a central cause of institutional fatigue and a phenomenon that begins even during undergraduate training. Burden sharing is a practice wherein responsibility for a difficult situation is passed down, often in exaggerated terms, to people with less, sometimes no power to address that situation. It could create a division between those most affected by a problem, and a distant authority figure depicted as the ones imposing that problem. Molly shared an example:

> I think I developed my fundamental mistrust of administration during my undergrad, because my professors would make comments like "Make sure everyone gets signed up, this class is on the chopping block, the district is looking to cut this class." Any time there was an unpopular decision that was out of the faculty control they brought in the administration as this kind of nebulous cloud of something that follows faculty and makes unpopular decisions.

In this case the burden of a district-level administrative decision is passed down through faculty to the students, while simultaneously teaching students to distrust external governance rather than engage with it.

As Julia and Molly progressed through graduate education and into faculty careers, the same patterns continued, as Julia explained:

> At the beginning of the year all the faculty gets together and you're thinking: "What are we going to teach?" and "I want to get in there!" And the Dean stands up and says "Money is really tight and I don't know if we will make it through this year, but there are going to have to be cuts." You could predict every year that he'd say the exact same thing. While these kinds of conversations were pitched as a form of democratization and transparency, after six, or nineteen years of the

same conversation without the dire predictions manifesting, those predictions started to be regarded as unnecessary fear-mongering, that nevertheless caused low spirits and desperate siloing as people tried to protect their jobs or specialist areas. The rhetoric was frustrating both because there was a lack of honesty, such as explicit numbers that could have backed up the nebulous threats of job loss and program cuts, and because faculty were in truth powerless to do very much other than be afraid, which led some to pass that fear onto their students. While this kind of language is common in many academic fields it is particularly pervasive in the arts because, as Julia put it: "I don't think math professors are really worried that the entire math program is going to get cut due to the economic downturn."

In thinking through how to have a more productive dialogue, one of the most interesting points Julia and Molly made was to remember that "hearing from everyone" is not the same thing as complexity. "If you're on multiple committees you spend the first twenty minutes of any meeting hearing exactly what's been said at every other meeting, and it's exhausting . . . get to the meat!" By summarizing content in emails and sharing information across committees rather than offering personalized recaps, institutional service could become more productive and less tiring. Rather than passing down fear without data, institutions could focus on realistic metrics and budgets, as well as strategies for actively engaging with external overseeing bodies. While they didn't have a clear answer for the point at which transparency becomes oversharing, the point was clear that fear, when linked to powerlessness, is not conducive to a healthy environment. If we value honesty and complexity we must also offer responsive actions that can take into account honest and complex individuals, especially when our institutions include those with additional vulnerability.

Major Takeaways

- Academic decisions are made in a hierarchical structure.
- The realities of that structure mean that information and power are divided.
- People can only work with the information and power that they have.
- These structures have to serve individuals with unique needs and obstacles.

To Be Vulnerable

A nonbinary professor and friend of mine once pointed out that while they are required to respect the names and pronouns of all students, students are not required to respond in kind. Similarly, at my own institution the Office of Disability Services offers students accommodations and support, but turn to the "Faculty" tab and all you will see is information about how to support students, rather than how to register for support yourself.[3] As has become appallingly apparent during the COVID-19 pandemic, teachers are broadly perceived as protectors of the vulnerable, providers of grace, rather than vulnerable individuals who might need grace themselves. This misperception can have tragic results: *Education Week* estimates that as of November 2021, 1,216 active or retired teachers of children aged three to twelve have been lost to COVID-19 ("Educators We've Lost" 2021).

Professors from marginalized populations do not become magically immune to systemic oppression. "Let me be clear," explains Susie E. Nam, "That we, as Women of Color and queer People of Color faculty, do this [put student well-being before their own careers] not because 'we've been there' but because we are still here, subject to the very same kinds of exploitation and oppression that our students face. The experiences of our students who are marginalized, neglected, or 'underserved' are closely linked to how our colleagues and administration manage to keep us all down and out" (Nam 2020: 173). While academic environments exist in the popular imagination as liberal spaces, even in departments where most of the professors are marginalized, the pressure to live up to institutional metrics can result in environments that are oppressive and inhumane. Andrew R. Spieldenner notes that these conditions are not solely external in their source: "The regimes of normativity act on us and determine what we can do and how we live. We resist, both individually and as a community. We create spaces where our differences are deliberately politicized, but we can still fall into normative ideas of professionalism and productivity. We are still learning to construct inclusive homes for our diverse communities" (Spieldenner 2019: 77). Inspired by these realities, I sought out honest descriptions of institutional vulnerability from two populations routinely disadvantaged by university structures: graduate students, and adjunct professors.

Steve Ha and Kathryn Holt were—at the time of recording—graduate students in the process of getting their PhDs in Dance Studies. Both taught general education and more specialized courses in addition to their own course load and dissertation writing. While the COVID-19 pandemic gave them a reason to stay indoors and focus on their writing, it also increased the burden on their general well-being, and particularly on their mental health: "Even before the pandemic I knew how to prioritize my own mental health, but the Department and University structure is really pushing back on me for it; when I say 'I need more time to do this thing' I get a lot of push back." During the pandemic mental health was identified early as a factor of concern, but this did not necessarily translate into structural change. "I feel like we get a lot of lip service to mental health, but [Departments need to be] a little more willing to shift and change their expectations of graduate students and what is actually feasible and healthy to ask of them."

When asked about specific problems contributing to mental health, both Steve and Kathryn identified the lack of rest time during the semester, a problem only exacerbated by the university's decision to eliminate spring breaks—a common choice to try and prevent the spread of COVID-19. While faculty did suggest days off and time for recovery, it was often accompanied by an ever-expanding list of tasks that needed to be done to succeed in the program. Factoring in the self-structured nature of a graduate program, it became all too easy for these tasks to dominate any time spare from structured assignments. Even when graduate students did take time off, the time was not necessarily restful: "I would just end up sitting there for two days doing nothing because I'm just so paralyzed with the anxiety over doing not doing work. I actually don't even get anything done anyway, and I don't enjoy the time I take off." The sudden loss of a spring break also had a major effect on burnout and mental fatigue. "By week nine, I remember feeling like, OK, ready to be done, but add six more weeks to the semester and I just I remember feeling like I was going to die, like I just wasn't going to make it."

What interventions could help with burnout? Kathryn and Steve suggested that rather than reminders of "Don't forget to take time off," faculty need to structure time off and independent workdays into their syllabi and then refrain from adding homework assignments during those times. Structured breaks could also be written into graduate writing schedules, with the understanding that these should be honored from both sides. Another suggestion would be for graduate students to have some recourse for mental health support outside of their academic advisers: "I get to a point where I'm afraid to ask for help because I feel scared or embarrassed that as a graduate student, I'm not performing my duty. It becomes really hard when the person that you're supposed to ask for help is also the person that's overseeing your progress, is monitoring your progress." Shame, and the need for relief from shame, is a recurrent topic in how to manage the emotional weight of the COVID-19 pandemic, which begs the question of how shame has become so deeply entrenched in academic environments. It also suggests that monitoring is needed to establish how graduate students and other faculty are perhaps being penalized for feeling exhaustion, guilt, burnout, and fear.

A final suggestion, discussed earlier, is for faculty to think realistically about the demands on a graduate student's life and the kind of labor that it is feasible to ask for. Most graduate students have to take on work in addition to their graduate assistantships (if they have one) in order to support themselves financially, and this is rarely factored in when appropriate workloads are considered. Because of the erratic nature of graduate hours, these second jobs are often service-industry positions, with large commitments in the evening or through weekends. If universities do not pay graduate assistants a living wage, what can be done to facilitate the dual use of their time? This question becomes even more pressing when we consider a group with greater impediments to their financial and economic security and even greater responsibilities within the university system, adjunct professors.

Independent artists Lexi Clark-Stilianos and Melissa Yes have worked extensively as adjuncts in Chicago, Illinois, and Birmingham, Alabama, respectively. Adjunct professors are instructors hired to teach required and elective courses on a flexible basis, and the majority of them receive no benefits, no health care, and no guarantee of employment from semester to semester (Krebs 2020). In 2015 data suggested that 75 percent of college-level teachers were considered part-time or contingent labor, earning an average of $20,000 to $25,000 a year (Dorfeld 2015: A8–9). This wage, however, is possible when juggling many jobs at once because of the low rate of adjunct pay. Melissa explained: "Most major state universities are going to pay somewhere between twenty-five hundred and four thousand dollars a semester for one, three credit hour class. That includes all the prep work, and then the time in class and then time grading and time outside of class sustaining those mentorship relationships with students." Even this rate, however, could drop dramatically according to Lexi: "I taught at a community college once that paid me sixteen-hundred dollars for a three credit. hour class. That's sixteen hundred dollars for the duration of the semester."

These low wages are neither guaranteed nor predictable, and adjunct contracts can be taken away at a moment's notice, like this example from Lexi: "One of [my classes] didn't run due to low student enrollment. . . . I still had to prepare that whole course over a month and a half time, and then I didn't get compensated for any of that prep work. . . . I get my contract, but then up until four or five days before the start of the Fall semester if that class doesn't hit whatever the enrollment is, then the class and all of that money is taken away from me."[4] This cycle, which repeats every semester, leads to adjuncts taking jobs from outside of their area of expertise just to make ends meet: "I teach three classes at one college and two at another. I bartend on the side. I started doing some tutoring . . . I've done some copywriting. I have at least eight jobs at any one time."

One unfortunate result of the additional labor adjuncts require to survive in their positions is that it prevents progression to a more secure position. As Melissa put it: "In order to get one of those jobs, you have to have a really good studio practice or research record." Working multiple jobs for subsistence wages means that adjuncts rarely have time for their own professional practice, especially since class prep time, grading time, and so on are required and yet not compensated. Lexi noted that this pressure made even available creative time disheartening: "Figuring out the three-hour chunk in a week that I've carved out to make my art and make it count, I have to get in that studio and don't waste a single second. If you don't come out like, say, Twyla Tharp[5] . . . then that time feels wasted." This constellation of forces keeping adjuncts employed in the lowest tiers of academia but unable to progress due to poverty conditions is called "The Adjunct Trap," and the overwhelming majority of those caught in it without time, pay, insurance, or a way out, are educators who have historically been marginalized in academia (Harris 2019).

The stress factors of adjuncting were exacerbated by the arrival of COVID-19. Lexi missed the camaraderie of a full-time environment, noting that as an adjunct, it is easy to get missed out when information goes around, or when people get together socially. The precarity discussed earlier increased as faculty grappled with whether classes would run, whether they would shift online, and what kinds of safety measures would be in place. Student enrollment dropped, summer classes were canceled, and people stopped going to in-person vocational classes, which dried up several sources of income. Grants were canceled, and those that ran as normal required an ongoing art practice and production cycle that few could sustain from their homes. Many adjuncts looked at the risk/reward balance of teaching for such low wages and so little benefit and decided that the additional risk of COVID-19 was too much—many universities struggled to fill adjunct positions as people looked for work that left them less vulnerable to exploitation.

Lexi and Melissa's episode of *How Do We Go Forward? How Do We Go Back?* caught a lot of attention from professors and students who didn't fully realize the vulnerability of adjunct life. In the discussion following their talk, Lexi and Melissa were asked not only what institutional changes could help reform the system but also what full-time faculty could do to support their adjunct colleagues. The most basic intervention they suggested was to give out adjunct contracts for, at minimum, one academic year, guaranteeing classes and income, to reduce the emotional stress of employment instability. Another suggestion they made was to educate students about the different levels of contracts and what they meant. Lexi said: "I made it a habit now of explaining to my students that I am an adjunct professor and making them understand what that is and that I am not as available to them as faculty that are full time because I am only on campus the days that I'm paid to be there for my office hours and for those classes." This is not to make students ask for less, but so adjuncts are not punished or looked down on for doing less than faculty whose contracts pay them for advising and mentoring.

Lexi and Melissa's vulnerability as adjuncts can only be addressed by institutional changes, and those changes can be made most swiftly with collective advocacy. Department chairs can be allies, making the case for longer adjunct contracts, for example. If adjunct class caps were removed, then they could teach more classes at one institution instead of moving between several, and could also qualify for benefits. Summer classes could be offered to adjuncts rather than tenure-track faculty. The counterpoint was raised that classes might not have enough enrollment to run, and Lexi suggested that then perhaps adjuncts could be paid to step into service positions or do research as guest artists for a semester, both of which would support the department and their career development. While they may not have the power to make some of these changes, contracted faculty can help bring them to broader departmental awareness. Faculty can also support adjuncts by inviting them into conversations about departmental issues, and paying them for that administrative time, so they can be involved more in the community of the department. Faculty and adjuncts can also support each other by sharing their salaries as a basis for negotiating a fairer wage for their labor.

The conversations around adjuncts and graduate students held several parallels that can be expanded across many vulnerable populations in the university. First, Steve Katherine, Lexi, and Melissa all pointed out that while an acknowledgment of vulnerability is useful, that acknowledgment must be met with structural support, not just with empathy and the well-meaning advice to take time for self-care. Second, work should be valued and fairly compensated. Third, the needs of the institution should be balanced with the needs of those serving the institution. Lastly, if universities work to meet the needs of their vulnerable populations, they will be rewarded with better teachers, better researchers, and a more committed community. These structural changes have always been important but are even more urgent during these times of increased precarity. We must move toward action if we want to see change.

Major Takeaways

- Rest structures need to be mandated, not recommended.
- Your source of mental health support should not be the person assessing your professional value.
- Adjunct positions need, at minimum, year-long contracts.
- Transparency about the realities of adjunct contracts could help reduce the precarity of these positions.

To Move Consciously

In 2021 I hosted the second year of *How Do We Go Forward? How Do We Go Back?* This time focusing on the need to radically change our communities as we look to restructuring and returning. To conclude this second summer, I invited the speakers of 2020 to return for a reunion talk to reflect on how their year had played out.

Some had seen major changes: Lexi Clark-Stilianos and Melissa Yes had both either left or were in the process of leaving academic teaching. A department chair from the Leadership roundtable who remarked in 2020 that her institution "cannot pronounce the words Black Lives Matter," had been removed from her position for supporting colleagues and students in their demonstrations for racial equality (Frank 2021). Others remained in the same institutional position but found that their work had changed substantially, and sometimes for the better. Benny Simon, who had previously spoken about Digital Classrooms, summarized many people's experiences: "There's an expectation of what a legitimate dance degree is supposed to be like, and when it wasn't that we all had to sort of figure out how to say, look . . . we're still dancing. It just looks and feels differently, and therefore, that can be just as legitimate as what we were doing before." Dance film, somatic, or wellness-based practices were not just adaptations to a pandemic but important additions to professional training. Emilia Stuart, now graduated, reflected on the success of student activism:

> We had more kids audition and come to Alabama than ever before . . . we really took the time to look at what we were able to do, and deconstructed that, and realized who's being heard. What systems have we just kind of put in place? Without all the glamour of performances, we got to look at the way that things were orchestrated.

Many of the queer values that proved so vital to shaping the *How Do We Go Forward? How Do We Go Back?* series, ended up being adopted far more broadly by institutions in their search for compassionate, flexible learning spaces.

As well as the structure of the programs themselves, there were marked changes in how the logistics of programs were administered, with again, a mix of positive and negative changes. As Rebecca Salzer, who spoke on Collaboration, put it: "There are so many things that we've been told were impossible that just happened over the last year and a half. Like free health care, for example, or like unlimited internet, things that we were told 'Oh no no no, that's not possible.'" What became logistically possible, and what did not, was another way of assessing departmental value systems. Molly Faulkner, who could not attend the reunion talk but who responded to prompt questions in writing, wrote that after eight months she was still waiting for the technology she desperately needed, and felt that the dance department was being sorely neglected. When money was available, there were specific limits on how it could be spent: "Why is it that I can spend $50,000 on zoom equipment, but I can't hire an adjunct? Or open a new tenure line?"

While most speakers had seen an uptick in Diversity, Equity, and Inclusion initiatives, limits had been seen in these areas also. "Just because we have a committee now doesn't mean we're now equitable and inclusive" was a common refrain. Similarly, marginalized faculty and students were, as they have been historically, overburdened with the responsibility for making change: "I have six Black peers, there's no one to pull from!" There was a strong undercurrent of frustration with tokenism: "I don't want to be the spokesperson for the department just because I am Black." Or: "To make an inclusion committee and pick the one Black Professor as the head of it, that doesn't fix anything . . . we all just saw right through it." Rather than wait for institutional solutions, many of my returning guests articulated a sense of personal responsibility and plans for action: "I have boundaries, I have expectations, I'm a lot more sound on what I know I can do and so coming back to school, it's like I have a finite amount of time, and I have a set amount of things that I want out of this. I think students will come back more empowered than they did before."

Major Takeaways

- We need to refocus on action.
- Legitimacy should not be our first concern.
- How we define success can profoundly affect how we serve our communities.

Conclusion

Two speakers from my original series, Lawrence Jackson and Ann Cooper Albright, summed up the precarious dichotomy of trying to move forward and backward at the same time. Ann, who is the Chair of Dance at Oberlin College, a Guggenheim scholar, the author of many fundamental texts in dance scholarship, and one of the world's leading practitioners of Contact Improvisation, put it like this:

> We're facing in two different directions. One of them is that we're trying to support our department and make sure that everybody gets the guest teachers they want to bring in and the opportunities and the performance conditions that are right for their work. And then you're also facing outward toward the

university and you're trying to articulate all the time why dance is a really important part of an academic institution.

The individuals caught in the middle of this pull desperately need principles of honesty, vulnerability, and equity to guide conversations about what actions can take them forward.

As Ann pointed out in her talk, recognizing the human at the center of the tangle is even more vital when so many of us are not talking to each other in person: "Now more than ever people are less and less involved in their own three-dimensionality—there's a lot more two-dimensional activity. And what does that do to our brains? What does that do to our reflexes?" Dancers and dance teachers are well equipped to think of the human body, but Ann also raised the caution that human, vulnerable, honest bodies can all too easily become sidelined underneath institutional concerns: "I'm missing the enzymes and people's sweat, I'm missing that bodily presence, and it makes me a little nervous in terms of the role of performance and dance and live bodies that we would create a situation where they were disposable."

How Do We Go Forward? How Do We Go Back? was founded in opposition to disposability, to try and hold on to individual voices rather than a bigger, homogenizing picture. Through the four practices outlined here: to speak freely, to value honesty and complexity, to be vulnerable, and to move consciously (as well as the individual details of how these practices manifested in a queer space of sharing), speakers found ways back to what mattered most to them, and forward through structural barriers, confusion, fear, and shame. I hope that through practices of queer sharing, more of us can participate in these conversations that are so vital to reshaping our futures together.

References

Brown, N. (2020), "Disclosure in Academia: A Sensitive Issue," in N. Brown and J. Leigh (eds.), *Ableism in Academia: Theorising Experiences of Disabilities and Chronic Illnesses in Higher Education*, 51–73, London: UCL Press.
Castagno, A. (2008), "'I Don't Want to Hear That!': Legitimating Whiteness through Silence in Schools," *Anthropology & Education Quarterly*, 39 (3): 318/314–33.
Dorfeld, N. (2015), "National Adjuct Walkout Day: Now What?" *College Composition and Communication*, 67 (1): A8–A13.
"Educators We've Lost to the Coronavirus" (2021), *Education Week*, November 5. Available online: https://www.edweek.org/teaching-learning/educators-weve-lost-to-the-coronavirus/2020/04 (accessed November 30, 2021).
Frank, B. (2021), "'It's Really Hard': GCU Dance Students Reckon With Firings, Shuffling in Department," *AZCentral*, January 13. Available online: https://www.azcentral.com/story/news/local/phoenix/2021/01/13/its-really-hard-gcu-dance-students-reckon-firings-shuffling-department/6595518002/ (accessed November 30, 2021).
Goldrick-Rab, S. (2017), "Poverty Is Largely Invisible Among College Students," *Talk Poverty*, November 7. Available online: https://talkpoverty.org/2017/11/07/poverty-largely-invisible-among-college-students/ (accessed November 30, 2021).

Harris, A. (2019), "The Death of an Adjunct," *The Atlantic*, April 8. Available online: https://www.theatlantic.com/education/archive/2019/04/adjunct-professors-higher-education-thea-hunter/586168/ (accessed November 30, 2021).

Jaschick, S. (2021), "Hannah-Jones Turns Down UNC Offer," *Inside Higher Ed.*, July 7. Available online: https://www.insidehighered.com/news/2021/07/07/nikole-hannah-jones-rejects-tenure-offer-unc-job-howard-u (accessed November 30, 2021).

Krebs, P. (2020), "Covid 19: How Adjuncts are Impacted," *University Business*, March 26. Available online: https://universitybusiness.com/covid-19-how-adjuncts-are-impacted/ (accessed November 30, 2021).

Larson, J., M. McNeilly, and T. Ryan (2020), "Free Expression and Constructive Dialogue at the University of North Carolina at Chapel Hill," *UNC.edu*, March 2, 27. Available online: https://fecdsurveyreport.web.unc.edu/wp-content/uploads/sites/22160/2020/02/UNC-Free-Expression-Report.pdf (accessed November 30, 2021).

Meek, J.B. (2021), "'Being Queer Is the Luckiest Thing': Investigating a New Generation's Use of Queer within Lesbian, Gay, Bisexual, Transgender, and Queer (LGBTQ) Student Groups," *Counterpoints*, 367: 187–98.

Nam, S.E. (2020), "Making Visible the Dead Bodies in the Room: Women of Color/QPOC in Academia," in Y. Niemann, G. Gutiérrez y Muhs, and C. Gonzáles (eds.), *Presumed Incompetent: Race, Class, Power, and Resistance of Women in Academia*, 171–9, Louisville: University Press of Colorado.

Spieldenner, A. (2019), "Considering the Queer Disabled/Debilitated Body: An Introduction of Queer Cripping," *QED: A Journal in GLBTQ Worldmaking*, 6 (3): 76–80.

Chapter 4

QUEER KINSHIP AS COUNTERNARRATIVE: A PARADIGM OF
PERSISTENCE FOR CROSS-DISCIPLINARY COLLABORATION

Shereen Inayatulla and David P. Rivera

Queer kinship is a paradigm within which the coauthors of this chapter approach our personal and professional collaborations. As faculty members working at the City University of New York (CUNY) with campuses situated on Lenapehoking (and referred to as the New York City borough of Queens), we view our collaborative endeavors as a way to intervene in the broad, often dismissive perceptions that circulate about our university and public higher education at large. Our kinship is simultaneously transparent and subtle; it enlivens our critical pedagogies, sharpens efforts to decolonize our professional identities, and fosters a mindful community committed to The Struggle to end oppression of all kinds. We recognize, also, the hubris surrounding decolonization efforts in our professional settings given the critiques advanced by Eve Tuck and K. Wayne Yang. In this chapter, we take a reflective dive into our process of kinship formation and consider how our alliance, while an embodiment of our cross-disciplinary intellectual work, is strategic, queerly ancestral, resistant to capitalist values, and affirming in ways that bristle against the institutional structures of individualistic, academic success.

Shereen Inayatulla (she/her/hers) is a queer, brown, cis woman, immigrant, and tenured faculty member of English at York College, whose areas of teaching and research blend composition, critical literacies, autoethnography, and queer theory. Her work with students interrogates the conventions and metrics of academic writing that are used as gatekeeping practices specific to CUNY and beyond. David P. Rivera (he/him/his) is a queer, gay, Latinx, cis man, counseling psychologist from a first-generation, poor background who is now a tenured faculty member at Queens College. His areas of teaching, research, and practice center critical theories, including Critical Race Theory, Queer Theory, Intersectionality, and DisCrit, as the basis for framing the impact of structural oppressions on wellness and psychological functioning. We met as board members in CLAGS: Center for LGBTQ Studies, which is the first university-based research center on sexual orientation and gender diversity in the United States and is housed within CUNY. This chapter documents, in a nonlinear fashion, how we parlayed our professional connection into a familial dynamic. With no identifiable blueprints to guide us, we were at liberty to create a familial structure that now evolves with fluidity but requires thoughtfulness and intentionality.

Queer kinship formations do not garner recognition as a form of labor the way familial structures endorsed by capitalist nation-states regularly do. By writing this chapter, we archive queer kinship as a sustainable and celebratory rebuke to neoliberal individualism and, in particular, its manifestations that pervade traditional notions of academic success. LGBTQ+ faculty who are Black, Indigenous, People of Color (BIPOC) are situated across CUNY but are often isolated and must labor to meet one another. Given this reality, there has been a serendipitous quality to our specific encounter, which inevitably affects how we carry ourselves into classrooms and workspaces with our LGBTQ+ students who are also BIPOC and also often isolated from their peers.

Notes on Our Process

Our kinship is anchored in imaginative approaches to community building and care. To mirror the early encounters of our relationship wherein a shared discourse developed exuberantly, our reflections in this chapter are presented through a dialogue containing ideas and concepts that permeate our queer kinship and professional connection. Our queer kinship is impossible to compartmentalize from all other aspects of our lives, most certainly including our professional endeavors. We come to queer kinship through a kind of rapid exchange of ideas; to observe our conversations is to be cycloned into discursive practices that are emotionally charged, philosophically wild, playful, absurd, at once geriatric and juvenile, euphemistic, protective, and anchored in mutual loyalty and a commitment to justice. The dialogue that follows enacts much of this. In writing this chapter, we aspire to the "ideal vision" of dialogue articulated in the collection *The Entrepreneurial University*, in which contributors express their initial desire for "stakeholders in education and culture" to have a "reciprocal" collaboration, "to expand . . . knowledge," and to "challenge the paradigms by which social and educational problems are positioned" (Quinn et al. 2014: 202–3). Although we are both positioned as academics, our personal histories and experience of queer kinship occupy ideologic space that reaches far beyond traditional academic pursuits. And yet, the matter of our queer kinship is entangled with our academic work, research, pedagogy, and the professional connection we share and cocreate.

We started our reflective dialogue in person then transcribed and revised it for written clarity, and it contains narrative retellings of the inseparable familial and intellectual connection we share. Like Quinn et al. (2014), our efforts at dialogue started as a way to "sidestep some of the more sterile conventions of academic writing" and embody "more spontaneity" (Quinn et al. 2014: 208). Yet, we also find that "In writing we are again caught between our dialogic drive and the messy reality of everyday life" (Quinn et al. 2014: 208). We are writing this chapter during the pandemic, through the tragically commonplace barrage of public, political, and personal crises, the nonstop pressures of academic and professional labor, domestic obligations, carework commitments, and the fundamental need for rest and self-care. Our understanding of carework is profoundly inspired by the book *Care Work Dreaming Disability Justice*, by Leah Lakshmi Piepzna-Samarasinha, who comes to this term at the intersection of "disability justice" and "femme emotional labor." For us, this term, fused as one word, operates at the nexus of physical and emotional community care with specific attention to our LGBTQ+ and BIPOC loved ones, who are routinely denied access to safety and material securities. Carework, as we see it, involves varied labors of love and vulnerability. It is also necessary for surviving the urgency and emergencies perpetuated by hostile, even deadly, material conditions of late-stage capitalism. Our collaboration on this chapter has been at once lopsided and invigorating, stagnant then rushed, sometimes simultaneous but often solo and piecemeal, too frequently interrupted by extraneous demands.

As part of our process, we choose to embrace interruptions and even exploit them in order to give shape to our dialogue. Inspired by Maddie Breeze and Yvette Taylor's work in which they strategically and creatively interrupt the conventions and trajectory of their book, we employ interruptions (and expand this to include *disruptions*) within our dialogue that follows in an effort to synthesize and reflect upon our process and offer context for our ideas about queer kinship. Breeze and Taylor (2020) posit interruptions as "a central methodological device in the book, as we work to interrupt and reconsider feminist conventions in taking up academic space across the career course, including by interrupting ourselves" (Breeze and Taylor 2020: xi). Later they explain that "Via our interruption methods, we endeavour to analyse *processes* of feminist academic self-formation, rather than simply performing and reiterating such processes in our methods" (Breeze and Taylor 2020: 16). For us, dialogue, interruption, and disruption are practices for embodying and further developing our queer kinship. The two of us are engaged in a rapid, tireless exchange of ideas, affirmations, and fantasies, always forming and performing the nuances of our relationship in ways that enrich or challenge the varied contexts through which we move about, ranging from the way we walk down the street to our professional undertakings.

Our primary goal is to present queer kinship as one formulation for disrupting neoliberal incentives such as competition, solo-accomplishment, and cursory collegiality that bolster faculty success in academic settings. In doing so, we aim to challenge misguided, dismissive, and elitist perceptions of what LGBTQ+ BIPOC within CUNY contribute to queer studies on a broader scale. Breeze and Taylor (2020) explain how their "methods re-focus on the routine and everyday aspects of feminist academic careers, including those quotidian 'documents of life'" (Breeze and Taylor 2020: 14). Likewise, we envision our practice of dialogue, interruption, and disruption as a site to be researched and from which to research, a site to be archived and from which to archive how queer kinship cannot be contained within only marginal states of existence.

Both of our disciplines, composition and psychology, centralize dialogue and reflection as tenets of reading, writing, healing, and carework practices. Above all, our professional work is anchored in social justice, which inevitably requires bringing our whole selves to classrooms, conferences, office hours, lectures, and scholarly research. While the idea of a "whole" self may be a fluid and subjective negotiation, we agree that our queer kinship is an unwavering aspect of who we are in most (if not all) spaces. In writing this chapter, we hold Breeze and Taylor's (2020) conceptualization of cowriting close: "collaborative re-working cohered around our technique of *interrupting* and fragmenting our accounts as we wrote them. This involved developing our initial material into fictionalised data fragements, [sic] by way of fabrication as ethical practice . . . and 'telling tales to speak embodied truth'" (Breeze and Taylor 2020: 18). They describe their process as allowing them "to develop partial, fragmented, *interrupted* career narratives as 'entangled data-stories' . . . unsettling smooth, coherent linear accounts of career progression" (Breeze and Taylor 2020: 18). Our dialogue in this chapter carries "fictionalized data fragments," also aware of "fabrication as an ethical practice." For us, fabrication is strategic and purposeful. It is an attempt at the documentation or archival work on queer kinship, which blurs personal and academic spheres of influence.

Queering Kinship: A Dialogue

Inviting readers into our rapid, unmetered, at times specialized, "insider," shared discourse lifts a curtain on our queer kinship in measured and strategic ways. We view this curtain lifting as adjacent to burlesque, and it reminds us of Joseph Pierce's (2019) analysis of family album photographs as artifacts through which queer reception comes to light: "The family album is not a queer object in and of itself. It is not an artifact that necessarily represents queerness either. . . . [T]he album serves to maintain patrimony and lineage; it registers hierarchical positions in proximity to and distance from sites of power; . . . it racializes bodies and partitions spheres of influence and access" (Pierce 2019: 143). We take this observation as incentive to document, craft, display, and maneuver our kinship for public consumption and private enrichment. We conceive of our kinship as both personal and academic, public and private, a performance wherein we control each movement, simultaneously veiling and offering glimpses of our relationship.

> SHEREEN: So, what does queer kinship even mean to us?
> DAVID: I think and feel so many things when I consider what queer kinship means to me.
> My mind first drifts to kinship and the sense of meaningful and persistent connection to my kinfolk that I rely on heavily to survive life. I also think about the contradictions that exist between normative, mainstream depictions and definitions of family and how the concept of family is experienced by queer people. I think about the *queering* processes by which we decolonize, depathologize, deconstruct, and ultimately redesign our conceptualization of family in order to help us

better navigate these contradictions and create kinship structures that advance our right to self-determination. One of the processes that we use to liberate ourselves from oppressive notions of family is *counternarrative* and the way it challenges oppressive discourses in written, spoken, and performed ways. Queer kinship feels safe to me. It provides me a support network that is more boundless than what a solely bio-kinship network can provide. Finitely defining queer kinship is impossible, in that the process of queering kinship is ever-evolving along with changing contexts and times.

Interruption....

Defining queer kinship can be as mercurial as defining queer theory (Dilley 1999). Just as queer theory is purposefully ambiguous in its definition (Monaghan 2016), our definition of queer kinship maintains a similar positionality. Rather than providing definitions that are prescriptive and linear in nature, queer theory challenges us to disrupt, dismantle, and invigorate our conceptualization of terms and concepts. As such, our definition of queer kinship is more about a process that is cocreated, ever-evolving, and positions liberatory concepts, such as self-determination, as foundational to the formation, maintenance, and impact of queer kinships. Survival and resistance are embedded in our definition in a fashion that runs parallel to and honors Indigenous *survivance* as applied by Indigenous scholar Gerald Vizenor (1999). Similar to survivance, queer kinship is a process that is deliberately imprecise, which yields limitless opportunities for community- and self-determination. The chronicling of our queer kinship provides an archive that, in the words of Joseph Pierce, "is both technology of past-making and iterative futurity" (Pierce 2019: 139).

> SHEREEN: You've mentioned that our kinship operates as a counternarrative, which I love and see manifesting in multiple ways. What specifically does counternarrative invoke for you?
> DAVID: We've been normed into specific ideas about the meaning and process of family and bio-kinship. Society prizes "blood," lineage, and nuclear structure as defining characteristics of the family. Our queer kinship is a direct challenge to these normed ideas about family and, in essence, creates a counternarrative to these oftentimes oppressive notions of family. Growing up queer in patriarchal, heteronormative environments means that we were exposed to a constant deluge of macroaggressions (i.e., structural oppressions) and microaggressions (i.e., subtle, covert discrimination) that simultaneously invalidated our existence and taught us the language of oppression. These oppressions become internalized when we don't engage in a process of challenging and interrogating them. Through our queer kinship, we are able to create new ways of knowing, experiencing, and relating to each other that defy the patriarchal, heteronormative notions of family and liberate us from the oppressions

we've internalized and can buffer us from the oppressions we continue to absorb. We're doing a counternarrative to what we've been taught, and the language we have learned through our counternarrative helps us express what we know to each other. And one of the ways that we know each other so well is because we had an underlying communication pattern or way of being that comes from our experiences persisting through oppression. This is paramount to our process of queer sharing.

Interruption...

We use the terms "family" and "kin" synonymously. In our conceptual discussions about this chapter, we've questioned and wrestled with the conflation of these terms and have come to enjoy their messiness. Kadji Amin explains that "chosen family" can "be regarded as a foundling form of queer kinship," and the varied and profound "energies it magnetizes ensure that a chosen family remains highly idealized as at once free from the contradictions of conventional kinship and uniquely capable of fulfilling the yearnings for love, care, and belonging that the romance of 'family' generates" (Amin 2017: 113). We also consider queer kinship to be an evolving process and one that can take on a multitude of qualities. We discussed processes such as the development of a shared queer knowledge garnered from our lived experiences with oppression and privilege dynamics. This shared queer knowledge translates into a common understanding of the oppressions and privileges that come along with being queer in this capitalistic, patriarchal, and heteronormative paradigm. The language, verbal and nonverbal, that we learn as queerly oppressed people is one that we oftentimes rely on to identify community members and to enter into emotionally connected, meaningful experiences with one another. Our conversation demonstrates how we use what we might call "queer language" as a primary way we communicate and share knowledge and experiences.

> SHEREEN: It seems like there are two counternarratives taking shape here: our kinship is itself a counternarrative in the ways you describe but also, the very act of documenting how it came to be (and continues to evolve) is a counternarrative to heteropatriarchal arrangements of family and academic collegiality defined/enforced by a capitalist nation-state. There's a lot here to unpack. More simply put, we are strategically coopting the terms "family" and "collegiality" toward our queer reality and the ways we connect to each other. Even the ways we talk to and about each other. This is evident in how we actively, consciously, and subconsciously blur kin categories and gender roles: I've called you Mom, Dad, Zaddy, and you've called me your sister and grandma! In professional contexts, I refer to you as my colleague, collaborator, colleague-friend, work-husband . . .

This appropriation of various terms is also woven throughout our interactions with other people; we sometimes refer to making/including friends in our social engagements as "throupling," and we are entertained by the unapologetically incestuous connotations of this. The discourse we use to describe our connection is filled with playfulness and mimicry, and at times it's even a rebuke to the strict ways that kin relations are socially policed. It probably isn't a stretch to consider how this also relates to our mutual love for "Dad Rock!"

Interruption...

We consider "Dad Rock" to be a subgenre of Classic Rock. We volley this term back and forth in our casual conversations, which sometimes elicits questions from bystanders. Dad Rock is an example of our shared lexicon, a term and type of music containing nothing inherently queer but to which we apply a queer lens. This genre of music spans the mid-1960s through the 1980s, and we delineate the label "Dad" to signify the "harder" side of Classic Rock. This can be conceptualized as a gendering of this musical genre, one that is simultaneously stereotypic and playful, as well as projections of our own gender identities and expressions. The labeling of "Dad" might also be a projection of our own complicated relationships with our biological fathers (i.e., daddy issues). This style of Rock was easily accessible (even ubiquitous during our childhood) in both of our communities of origin in the rural Rocky Mountain and urban prairie land of so-called Canada, which resulted in a common understanding and shared love of this style of music. A significant part of our specialized discourse is anchored in Dad Rock. The music itself and our relationships to it are layered and far from uncomplicated; we share a critical sentimentality, a somewhat twisted but also unmistakable nostalgia for local radio stations that now play Dad Rock on an unending loop, likely appealing to listeners of our generation (many of whom are themselves now dads/parents).

> DAVID: Our mutual love for Dad Rock is interwoven into our queer kinship!
> SHEREEN: I love that we call it Dad Rock to begin with! There's a queer commentary to be made about this classification itself—the playful "daddy" connotations are spilling over here. What we are referring to includes Classic/Arena/Hard Rock, genres that fuel and reify the totally ubiquitous, unflinching white cis emblems of individualism and toxic masculinity. My brown, immigrant father neither listened to nor tolerated Dad Rock. So, when we use Dad Rock as a soundtrack to our kinship, it feels like yet another counternarrative or appropriative act—for me, it's a rebellion against the intended audience and my own upbringing. You and I spend countless hours together (in both domestic and public spaces) with Dad Rock playing in the background and inducing all kinds of mixed nostalgia, but what we bring to and embody in these spaces is our humanity and love for each other, which feels like the farthest thing from toxicity.
> DAVID: I also love that we're queering Dad Rock as the soundtrack to our kinship! I'm thankful to have inherited my love for Dad Rock from my mom, who I'm sure initially embraced it as an act of rebellion in her

youth. So, in a way, I inherited some queerness with my appreciation for Dad Rock. It also reminds me of our relative shared proximity to the Great Plains and a shared geographic and topographic knowledge that is part of our kinship. It [our attachment to Dad Rock] was based in prairie life, it was based in sagebrush and knowing what that looks like and how it's gorgeous in its multitudes. This gorgeous scenery juxtaposed with our constant experiences with oppression is something that we both know and can communicate and understand without too much interpretation. We had to navigate predominantly white, heteronormative contexts since our earliest moments of awareness, and this shared experience is also salient to our kinship. Our queerness and brownness were silenced so much by people within our bio-families and in our communities. We know what that's like, and we both were silenced so much and we also learned how to persist whilst being silenced. We persisted so much that we both ended up in professions that are all about communicating!

SHEREEN: Yes, this connection between land, sound, and our discourse communities makes sense. We both come from places that were (or still are) predominantly white, where landscapes are scarred by the continued violences of colonization. My birthplace, which is on Treaty One territory, the homelands of Anishinaabeg, Cree, Oji-Cree, Dakota, and Dene peoples, and Métis Nation, is often associated with farmlands that stretch into the horizon, and little popular thought is given to how this farmland is a marker of settler colonial history. The land is a site where truth is buried and concealed, but it also resists (perhaps via drought and various geological phenomena) in ways that reveal its real history.

There is a profound link between Dad Rock and both of our childhood landscapes— they (both the music and the land) attempt to conceal the inverted realities resulting from and used to justify colonial destruction. But I'm learning to be hypervigilant of this inversion and insist on flipping it to see reality as it actually is. This very act of flipping the falsehood is itself writing a counterstory. The counterstory bears truth. Especially as I consider how counterstory shapes my professional and personal work with storytelling. Aya Y. Martinez puts it beautifully: "As an interdisciplinary method, CRT [critical race theory] counterstory recognizes that the experiential and embodied knowledge of people of color is legitimate and critical to understanding racism that is often well disguised in the rhetoric of normalized structural values and practices" (Martinez 2014: 69).

As a settler-immigrant, I have a responsibility to speak to these truths about the land of my birthplace by unearthing what has been buried, even though those who claim to "own" the land attempt to hush this type of effort. So, the counterstory in this case *is* the story, the history, the record that has been selectively, strategically muted; however, it is reverberating in and through the land, in and through the knowledges we carry as BIPOC. I don't think it's too big of a leap to declare that this way of understanding counterstory is also how I hear and respond to Dad Rock—what it conceals about toxic white masculinity, colonial hubris, and class markers—how it is meant to pacify and silence BIPOC *and* misappropriate our rhythms and sounds. There's just so much worth exploring here . . .

Interruption. . .

Aja Martinez (2014) positions "counterstory" in ways that inform the field of composition and its relationship to academia. This work, which takes up CRT at its core (but in a cross-disciplinary manner), seems particularly exigent at the present moment when CRT is misunderstood and under violent siege on such a broad scale. Martinez distinguishes "counterstory" as a method that departs "from fictional storytelling," explaining, also, that it "critically examines theoretical concepts and humanizes empirical data" (Martinez 2014: 69). As a note of personal documentary, our "buddymoon" (a cabin trip the two of us took to the Adirondacks) offers a "counterstory" to the celebratory outcomes of traditionally cis, hetero, couplings, which so frequently culminate in weddings and honeymoons. Of our own volition, we queered the idea of a "honeymoon" around the genesis of our kinship, taking a celebratory getaway that we named a "buddymoon," another term deposited into the shared lexicon. Our photos documenting this getaway read to many people as romantically confusing. On the one hand, it seemed clear that this wasn't a romantic couple's getaway to people who know us, and yet, on the other hand, our pictures spilled over with something oddly akin to a honeymoon! We delighted in the confusion it created.

> DAVID: There are multiple and overlapping silences that impact our queer kinship. We have the aggressions and silencing we endured directly and personally that we are resisting with our kinship, and we are addressing the historical, structural, and institutional silencing that predated us by intentionally taking a critical and historical lens on how we live life, including our kinship. Because of our shared processes of being silenced and living in environments wrought with historical silencing, we had to learn a language to persist through all the invalidating silence. We've learned a way to persist in these environments that actually helped us to grow and flourish through all the oppression. Even though we've left our homes of origin, we keep with us the initial language and processes we learned to resist oppression as our child-selves and we can recognize this in each other. We can catch the glimmers of queerness in each other that are most often unseen and ignored by others. It's a connection and understanding that happened before we even first spoke to each other. Because our mere existence has been silenced, queer people needed to develop a way of knowing each other without the use of dominant discourses. This is what's really going on. Mastering oppression means that we know how to undo and undesign it, and that's what we do through our work and our queer kinship.

SHEREEN: Wow. That's shockingly beautiful. I would add that we also recognize and discuss how queer kinship carries different significance to each one of us because we have divergent relationships and attachments to biological family. Our queer kinship overlaps the more general domain of "chosen family," although for me, these are not always synonymous terms (I see "chosen family" as a broader relationality that doesn't exclusively involve queer kinship).

The way we experience chosen family can at times elicit guilt and shame, especially where we encounter bio-fam as supportive and loving (we could liken this to survivor's or thriver's guilt). But guilt and shame can also get kicked up where we do *not* experience biological family as supportive and loving. So, decisions to go no- or low-contact with bio-fam can feel very fraught and alienating. Within the latter context, the most reliable family often becomes queer kinship/chosen fam. Amin describes it best: "Chosen family channels both the longings generated by exile from the heterosexual family and the critical injunction to not repeat its hierarchies and exclusions into the creation of a novel form of kinship" (Amin 2017: 113).

There's a tension operating for us between chosen and biological family, which feels like an unsettling construction of yet another binary. To be sure, this tension also feels joyful, liberating, and transgressive, like an invitation to centralize chosen kin/friendship over compulsory romantic couplehood and bio-fam. The joy you and I feel in our queer kinship is often so unbridled and explosive that bystanders find it disorienting! There have been so many instances where people assume our relationship to be something beyond what it actually is, often something that fits socially sanctioned scripts for intimacy. I think we exhibit a kind of closeness that many reserve exclusively for romantic, sexual partnerships. Of course, this reflects how deeply compulsory couplehood cuts through the collective psyche, limiting imagination and erasing creative ways of forming relationships. In our case, though, the joke's on those who make these assumptions because it's not like not we're *not* in love! You and I both experience friendlove (and beyond) as falling in love. For us, friendlove carries the physical, emotional, social, psychological transformations widely attributed to romantic love. So, the fact that "falling in love" is commonly ascribed to romance and sex is not our concern!

DAVID: Yes, I'm in love with what you just said. The misguided and oppressive projections others make on our kinship are not our concern! When we absorb these projections as something that is our doing, it can induce feelings of guilt and shame, and when not checked and processed these can become internalized oppressions. Guilt and shame don't have to be "debilitating." I think both of us have understood it to be debilitating in some ways where it's pulled us back from actualizing our fullest potentials. These feelings can cause us to question ourselves in ways that are undercutting to our self-determination. But we understand it has a purpose, like there's a working through the guilt and shame to get to a place of power, which comes to our kinship. In a way we are reconceptualizing oppressive language, like "debilitating." We recognize the inherent ableism in the term "debilitating," especially how it is used in mainstream communication to oppress queer communities. It wasn't too long ago that my profession (psychology) purposefully conceptualized being queer as debilitating and pathological by considering "homosexuality" a legit mental disorder. Even though the diagnostic category was removed from the DSM (Diagnostic and Statistical Manual of Mental Disorders) in the 1970s, the damage to our queer communities stemming from this misguided diagnosis still persists. In reconceptualizing oppressive language and concepts via our kinship, we are not only helping each other to resist oppression, but we are also adding to a larger, community-oriented process of resistance.

Kinship means we have an everlasting source of support that is constant and will buttress us through our hardships, but it will also challenge us to grow. The power of kinship won't let us just devolve into whatever mediocrity might be an acceptable answer at the time. Queer kinship will push us to find the path that will elevate us as individuals and also elevate our kinship and our queer communities. So, we have collectivism as a major tenet in how we understand each other, which means that through collectivism your learning is always evolving. It's never devolving.

Interruption...

Our dialogue reveals our own understanding and direct experiences of subjugation, which have resulted (in part) in our ability to resist and dismantle oppressive circumstances in our personal and professional lives. A key ingredient of our ability to resist, dismantle, and even "master" oppression, is our queer kinship and the existing and ever-developing, shared discourse that allows us to enter into deeply meaningful and critical conversation about our lived experiences. This particular quality of our queer kinship is necessary for the fostering of survivance that is both a process and function of our queer kinship. As we chronicle, the oppressions play out across multiple sources, including within our biological families of origin. While our experiences with our biological families are qualitatively different, there are tensions that we both experienced from our biological families as we created and maintain our queer kinships. How we manage the resulting guilt is an example of how our queer kinship is a transformative force on how to negotiate life. Our queer kinship allows us to enter into a validating, reiterative process of conceptualizing challenges and threats that moves us to maximize our personal and community strengths and situate ourselves in relation to others.

SHEREEN: Our discussion about guilt, shame, and hardship offers a realistic segue into examining our academic lives. I find myself having to consciously resist feelings of guilt and shame (usually having to do with capitalist notions of "productivity") on an ongoing basis. I think it's too frequently assumed that earning tenure lessens these pressures around "productivity," but that certainly has not been my experience, which I think says a lot about what queer/brown/immigrant/child-free/femmes at my rank are denied by the institution or society on a broader scale. I get asked to do much more with much less at every turn, and so I must sharpen my resolve to say no and to choose where to spend my energy very strategically.

I often rely on our queer kinship as a space to seek refuge from the academic grind, a space to strategize, vent, troubleshoot, problem solve, organize, drum up creative ideas, unwind, and refuel. This queer kinship also shapes and fortifies our professional collaborations—there are so many surprising intersections in what we research and do. We both centralize queer BIPOC knowledges in our research, teaching, and approach to service even though our work sometimes manifests in wildly dissimilar contexts. I didn't necessarily expect to seek and create opportunities for such a close collaboration outside of my field or the humanities more broadly, so our alliance is especially energizing. And the more we collaborate, the more I notice that forming or sustaining cross-disciplinary queer kinship within academia seems fairly anomalous. It shouldn't be, but it is.

DAVID: Yes, collaborating on this specific writing project is resisting the ways academia has structured how "we are to be" as faculty. The higher education system is set up to be purposefully siloed, which is a mechanism of control. When we are siloed as individual scholars, by program/department, by college/university, and especially by discipline, we lose the capacity for meaningful connection. This is an especially harmful dynamic for queer faculty, in that we are less likely to find points of meaningful and queer connection in our siloed programs and departments. And when we add on the other layers of sociocultural identity, such as both of us being people of color, the opportunities for mirroring and connection are even more difficult to find. When we lack the opportunity to connect with people who share our backgrounds and who even look and sound like us, it can lead to a sense of isolation and even professional identity diffusion. This can result in someone questioning their place, role, and value at the institution. The academic silos we often find ourselves in also induce the unnecessary and malignant nature of competition that pervades academia. Our queer kinship provides me with all the valuable processes you just mentioned. Even just focusing on our process of cowriting this chapter, I've benefited from our ability to be candid with one another and from being understood as a full person, and not just as a scholar. This allowed me to bring myself more fully into this project because of the very dynamic of our queer kinship. You provide me with mirroring that is validating and affirming, and necessary for me to express myself with less editing, as well as to grow and develop as a scholar and human being.

>SHEREEN: What you're saying here is absolutely true. One of the most challenging aspects of academic labor is how isolating it can be or is designed to be. I think it takes so much effort to locate and follow through with meaningful collaborations.
>
>It's true that you and I both do a lot of cowriting with colleagues in our respective fields, but coauthoring publications is one of the obvious areas of academic work that is valued and rewarded. There should be so many more opportunities to share and cocreate, and maybe there are, but I don't think they hold recognizable kinds of "currency." And there it is again: "currency," another term entwined with (if not entirely born out of) a capitalist paradigm.

You and I have certainly interrogated our disdain for "recognizable academic currency." (I have also had to examine my reliance on it for bread and butter survival!) And we never cease to question how the power to "recognize" or "dismiss" fuels the larger academic gatekeeping mechanisms in the first place. All of these considerations help us determine what we choose to accept or disrupt within our professional work and where we can insist upon sharing resources (instead of competing for them) as an act of resistance. In part, this is what queer kinship does for our academic lives, it gives us options for how to intervene in the "business as usual" systems that often leave us feeling dehumanized, right?

Reflection

This chapter emerged from casual conversations about how much we treasure and protect our queer kinship. There was no outline, no strict agenda, no burning question at the outset. We didn't have a roadmap for how to explore our kinship and make it a site of inquiry. In many ways, the very methodology (or lack thereof) in the construction of this chapter was queer, unconventional, and nonnormative. Our conversation started in person and felt very organic. After fully transcribing the recording of it, the drafting process took a more solitary approach. Apart from two in-person writing sessions and using a shared online document, we didn't cowrite or consult with each other in a simultaneous cogenerative way. Instead, we drafted this chapter from the separate spaces of our respective homes, working on different sections at different times. And yet, the dialogue format sustained itself, remaining mostly untouched through our revisions process, which involved more in-person cowriting focused on the interruptions, methodology, and reflections. Neither one of us has approached scholarship in this fashion before, and our process here is itself a counterstory, mirroring again what Martinez describes as "a hybrid form of scholarly inquiry" and "storytelling" (Martinez 2014: 69).

Our conversation revealed a strong emotional quality of queer kinship. Throughout our dialogue, we mentioned emotions such as love, guilt, and shame. Lynch argues that "through our interdependencies and vulnerabilities we exercise judgments, judgments that are deeply affectively driven" (Lynch 2010: 61). Witnessing and validating our emotional experiences, especially the emotional by-products of experiencing academic oppression, are necessary for counteracting the emotionally stifled academic climates that we regularly navigate. Academia overly prizes and celebrates productivity in scholarship and teaching endeavors. And, as our conversation disclosed, the lived experiences of queer scholars can be an arduous journey due to the demand for our time and talents compounded by the perceived abundance of time and energy some of us are assumed to have as single and child-free people, for example. This creates pressure and saps our emotional, physical, and creative energies in ways that can lead to wellness compromises when our institutions fail to recognize and validate this injustice. Queer kinship recognizes this unsustainable, often dehumanizing dynamic, and our validation and affirmation of our emotional experiences serve as an academic counter-practice.

Another theme that emerged was how queer kinship in academia promotes interdisciplinary sharing and collaboration. Because our queer kinship is experienced holistically, it has impacts on both our professional and personal lives. The content and quality of our shared experiences often blend the professional and the personal. We alluded to the collectivistic nature of queer kinship, which we purposefully apply toward integrating the personal and the professional. This in turn creates a specific kind of intimacy in our relationship that opens up space for opportunity and possibility. And this same collective quality promotes our interdisciplinary sharing and collaborations due to the blurred or dissolved boundary between our professional and personal lives.

Perhaps our dialogue and reflections can serve as a template for interdisciplinary work: one that is committed to collaboration within a paradigm of abundance rather than scarcity. Approaching our professional and personal spheres with a mindset of abundance is an act of resistance against capitalism that tells us we never have or do enough, we are never adequate. This interplay between abundance and scarcity manifests at the local level of our academic institutions, where resource deprivation and the pressures placed on queer, BIPOC students, staff, and faculty create often invalidating working and learning conditions. Abundance/scarcity also shapes the material realities of the queer lives we embody, being cast as "too much" (hypervisible, overly sensitive, dramatic, unsubtle) and "not enough" (selfishly solitary, avoidant of domestic/marital/parental responsibilities for upholding the nation-state) in all facets of our private and public existence. We are reminded of Amber Jamilla Musser's descriptions of "excess," the space of being emotionally excessive, in her analysis of affect and sensation (Musser 2018: 124).

In this chapter we described how we use queer kinship as a paradigm and process for our personal and professional collaborations. In addition to offering perspectives and reflections on queer kinship via our conversation, we also discussed a queered methodology for qualitatively revealing queer phenomena. Given the purposefully ambiguous and imaginative nature of queerness, queer theory, and queer studies, it was fitting to use an unconventional and nonnormative process for coauthoring this chapter on queer kinship. Our counterstory challenges the inherently capitalistic, patriarchal, and heteronormative academic structures and processes we navigate by providing examples of how we benefit from our queer kinship to decolonize and depathologize our professional work and our lives. We've come to understand the centrality of queer kinship in our lives as a force that gives us the power to resist oppression and persist toward actualizing self-determination and optimizing our fullest potentials.

References

Amin, K. (2017), *Disturbing Attachments: Genet, Modern Pederasty, and Queer History*, Durham, NC: Duke University Press.

Breeze, M. and Y. Taylor (2020), *Feminist Repetitions in Higher Education: Interrupting Career Categories*, Cham, Switzerland: Palgrave MacMillan.

Dilley, P. (1999), "Queer Theory: Under Construction," *International Journal of Qualitative Studies in Education*, 12 (5): 457–72.

Lynch, K. (2010), "Carelessness: A Hidden Doxa of Higher Education," *Arts and Humanities in Higher Education*, 9 (1): 54–67.

Martinez, A.Y. (2014), "A Plea for Critical Race Theory Counterstory: Stock Story vs. Counterstory Dialogues Concerning Alejandra's 'fit' in the Academy," *Composition Studies*, 42 (2): 33–55.

Monaghan, W. (2016), *Queer Girls, Temporality and Screen Media: Not "just a phase,"* London: Palgrave Macmillan.

Musser, A.J. (2018), *Sensual Excess: Queer Femininity and Brown Jouissance*, New York: New York University Press.

Piepzna-Samarasinha, L.L. (2018), *Care Work Dreaming Disability Justice*, Vancouver, BC: Arsenal Pulp Press.

Pierce, J.M. (2019), *Argentine Intimacies: Queer Kinship in an Age of Splendor, 1890–1910*, Albany: SUNY Press.

Quinn, J., K. Allen, S. Hollingworth, U. Maylor, J. Osgood, and Rose, A. (2014), "Dialogue or Duel? A Critical Reflection on the Gendered Politics of Engaging and Impacting," in Y. Taylor (ed.), *The Entrepreneurial University*, 202–22, London: Palgrave Macmillan.

Tuck, E. and K.W. Yang (2012), "Decolonization Is Not a Metaphor," *Decolonization: Indigeneity, Education & Society*, 1 (1): 1–40.

Vizenor, G.R. (1999), *Manifest Manners: Narratives on Postindian Survivance*, Lincoln, NE: University of Nebraska Press.

Part II

FAILURE AND RESISTANCE IN DIVERSITY WORK

Chapter 5

UNAFFILIATED: THE DELEGITIMIZATION OF SCHOLARS OF COLOR OUTSIDE OF ACADEME

Monalesia Earle

Introduction

The mutually constitutive relationship between academia and scholarship has its inverse in the systematic stratification of independent researchers from those within academe. While much has been written about the lack of opportunity for scholars of color who are granted conditional entry into the academy (Baez 2000; Stanley 2006; Doharty, Madriaga, and Joseph-Salisbury 2020) this chapter focuses primarily on those who have little to no access at all. By applying a queer(ed) Black framework to examining the multiple and fraught inflection points for scholars of color attempting to gain employment in academe, this chapter underscores the peculiar tension between Black scholarly achievement with its anticipated rewards of academic affiliation and recognition, against the intransigence of higher education gatekeepers in recruiting them. Moreover, the peculiar entanglements of white institutions and Blackness in all of its historically raced permutations bring into sharp relief what I suggest is a racist "anti-agenda" undergirding nearly every aspect of entry into higher education.

It is well documented that the machinations of historically white educational institutions across the globe have their antecedent in colonialist practices that are meant to affirm whiteness in all of its brutal and self-reflexive forms (Hode and Meisenbach 2016; Kumalo, 2018; Heleta 2020). Evidenced through hiring practices that are not always transparent, the language used to support the exclusion of scholars of color changes over time, but the outcome remains the same: a lack of diversity within academia, the devaluing of important research, the creation of an outsider professional class, and the use of hiring committees comprised of "a small number of faculty [. . .] leaving room for biases and discriminatory practices to creep in, often masked as 'fit'" (Sensoy and DiAngelo 2017: 559). Such implicit bias hiding behind the mask of plausible deniability is far too common in recruitment and hiring practices. Indeed, racism in hiring has become less overt, creating a convenient, although according to Pollard (1999), a possibly unconscious way to justify discriminatory practices.

In building on the work of Kovel (1970), Pearson, Dovidio, and Gaertner (2009) examine how "aversive racism" is operationalized in academe. Essentially another form of plausible deniability, this type of discrimination continues to operate across disciplines. Dovidio and Gaertner compare openly racist perceptions of Black people expressed by political conservatives, to the less openly racist views held by political liberals. Those who fall into the "aversive racism" column "openly endorse non-prejudiced views, but [their] unconscious negative feelings and beliefs get expressed in subtle, indirect, and often rationalizable ways" (Dovidio and Gaertner 2009: 317).

A case could be made that aversive racism is perhaps one of the most pernicious forms of discrimination, not only because of the incredible harm that it does but also for many people of color who have had lifelong experiences of being at the receiving end of these practices, there is almost an element of self-doubt that comes into play when one is constantly told that they are imagining racism where none exists. Sensoy and DiAngelo (2017) also offer examples of these discriminatory practices. They noted that in a department in which one of them taught, the department went seventeen years without hiring a single Black faculty member. A similar case was noted by Cecily Jones (2006), a faculty member at a UK university who reported that from the time of her appointment in 1999 to a period of seven years later, and "despite the implementation of equality of opportunity action plans aimed at increasing BME representation among faculty [...] no other African Caribbean female has been appointed to an academic post" (Jones 2006: 149).

Recent data published by the Higher Education Statistics Agency (HESA) in the UK reveals that out of 21,000 professorships held in the UK for example, only 140 of those are held by academics identifying as Black (Adams 2020). To put numbers such as these into a local context, in 2018, and in one fell swoop, one UK university promoted twelve educators to the professorial level. Based on their faculty photos (which should not be taken as a definitive indicator of their race or ethnicity), all appear to be white. This is not necessarily an indictment of this particular university, as it now currently has on offer certificates and diplomas in diaspora studies. But it does highlight the continuing disparities in career advancement for Black faculty both nationally and internationally, and across a range of academic disciplines. In the field of medicine, for example, a "minority tax" or "cultural tax," places an unequal burden on faculty of color to take on additional responsibilities that do not necessarily result in career advancement (Rodríguez, Campbell, and Pololi 2015). Statistics, longitudinal studies, interviews, and historical data notwithstanding, it is anecdotal information like this that speaks most forcefully to the reality of scholars of color who are routinely overlooked at the interview stage and beyond.

"Credentialing," as Victor Ray (2019) explains it, is yet another way that historically white institutions screen out applicants of color. In this case, the "credential" is whiteness, which, Ray argues, provides "access to organizational resources, legitimizing work hierarchies, and expanding white agency" (Ray 2019: 41). Underresearched yet inseparable from the countless ways in which scholars of color are relegated to the margins, is the matter of citations: whose work is cited and thereby valued, whose work is ignored and thereby devalued, and how the inability to build credentials has a direct correlation to the lack of mentoring, biased job screening processes, and a host of other discriminatory tactics that unaffiliated scholars of color routinely encounter.

> In addition to publication, citation is taken as an assumed proxy for measuring impact, relevance, and importance, with implications not only for hiring, promotion, tenure, and other aspects of performance evaluation, but also for how certain voices are represented and included over others in intellectual conversations. (Mott and Cockayne 2017: 2)

Recent scholarship that interrogates the hierarchies of inclusion and exclusion in educational institutions has its discursive foundation in the idea that whiteness "suggests a milieu rooted in both past and present structural, political, and cultural practices and norms that has implications for admissions, faculty advising, and racially hostile campus environments" (Corces-Zimmerman, Thomas, and Cabrera 2021: 12). Thus, the reification of whiteness as an extension of white supremacy, as Corces-Zimmerman et al, go on to suggest, finds ways to reinvent itself as the ideological and policy-making norm.

Although obsolescence is a long way off from being the watchword signaling the dismantling of white power structures, the irony is that the constant reinvention of whiteness anticipates its own irrelevancy. This in turn often results in increasingly strident expressions of entitlement, as well as a more intrusive surveillance regime directed at Black scholars who may be perceived as threats to the status quo. Thus, the reality is that whether one is within the academy or on the outside looking in, the mechanisms of white privilege function in similar ways: bias in recruitment and selection; few opportunities for mentoring; inequity in promotions and tenure for those who are eventually hired; little job security; guest lecturing stints that never result in even temporary employment; and, lack of access to important career-making networking opportunities. This unfortunate reality is all to the detriment of the unaffiliated. These exclusionary practices both within and outside of academe have effectively created a permanent professional underclass whose contributions are either devalued or largely ignored.

For scholars of color who fall into these categories, there is ample evidence pointing to their disproportionate representation at the "bottom tiers of academia" (Lomax 2015). Furthermore, the power and deference accorded to whites in the upper echelons of the higher educational system "creates insiders and outsiders, marking boundaries that exclude, disqualify, and oppress" (Duncan 2014: 52). This "epistemic exclusion" occurs when "faculty of color are deemed illegitimate members of the academy, and thus their scholarship is devalued" (Settles et al. 2020: 1).

Equally if not more important to future career progression, mentoring as well as networking is seen as a form of "social capital" that is routinely available to white students but largely unavailable to students of color (Walton and Cohen 2007: 82). Even when students of color are able to secure funding to attend college or university, their access to quality mentorships are limited, due in no small part to the anti-Black sentiment that is inextricably bound up in complex matrices of imperialism that preserve the white status quo by systematically silencing Black voices.

The Making of the Unaffiliated

Before proceeding I want to briefly explain my usage of the term "unaffiliated." General definitions notwithstanding, being unaffiliated depends upon the contexts within which it derives (and ultimately signifies) its meaning. If, for example, a group of activists is unaffiliated with the power structures that systematically oppress citizens, then their legitimacy as nongovernmental actors is perceived by those who are also outside of the system to be valid. Yet if legitimacy via affiliation is conditioned upon having a seat at the table in order to influence policy, seek advancement, or simply to be taken seriously, then being part of the inner circle becomes much more than an ideological exercise in decentering whiteness from its entrenched position on the world stage. It also becomes essential to being *seen* and *heard* in decision-making processes.

As I will show in this chapter, the unaffiliated are not only excluded through biased recruitment processes, lack of access to formal networks, or through their "queer(ed)" (read: too "ethnically" oriented) research interests but for those who are eventually hired, their de facto unaffiliated status *within* academia is also problematic. To borrow a phrase from Saidiya Hartman (2019: xvii), the unaffiliated are "surplus [scholars] of no significance". Being an outsider on the inside of academe tends to amplify identity markers that swing the pendulum of belonging toward either acceptance or rejection, thereby ensuring that what remains constant is the performative power of whiteness.

Following insights derived from centuries of whiteness and its epistemological conceit, coupled with the "tumultuous legacy of race and gender relations in America, African American women suffer the 'double whammy' of being both Black and female in academic environments that place little value on either trait" (Holmes 2008: 104). Moreover, where doubt is sowed around a constellation of perpetual "otherisms," and gaining admittance to academia as students or faculty is rife with seemingly insurmountable roadblocks, once inside, "our presence [. . .] marks a deviance from the bodies that are seen to occupy the academe as well as the way in which knowledge has been produced" (Johnson and Joseph-Salisbury 2018: 149). We are positioned as outliers, as the "queer(ed)" (read: Black, brown, undesirable, undisciplined) imposters in white spaces. Black achievement is routinely scrutinized against racist stereotypes and metrics that are historically intertwined with whiteness functioning as the ultimate arbiter of intellectual worth.

Described by Bernal and Villalpando (2010) as the "apartheid of knowledge," the unfortunate stratification of intellectual ability between whites and people of color is historically entrenched. Under cover of purportedly objective "assessment metrics" such as the Research Excellence Framework (REF) in the UK, which measure: outputs (originality, significance, and rigor), impact (reach and significance), and environment (vitality and sustainability), the unaffiliated have no formal standing to compete, or even contribute to, a university's academic ranking. Ultimately the disenfranchisement of unaffiliated scholars of color by the very systems through which many obtained their postgraduate degrees, underscore the contradictions built into the very fabric of historically white institutions (HWUs).

Originally founded upon principles enshrined by white settlers to control access to knowledge and power, Dancy, Edwards, and Davis (2018: 178) note that the "academic model is still essentially a colonial one". Perhaps not since the establishment of Historically Black Colleges and Universities (HBCUs) in America, whose purpose was to remedy the widespread racial animus that saw Black students largely denied admission to established higher education institutions, has this colonial mindset been so starkly evidenced than in the current moment of extreme political and cultural fracture. Couched in more nuanced language than the overt racism of old, including the gatekeeping measures and metrics previously mentioned, the wholesale effect is the same: Black scholars are not considered intellectually equal to white scholars.

Beattie, Cohen, and McGuire (2013) note that "BME individuals not only have to send, on average, 74% more applications than Whites to secure an interview, but that once in employment BME staff face lower hourly earnings and lower levels of occupational attainment, compared to equally qualified White staff" (Beattie, Cohen, and McGuire 2013: 172). For those few who are eventually offered academic posts, "underlying it all is the message that faculty should be grateful to have been hired in the first place" (Duncan 2014: 46). Implicit in this statement is that faculty of color almost always start from a deficit position, and once inside the academy, there is an expectation that they demonstrate their gratefulness by staying quiet and unseen.

This chapter aims to take up and build upon important conversations put forth by unaffiliated scholars of color, both in the UK and the USA, although race-based hiring practices in academia are also a troubling holdover in many previously colonized countries. Recognition for scholars of color often flows from a temporary and conditional belonging, and rarely results in permanent membership in the overwhelmingly white environs of academia. Moreover, this chapter concerns itself with the coded white-centric language that sets up critical and social divides between those on the inside of higher education institutions and those who struggle to be included. Inextricably tied to a much coveted "naming" (lecturer, professor, teaching or research fellow, postdoc, reader), academic language equates to *belonging* and belonging bestows certain benefits, recognitions, funding, and honorifics that remain mostly out of reach for the unaffiliated. For those without access to the right networks, mentorships, fellowships, titles, or positions—all typically gained through employment or postdoctoral work linked to academe—they find themselves pushed even further to the outer margins.

Research has shown that in spite of the intense focus and sacrifice it takes to complete years of original research that culminates in a doctoral degree and eventual publication of one's work with a reputable press, scholars of color are still deemed not good enough to secure postdoctoral positions in higher education. Thus, this coveted "naming" that is essential to advancement, becomes time-limited and conditional, and loses its relevance the longer one remains unaffiliated. Evidence from multiple field studies suggests that being unaffiliated results in a cumulative effect whereby minorities who gained ground by virtue of being accepted onto (and completing) rigorous doctoral programs, experience an alarming return to what Zwysen and Longhi (2016) describe as an "ethnic penalty" that alongside wage and employment penalties, coalesce to significantly lessen their career chances (Zwysen and Longhi 2016: 1).

In their analysis of hiring disparities between whites and Blacks in higher education, Mickelson and Oliver (1991) point out the unspoken importance of patronage, and how this is advantageous to white students who are more likely to come from privilege or who have been groomed to expect preferential treatment based on their social networks. "To the degree that minorities are found less often at top institutions, and to the degree that they are left out of prestigious patronage networks, then 'the institution as proxy' process will tend to exclude perfectly qualified African American candidates" (Mickelson and Oliver 1991: 193). Put another way, the authors point to coded language that allows universities to escape close scrutiny over discriminatory hiring practices.

When search committees put forth claims that there are simply no qualified applicants of color to be found, Mickelson and Oliver (1991) assert that what they are really saying is that "'properly sponsored and credentialed' minority Ph.D.s cannot be found" (Mickelson and Oliver 1991: 193). Current research shows that discriminatory trends in hiring have not significantly changed over many decades. In pulling back the curtain on the sleight of hand used by recruitment and hiring committees to justify the rejection of otherwise qualified applicants of color, we can better understand Onwuachi-Willig's (2010) focus on two specific types of discrimination. "Complimentary" discrimination treats the minority candidate as overqualified and likely to not be interested in offers from low-ranking institutions, whereas "complementary" discrimination locks out less-qualified candidates. In other words, one purportedly "positive" discriminatory action causes an opposite and unequal discriminatory reaction.

Thus the struggle to be validated through hiring processes, research output, participation in academic conferences, and competition for fellowships that are linked to higher education affiliation intensifies when paired with systemic racism and a presumed intellectual unfitness—whether it be the twin discriminations of overfitness or underfitness. The further underlying conundrum is that if unaffiliated scholars are denied access to the networks and sponsorships required in order to fairly compete for fellowships and grants because of their unaffiliated status, those rewards will remain closed to them.

Here, mentoring plays a crucial role in helping minority applicants negotiate their way through the daunting process of the academic job search, but to also safely navigate treacherous waters within the academy. What might be routine for many middle-class white applicants who come from families where pursuing higher education is a given, minority students and scholars may not have the "formal and informal support structures" that lay the groundwork for academic careers (Arday 2017: 7). The author goes on to note that mentoring relationships are, in effect, one of decoding, of "understanding the topography of academia" (Arday 2017: 7). The significance of these relationships cannot be overstated, as they have the potential for mapping out entry routes into successful career paths.

Brunsma, Embrick, and Shin (2017), citing Gasman (2016), make the case that not only do "departments [not] want faculty of color" but a typical reason put forth for not hiring minorities revolve around a belief that "([. . .] they are not qualified—namely, they did not get mentored by a prominent 'white' person in the field)" (Brunsma, Embrick, and Shin 2017: 8). This type of shortsighted reasoning is not uncommon, as it has a long history that is firmly grounded in racial elitism. And while those scholars who attend HBCUs stand a better chance of accessing mentorships and building important networks that will stand them in good stead later on in life, these opportunities are largely unavailable in predominantly white institutions of higher learning.

What we know is that HBCUs are in a unique position to offer students of color what Flowers III, et al. (2015) refer to as "othermothering," a more holistic and nurturing approach that is distinct from traditional mentoring. In citing Kram (1983) and James (1993), Flowers et al. note that whereas mentoring is often seen as a "formalized relationship between an individual and a person of authority," othermothering is layered and quite nuanced. It is a community practice drawn from centuries of teaching Black and brown children not only how to navigate the often unwelcoming landscape of a white-dominated world but how to also keep hold of the very essence of who they are (Flowers et al. 2015: 60).

Naming—a Matter of "Degrees"

The historically exclusionary practices in the recruitment and retention process in higher education institutions guarantee that the status quo will be preserved and that those seeking entry must be able to understand layers upon layers of coded language in order to secure even conditional membership. In the recruitment process side-by-side comparisons of professional degrees, experience, publications, conferences, and pre-postdoc teaching assignments are misleading if considerations of race, gender, social class, and age are excluded. Thus, the extent to which these factors—if they are taken into account at all—result in a level-playing field for scholars of color is the basis of much debate.

In an illuminating paper coauthored by Johnson-Bailey and Cervero (2008), the institutional divide between white professors and Black professors is laid out in a way that mirrors the harmful stereotypes about people of color that are perpetuated across many social, educational, cultural, and political settings. Cervero drafted a list of privileges afforded to white professors alongside lesser privileges afforded to Black professors. Building the list around two major themes (relationships with colleagues and students, and relationship with the institution), it was in the context of race and gender privilege that equity (or the lack thereof) was measured. For purposes of illustration only a few of the thirteen points listed by Cervero will be noted (Table 5.1).

According to Elizabeth J. West (2020), "naming [. . .] is the conduit to existence or being" (West 2020: 2). And while the points on Cervero's list underscore parallels to racist practices and language that people of color also encounter outside of the academy, we know that the tentacles of racism find root at the very moment a child of color is born. "It's a (black) boy or a (black) girl." Oft cited and reframed through multiple viewpoints, J. L. Austin's *How to Do Things with Words* (1962) is a reminder of how naming (or un-naming) something brings it into or out of existence as the thing or the something that it has been called. Not only are Black children—like everyone else—assigned a gender at birth, but they have also been assigned to a racial category, either or both of which has been considered throughout history to be immutable.

As Sigrid King notes (1990), in African American traditions naming has always been critical, largely due to the power it confers (King 1990: 683). Django Paris (2019) underlines this in much starker terms by carefully breaking down the coded discourse of erasure that is endemic in white-dominated educational and social institutions. Indeed, calling institutions out of *their* name(s) is crucial to interrupting the deficit model upon which Paris insightfully notes, "hegemonic classifying regimes" turn (Paris 2019: 218). But where the power to name is held by

Table 5.1 Table of Privileges

Academic life with race and gender privilege	*Academic life without race and gender privilege*
White male professors are considered intellectual and well suited for the professoriate.	Black women professors are not seen as intellectuals who are well suited for the professoriate, and their membership in the academy is seen as a credit to their gender and their racial group.
In an academic life automatically advantaged with race and gender privilege, it is difficult for a white male professor to come up with a list of what academic life is like with race and gender privilege.	In an academic life without race and gender privilege, Black women professors are considered outsiders and are viewed with the stereotypical societal lens that characterizes them as hostile, emasculating, and intimidating.
White male professors are seen as producers and disseminators of knowledge.	Black women professors are seen as not contributing to the knowledge base in academia and instead are often viewed as affirmative action cultural representatives.

Source: Johnson-Bailey and Cervero (2008: 321).

those whose intentions are to oppress and subjugate others, it is also often linked to preconceptions about intelligence and worthiness. This in turn often becomes the precursor to disproportionate treatment in nearly every aspect of a person's life. Thus whereas Cervero has likely been what I describe as *privileged into* his position by dint of birth, possibly class, and certainly his whiteness, his Black colleague (and multiple other Black faculty throughout time) has been "other-named," relegated to an epistemological caste system, devalued, and largely ignored.

When I suggest that in a so-called post-racial world where exclusion and discrimination are masterful and paradoxical arts that are measured in "degrees," what I am getting at is that the degree to which naming equates to power and the control of knowledge; to one's inclusion or exclusion; to legitimacy or marginalization, there is a direct correlation to the erasure that begins at the very moment of our (un)naming.

Naming sets the stage for future personal and social relations, educational and job opportunities, as well as the types of interactions one has with legal systems and government entities. Naming determines not only the amount but also the quality of opportunities for attainment of the most basic tools (and language) required to navigate the coded routes both into higher education and beyond. It is measured in increments, and we know it as a terrible farce dressed up in the costumes of masters and doctorates and professorships. It is crudely nuanced, precisely because it is conditioned upon the underlying premise that the degree to which we are members of humanity, holders of important knowledge, or equals to white scholars, is a direct correlation to the degree to which we really are not.

A close interrogation of the (un)namings: (minor)ity, non-white, imposter, other, through which scholars of color are unfairly measured, is made explicit in *Presumed Incompetent: The Intersections of Race and Class for Women in Academia* (2012). The title of the book lays bare the unmistakable message that the path to recognition for scholars of color, whose already hyphenated identities create an almost insurmountable critical divide, is nearly impossible to successfully navigate without great personal cost. Moreover, if institutions were truly committed to widening the critical frame that has for centuries shaped our understanding of the world, this would go some way in filling in the historical gaps that systematically erased our voices and contributions.

It has never been the case that researchers of color who work just as hard, and often harder than their white counterparts in earning postgraduate degrees, experience truly race-blind equity in the job market. No longer is it just a matter of how many degrees one holds that is a measurement of worthiness or legitimacy, but rather the "degrees" of systemic inequalities that the unaffiliated must constantly navigate. Increasingly, the specialization of university jobs requiring additional certifications that are sometimes only indirectly related to advertised positions often results in further marginalization of unaffiliated researchers from important professional networks that can lead to employment in higher educational settings.

Job seekers are either filtered out at the start of the application process or at the shortlisting stage. And for the few who make it to interview and on to teaching posts, the struggle for recognition and advancement is a constant grind. For many researchers who find themselves at arguably the most productive point in their professional careers, the social and economic disparities holding them back start long before the academic job search begins. Indeed, in their introduction to *Presumed Incompetent: The Intersections of Race and Class for Women in Academia*, Harris and González point out that for students who come from a "working-class or impoverished background, whether they are students of color or not, college and graduate school is a mystifying—even hostile—place, full of opaque cultural codes and academic challenges for which they are poorly prepared" (Harris and González 2012: 2). Their assertion is borne out by multiple studies, reports, and first-hand experiences, and it is no accident that the "social risks impacting black women's lives beyond academe simultaneously influence their experiences within it" (Lomax 2015). What then is the discursive work that needs to be done in relation to dismantling the privileged routes into academia, and once inside, what is the work that needs to be done to avoid becoming unaffiliated within other legitimized affiliations?

On the Outside Looking in(to) the Abyss

"Legitimate" scholarship as defined through measurements that are constructed through inherently biased processes reinforces the "insider/outsider binary" that privileges certain people, groups, or systems over others. This particular binary is, as Iverson (2012) explains, "further reinforced by situating the diverse individual in comparison and opposition to a 'majority' or 'norm'" (Iverson 2012: 166). In other words, gaining entry into academia does not automatically eradicate class or racial disparities. Instead, and almost always to the benefit of the university, it makes the largely unspoken case for preserving racial and epistemological hierarchies. In this way, scholars of color who are fortunate enough to be on the "other" side of the looking glass are really just staring into another racially charged abyss. Thus the question here must be: if the work of decolonizing curricula, insisting that recruitment and selection panels are more representative of multicultural communities, and expanding reading lists to offer a more trans-historical context has a singular command, it would be to mine the silences for that which is left unsaid and ignored.

"De-Blacking" the Ivory Tower

For scholars of color the journey to employment and recognition in academia is paved with multiple hurdles that begin, and almost always end with, the diminishment of our authentic selves in service to an established white-centric norm. For example, the necessity of having to "de-Black" oneself in order to be competitive with white scholars seeking postdoctoral opportunities finds its correlation in reports of interracial couples having to "de-Black" their homes in order to get a fair market appraisal, or lesbians feeling the need to "de-dyke" their spaces when disapproving relatives visit, or transgender men and women needing to "de-trans" to accommodate hetero and/or homonormative sensibilities.

In the case of job seekers, scholars of color have been known to create the most race-neutral descriptors as possible in their applications, in order to escape "detection" as a person from an "undesirable" minority group. Ultimately the abrading of Blackness to fit into a more "normative" (white) academic framework benefits no one, least of all scholars of color whose research is no less rigorous as that which is produced by their white counterparts. Pointing to various field studies where job résumés are scrubbed of identifying racial markers, Kang et al. (2016) note that "résumés containing minority racial cues, such as a distinctively African American or Asian name, lead to 30% to 50% fewer callbacks from employers than do otherwise equivalent résumés without such cues" (Kang et al. 2016: 2). The authors go on to assert that since recruitment is positioned at a critical stage in the furtherance of professional attainment, discriminatory hiring practices effectively hinder access to positive career prospects for racial minorities (ibid).

Thus the exceptionally fraught—and for historically white educational institutions that continue to discriminate against scholars of color in postdoctoral hiring practices and faculty promotions—the seemingly irresolvable contradiction between Blackness and intelligence; Blackness and worthiness; Blackness and ability, seems to stubbornly endure. It may seem counterintuitive to intentionally strip away the very characteristics that make us unique, yet historically the (Black, queer[ed], feminist, nonconforming) unaffiliated, have always held contradictory positions.

Whether on the inside of the academic-industrial complex or on the outside looking in, at the forefront of scholarship or permanently relegated to the margins, at the most basic level, scholars of color have been conditioned to navigate the frustrating reality of a Duboisian double consciousness, where even our most basic freedoms have been abridged and "surreptitiously underwritten by whiteness" (Michael and Schulz 2014: vii). We have been conditioned to navigate the egregiousness of a Blackness denied, in service to the illegitimacy of an all-consuming colonizing gaze. For as long as institutions of higher learning have existed, the marginalized have understood that when one's worth is measured against systems that align competence and knowledge with whiteness, then centuries of epistemic arrogance solidify to form pathologizing frameworks through which oppressive tactics are allowed to flourish. Yet it could also be said, and perhaps this is the overarching takeaway, that centuries of experience in negotiating multiple identities and striving to overcome structural disadvantages uniquely position unaffiliated scholars to contest the ostensible inclusiveness of academe by creating more generative spaces that find their propulsive, eloquent, and authentic voices from the very margins to which the unaffiliated have been consigned.

References

Adams, R. (2020), "Fewer than 1% of UK University Professors are Black, Figures Show," *The Guardian*, February 27. Available online: https://www.theguardian.com/education

/2020/feb/27/fewer-than-1-of-uk-university-professors-are-black-figures-show (accessed March 7, 2022).

Arday, J. (2017), "Exploring Black and Minority Ethnic (BME) Doctoral Students' Perceptions of an Academic Career," *University and College Union Executive Summary*.

Austin, J.L. (1962), *How to Do Things with Words*, Oxford: Oxford University Press.

Baez, B. (2000), "Race-Related Service and Faculty of Color: Conceptualizing Critical Agency in Academe," *Higher Education*, 39 (3): 363–91.

Beattie, G., D. Cohen, and L. McGuire (2013), "An Exploration of Possible Unconscious Ethnic Biases in Higher Education: The Role of Implicit Attitudes on Selection for University Posts," *Semiotica*, 197: 171–201.

Bernal, D.D. and O. Villalpando (2002), "An Apartheid of Knowledge in Academia: The Struggle over the 'Legitimate' Knowledge of Faculty of Color," *Equity & Excellence in Education*, 35 (2): 169–80.

Brunsma, D.L., D.G. Embrick, and J.H. Shin (2017), "Graduate Students of Color: Race, Racism, and Mentoring in the White Waters of Academia," *Sociology of Race and Ethnicity*, 3 (1): 1–13.

Corces-Zimmerman, C., D. Thomas, and N.L. Cabrera (2021), "Historic Scaffolds of Whiteness in Higher Education," in K.R. Roth and Z.S. Ritter (eds.), *Whiteness, Power, and Resisting Change in US Higher Education: A Peculiar Institution*, 9–32, London: Palgrave Macmillan.

Dancy, T.E. II, K.T. Edwards, and J.E. Davis (2018), "Historically White Universities and Plantation Politics: Anti-Blackness and Higher Education in the Black Lives Matter Era," *Urban Education*, 53 (2): 176–95.

Doharty, N., M. Madriaga, and R. Joseph-Salisbury (2020), "The University Went to 'Decolonise' and All They Brought Back Was Lousy Diversity Double-Speak! Critical Race Counter-Stories from Faculty of Colour in 'Decolonial' Times," *Educational Philosophy and Theory*, 53 (3): 233–44.

Duncan, P. (2014), "Hot Commodities, Cheap Labor: Women of Color in the Academy," *Frontiers: A Journal of Women's Studies*, 35 (3): 39–63.

Flowers, A.M. III, J.A. Scott, J.R. Riley, and R.T. Palmer (2015), "Beyond the Call of Duty: Building on Othermothering for Improving Outcomes at Historically Black Colleges and Universities," *Journal of African American Males in Education*, 6 (1): 59–73.

Gasman, M. (2016), "An Ivy League Professor on Why Colleagues Don't Hire More Faculty of Color: 'We don't want them,'" *Washington Post*, September 26, https://www.washingtonpost.com/news/grade-point/wp/2016/09/26/an-ivy-league-professor-on-why-colleges-dont-hire-more-faculty-of-color-we-dont-want-them/.

Gutierrez y Muhs, G., Y.F. Niemann, C.G. Gonzalez, and A.P. Harris (eds.) (2012), *Presumed Incompetent: The Intersections of Race and Class for Women in Academia*, Utah: Utah State University Press.

Hartman, S. (2019), *Wayward Lives, Beautiful Experiments: Intimate Histories of Riotous Black Girls, Troublesome Women and Queer Radicals*, London: Serpent's Tail.

Heleta, S. (2020), "Coloniality, Knowledge Production, and Racialized Socio-Economic Inequality in South Africa," in M.E. Ruprecht Fadem and M. O'Sullivan (eds.), *The Economics of Empire: Genealogies of Capital and the Colonial Encounter*, 181–97, London: Routledge.

Hode, M.G. and R.J. Meisenbach (2016), "Reproducing Whiteness Through Diversity: A Critical Discourse Analysis of the Pro-Affirmative Action Amicus Briefs in the Fisher Case," *Journal of Diversity in Higher Education*, http://dx.doi.org/10.1037/dhe0000014.

Holmes, S.L. (2008), "Narrated Voices of African American Women in Academe," *Journal of Thought*, Fall–Winter: 101–24.
Iverson, S.V. (2012), "Constructing Outsiders: The Discursive Framing of Access in University Diversity Policies," *The Review of Higher Education*, 35 (2): 149–77.
James, S.M. (1993), "Mothering: A Possible Black Feminist Link to Social Transformations?" in A.P.A. Busia and S.M. James (eds.), *Theorizing Black Feminisms: The Visionary Pragmatisms of Black Women*, 45–56, London: Routledge.
Johnson, A. and R. Joseph-Salisbury (2018), "'Are You Supposed to Be in Here': Racial Microaggressions and Knowledge Production in Higher Education," in J. Arday and H.S. Mirza (eds.), *Dismantling Race in Higher Education: Racism, Whiteness and Decolonising the Academy*, 143–60, London: Palgrave Macmillan.
Johnson-Bailey, J. and R.M. Cervero (2008), "Different Worlds and Divergent Paths: Academic Careers Defined by Race and Gender," *Harvard Educational Review*, 78 (2): 311–22.
Jones, C. (2006), "Falling Between the Cracks: What Diversity Means for Black Women in Higher Education," *Policy Futures in Education*, 4 (2): 145–59.
Kang, S., K. DeCelles, A. Tilcsik, and S. Jun (2016), "Whitened Resumes: Race and Self-Presentation in the Labor Market," *Administrative Science Quarterly*, XX: 1–34.
King, S. (1990), "Naming and Power in Zora Neale Hurston's *Their Eyes Were Watching God*," *Black American Literature Forum*, 24 (4): 683–96.
Kovel, J. (1970), *White Racism: A Psychohistory*, New York: Pantheon.
Kumalo, S.H. (2018), "Explicating Abjection—Historically White Universities Creating Natives of Nowhere?" *Critical Studies in Teaching & Learning*, 6 (1): 1–17.
Lomax, T. (2015), "Black Women's Lives Don't Matter in Academia Either, or Why I Quit Academic Spaces that Don't Value Black Women's Life and Labor," *The Feminist Wire*. Available online: https://thefeministwire.com/2015/05/black-womens-lives-dont-matter-in-academia-either-or-why-i-quit-academic-spaces-that-dont-value-black-womens-life/ (accessed March 24, 2022).
Michael, L. and S. Schulz (2014), "Unsettling Whiteness: Disruptions and (Re)Locations," in L. Michael and S. Schulz, (eds.), *Unsettling Whiteness*, vii-3, Oxford: Inter-Disciplinary Press.
Mickelson, R.A. and M.L. Oliver (1991), "The Demographic Fallacy of the Black Academic: Does Quality Rise to the Top?" in W.R. Allen, E.G. Epps, and N.Z. Haniff, (eds.), *College in Black and White: African American Students in Predominantly White and in Historically Black Public Universities*, 177–96, New York: State University of New York Press.
Mott, C. and D. Cockayne (2017), "Citation Matters: Mobilizing the Politics of Citation Toward a Practice of 'Conscientious Engagement,'" *Gender, Place & Culture: A Journal of Feminist Geography*, 1–22, doi:10.1080/0966369X.2017.1339022.
Onwuachi-Willig, A. (2010), "Complimentary Discrimination and Complementary Discrimination in Faculty Hiring," *Washington University Law Review*, 87 (4): 763–800.
Paris, D (2019), "Naming Beyond the White Settler Colonial Gaze in Educational Research," *International Journal of Qualitative Studies in Education*, 32 (3): 217–24.
Pearson, A.R., A.F. Dovidio, and S.L. Gaertner (2009), "The Nature of Contemporary Prejudice: Insights from Aversive Racism," *Social and Personality Psychology Compass*, 3 (3): 314–38.
Pollard, D.A. (1999), "Unconscious Bias and Self-Critical Analysis: The Case for a Qualified Evidentiary Equal Employment Opportunity Privilege," *Washington Law Review*, 74 (4): 913–1031.

Ray, V., (2019), "A Theory of Racialized Organizations," *American Sociological Review*, 84 (1): 26–53.
Rodríguez, J.E., K.M. Campbell, and L.H. Pololi (2015), "Addressing Disparities in Academic Medicine: What of the Minority Tax?" *BMC Medical Education*, 15 (6): 1–5.
Sensoy, O. and R. DiAngelo (2017), "'We Are All for Diversity, but . . .': How Faculty Hiring Committees Reproduce Whiteness and Practical Suggestions for How They Can Change," *Harvard Educational Review*, 87 (4): 557–80.
Settles, I.H., M.K. Jones, N.T. Buchanan, and K. Dotson (2020), "Epistemic Exclusion: Scholar(ly) Devaluation that Marginalizes Faculty of Color," *Journal of Diversity in Higher Education*, 1–16, http://dx.doi.org/10.1037/dhe0000174.
Stanley, C.A. (2006), "Coloring the Academic Landscape: Faculty of Color Breaking the Silence in Predominantly White Colleges and Universities," *American Educational Research Journal*, 43 (4): 701–36.
Walton, G.M. and G.L. Cohen (2007), "A Question of Belonging: Race, Social Fit, and Achievement," *Journal of Personality and Social Psychology*, 92 (1): 82–96.
West, E.J. (2020), "Community and Naming: Lived Narratives of Early African American Women's Spirituality," *Religions*, 11 (426): 1–15.
Zwysen, W. and S. Longhi (2016), "Labour Market Disadvantage of Ethnic Minority British Graduates: University Choice, Parental Background or Neighbourhood"? *ISER Working Paper Series*, 2016 (2): 1–82, University of Essex, Institute for Social and Economic Research (ISER), Colchester.

Chapter 6

BEYOND BOX TICKING AND BUZZWORDS: A QUEER, WORKING-CLASS, ANTI-RACIST, ANTI-ABLEIST SHARING IN UK ACADEMIA

Leanne Dawson

I was invited to write this chapter on sharing in academia at a time of feeling so very dismayed with UK universities. Feelings caused, in part, by institutions shouting loudly and publicly about their work on EDI (Equality, Diversity, and Inclusion), as it is known in the UK context, while using their EDI policies, initiatives, and research as a smokescreen to maintain their status quo of privilege and distract from a range of -isms, -phobias, and abuses of power within. There is not nearly enough of the good kind of sharing in academia, which—as we will see as this chapter progresses—accompanies serious issues around EDI.

Much sharing is done for promotion, in the sense of publicizing (both individuals and institutions) and career advancement, rather than to make something equal or for many people at different levels to positively benefit from what is shared. We academics share our research via publications not only to improve a body of knowledge but also because our jobs demand such dissemination. And we share for ourselves, for who can deny the buzz of finally pressing send on a publication and subsequently seeing it in print? We share with students when we teach, just as they share their knowledge with us, but while some of us find teaching and exchanging knowledge (it really is a two-way street) with students to mostly be a pleasure, others treat it as a nuisance intruding on research time or management duties.

Furthermore, with the rise of social media, many academics have larger audiences than ever before, and because platforms such as Twitter can be brilliant for gathering support and creating change, there has been an increase in academics jumping on bandwagons and sharing as performative allyship to boost their own profiles or social capital, rather than a real dedication to equality. A key example is the Black Lives Matter movement, which has seen a great deal of performative allyship from UK academics and institutions since the killing of George Floyd, with these supposed allies using social media to denounce racism, while failing to try to make any changes, small or large, in their own academic programs and institutions.

This performative sharing ties, in recent years, to an increased pressure within UK academia to share our research beyond the academy via "Knowledge Exchange" (KE) and "public engagement" leading to "Impact." KE is UK academic jargon for sharing academic research and findings beyond academia with the aim of improving—or impacting—financial, social, health, political, cultural (and so on) situations outside of higher education (HE). KE has long been undertaken by the more ethical among us to positively benefit others before it was repackaged, given fancy names, and turned into an issue of metrics for institutional benefit. In the current climate, it is too often a box-ticking exercise to performatively demonstrate the public good and, therefore, the value of academic research for promotion documents, and job and funding applications, because of the Research Excellence Framework (REF).

The Research Excellence Framework, a data collection and rating exercise undertaken by the four UK higher education funding bodies (Research England, the Scottish Funding Council, the Higher Education Funding Council for Wales, and the Department for the Economy, Northern Ireland) assesses the supposed quality of published research and, more recently, of KE/Impact in UK higher education institutions and subsequently funds universities according to the results of their own exercise (for more on the challenges of impact and its presentation for REF versus reality, see Quinn et al. 2014). Without demonstrable KE and Impact, universities would receive no funding. There was, unsurprisingly, a sudden surge of academics clamoring to work with people and places beyond universities when KE and Impact was added to the REF agenda and to research council funding award applications. However, this cherry-picked sharing of findings beyond the academy for personal and institutional gain ("Impact") coincides with a further closing off of access to/creation of knowledge within the academy thanks to increasing tuition fees and the significant costs of student accommodation, as well as the rise of casualization with a large number of short, fixed-term contracts not paying academics for their research time and not allowing many academics to continue in academia longer term. As we will see throughout this chapter, KE leading to what universities neatly package as Impact is often the antithesis of queer working-class sharing because specific people and institutions claiming to share often benefit significantly more than those being shared with.

Throughout this chapter I bring class and race into queer theory, coupling Bourdieu's work on class and capital (1984) with Halberstam's writing on queerness and temporality (2005), to theorize a new, queer, working-class, anti-racist, anti-ableist academic sharing that stands in opposition to what I coin a self-serving "straight sharing." I illuminate how straight sharing in universities disguises how heterosexist, white supremacist, ableist, and classist power functions, and how such selfish sharing is failing too many people. To do this, I consider some of the current "sharing" trends and buzzwords in UK academia, which also involve EDI: Widening Participation, Decolonizing the Curriculum, and Knowledge Exchange/Impact, all of which include an element of sharing knowledge with those who are not currently part of or were not traditionally part of UK academia, and which are too frequently box-ticking exercises incongruent with their host institution's

EDI practice, especially that of more elite universities. I do not address "Athena SWAN" in this chapter, but I intend to give this significant attention in future work. Throughout this chapter, I employ Pereira's academic "corridor talk" (2017), a feminist methodological practice of sharing knowledge, usually informally, although here I am formalizing it because privilege is too often upheld by both silence and silencing, which stands in the way of fairness and transparency. I have written this chapter with the intention of helping to create change in order to make universities, particularly those considered elite, a more comfortable space for those they often exclude or treat poorly including: working-class people; Black, Indigenous, and People of Color (BIPOC); and those with disabilities. With this goal in mind, I offer suggestions of practical changes that universities, and those who hold any power within them, can start to make now.

Queering Sharing in the Academy

We need to consider the ways in which universities, spaces which claim to share knowledge, in reality exclude people from gaining knowledge and accompanying benefits. As the call for contributions for this book made clear, "if queer theory has been a major intellectual driver of liberatory politics in the university it has not been successful in challenging the increasing marketisation and capitalist instincts of higher education." The increased marketization of HE, including tuition fees and hugely expensive private accommodation packages, can make attending university out of reach for many, despite policies such as "Widening Participation" for students from what are technically known as "deprived" areas—although this terminology is problematic—as well as those who are care-experienced, and students of color, claiming to make them more inclusive. Universities have long been spaces for middle- and upper-class people, especially men historically, and many of them remain overwhelmingly inhabited by white, wealthy people. We must never forget that because of systemic and other racisms, many BIPOC are in poverty. Out of the "nontraditional" students who do enter university in the UK, many of these attend post-92 universities, that is institutions formerly known as "polytechnics" and granted university status in 1992, and which, as with spaces such as community colleges in the US context, are often unfairly viewed as inferior.

Queer, Trans, Black, Indigenous, and People Of Color (QTIBOPOC), many of them in poverty, helped to kick off the modern gay rights movement, thanks to the Stonewall Riots in New York City in 1969. In the AIDS crisis of the 1980s, the term "queer" was reappropriated from its use as a homophobic slur and employed by LGBT+ people uniting to care for those with HIV and AIDS. The latter were purposefully failed by white supremacist and homophobic governments, including the Republican Reagan administration in the US and Thatcher's Conservatives in the UK. In this time period, the white supremacist, heteronormative academy has profited handsomely from gay and lesbian studies, which then gave way to queer studies, with these (alongside women's studies and

Black studies) emerging out of activism to become academic fields. In addition, a handful of big—often wealthy and white—names are celebrated in queer theory without adequate recognition of the grassroots collective work that got us here and of the less privileged activists and carers whose labor, physical and emotional, was used as a springboard.

A dominant trend in queer theory in the past two decades is work on temporality, and one of the biggest names is Jack Halberstam, who reconsiders the aforementioned AIDS epidemic to rethink time. Even as it resulted, and too often continues to result, in death and a "constantly diminishing future," AIDS also created "a new emphasis on the here, the present, the now" (Halberstam 2005: 2). Halberstam claims "queer uses of time and space develop, at least in part, in opposition to the institutions of family, heterosexuality, and reproduction.... If we try to think about queerness as an outcome of strange temporalities, imaginative life schedules, and eccentric economic practices, we detach queerness from sexual identity" (Halberstam 2005: 1). Since the AIDS crisis, we have witnessed a decidedly unqueer politics, which focuses on family and conservative values, including the legalization of same-sex marriage (and the consumerism and tax breaks associated with this) alongside various forms of legally recognized parenthood, including assisted reproduction, adoption, and birth certificate inclusion for same-sex parents. Meanwhile, truly queer issues such as the disproportionate number of homeless LGBTQI+ youths and, in the US context, the horrifically high murder rates of Black trans women have not received the political, legal, and economic attention they deserve. So, the progress in health care, coupled with the normalization of a certain kind of respectable gay homonormative subject (Duggan 2003), reinforces the nuclear family, gay or straight. Those normative, cis, monogamous, married, white, hard-working, "good" citizens supposedly contribute to the economy and society in a way that single queers, people with disabilities, single mothers (whose children former UK prime minister Conservative Boris Johnson referred to as "ill-raised, ignorant aggressive and illegitimate") and suchlike do not. I return to the unearned rewards of normativity shortly when I theorize "straight sharing" in more depth.

Queer temporality, rethinks the present and the future. This is highly relevant to class because being in poverty is so often about the present: needing to locate the food, money, warmth, shelter, and so on in order to be able to survive for that day, with nothing or very little to save or invest in the future. In addition to this, society is set up to stop those in poverty from "achieving" what middle-class+ people do, without the aspirations of a "successful" (in the capitalist sense) future of a university education, a professional and highly paid career, and a portfolio of assets intended to create and hoard even more wealth for oneself and future family generations.

Sociologist Pierre Bourdieu (1984) breaks capital down as *economic capital* (income and wealth), *social capital* (social ties and networks), and *cultural capital* (education, intellect, style of speech), which together "offer advantages to achieve a higher social-status in society" (Crew 2020: 1). Privilege leads to more privilege. When we think of Bourdieu's forms of capital, these are about the accumulation and select sharing (which is also a form of exclusion) of wealth, assets, cultural capital, and networks, often for future use. Bourdieu (1977) speaks of "habitus," which are norms, values, habits, and inclinations within a social class or group, as well as personal experiences, and argues that the two most influential forces are the family and the education system. A field (Bourdieu 1984) is a competitive space with its own rules and patterns of behaviour and "in academia, it is middle-class dispositions and forms of capital that monopolize the field" (Crew 2020: 12). That certain types of capital and privilege dominate a field means that the field is not shared but rather represents a space in which inequality is maintained.

A middle-class+ logic of investing in select people and their future is very relevant to universities and the traditional passing down ("sharing") of knowledge and cultural capital, which helps to maintain or improve social, economic, and cultural capital. There is so much *talk* about equality, diversity, inclusion, and decolonizing universities because many UK institutions are such homogenous, exclusionary sites of privilege. Those who are not wealthy, not white, and not without disabilities are often made to feel unwelcome in many institutions, while opportunities continue to be passed between the most privileged groups. Queer theory has not been successful in challenging the increasing marketization of the university, in part because class and socioeconomic realities are too frequently absent from queer theory, likely because most academics do come from economic privilege (while working-class academics are here despite, not because of, where we came from). Halberstam—a professor whose father was also a professor—does not appear to lose much sleep over the "eccentric economic practices," "imaginative life schedules," and "strange temporalities" he refers to when theorizing a queer temporality. These, in reality, often occur out of necessity when someone is living hand to mouth in poverty and being kept at the bottom of a pyramid of privilege.

Halberstam's starting point implies that straight economic practices include, as default, finances and economic stability that can be passed between generations, but for many working-class people there simply is no money for insurance, healthcare, wills, property, or children's university fees. He declares,

> the time of inheritance refers to an overview of generational time within which values, wealth, goods, and morals are passed through family ties from one generation to the next. It also connects family to the historical past of the nation, and glances ahead to connect the family to the future of both familial and national stability. In this category we can include the kinds of hypothetical temporality—the time of "what if"—that demands protection in the way of insurance policies, health care, and wills. (Halberstam 2005: 5)

He states that "within the cycle of the Western human subject, long periods of stability are considered to be desirable, and people who live in rapid bursts (drug addicts, for example) are characterized as immature and even dangerous" (Halberstam 2005: 4–5). We must be aware that a hedonism of free or cheap thrills in the here and now can be used when there is no easy, wealthy future to look forward to. Indeed, addiction is so often bound to what is too often formally referred to as "deprivation" and an escape from circumstances, but Halberstam instead uses this to call for a queer temporality with rapid bursts and pleasure in the present. These bursts of pleasure and temporary highs stand in opposition to schedule, routine, and practicing delayed gratification, which is typically middle class and which can ensure future generations of one's own family will be socially and economically provided for. Without an adequate consideration of the sociopolitical reality of precarity, poverty, and addiction, living in rapid bursts with no future is sexy and fun in theory, while in practice, as a day-to-day reality, it is anything but.

I propose we couple this theory of queer temporality with socioeconomic reality. A queer working-class, anti-racist, anti-ableist sharing, forms of which many less privileged people have been partaking in beyond the academy for years, is a way to slow down the current dominant system of straight sharing. Straight sharing is synonymous with selfish sharing; the person or institution doing the sharing reaps most of the rewards or even performatively pretends to share while squirreling away most/everything for themselves. Although it has as its foundation hetero- and (now) homonormativity, straight sharing is not about heterosexuality (many straight people are also in poverty) but rather about straight lines of sharing, which means that white wealthy people repeatedly profit most. It is also to note that straight sharing is coded white, in that the creation of (further) intergenerational wealth included the enslavement of Black people and that racial capitalism frequently prevents Black families from building intergenerational wealth. Straight sharing creates a future for a specific type of privileged subject. It is a stratification of hierarchies and those who thrive within capitalism (white, middle-class+, no disabilities, part of certain cliques) based on the passing of power to those who share the characteristics of privilege. Straight sharing is classist, racist, ableist, transphobic, and sometimes homophobic. Straight sharing is also about the future of the "nation," with white, wealthy, heterosexual, capitalist citizens procreating and perpetuating their privilege alongside their own, their families', and their countries' futures.

Reproduction of knowledge in the university follows lines similar to heterosexual reproduction and the reproduction of the nation, resulting in the passing down of wealth and knowledge to further generations. Straight sharing has a clear goal of investing in the present for the future and of passing down privilege along certain lines. In academia, this plays out as the PhD supervisor calling up their friend to let them know their former student is applying for a job at their university and seeking assurances they will get it; it is faculty hiring new staff in their (wealthy, white) likeness; it is the universities labeled as elite that prioritize accepting students from supposedly elite public schools, even if their performance at the school was far from elite and with their acceptance made possible only by family wealth, while the state school students suffer manifold under the university structure and at the hands of staff and fellow students. Often, the academic and the familial align: children of alumni being accepted and offered preferential treatment over their better-performing counterparts from poverty; the professor who knows how to play the system and contacts a university to demand that rules are bent or broken for their offspring who studies there; the underperforming spousal hire, who has not published in decades and receives no students signing up to their courses, yet has somehow managed to obtain prestigious positions in the same section of every university their professorial spouse has worked at. Straight sharing, academia, and the nation align, with a key example being the large percentage of UK Conservative prime ministers who studied Philosophy, Politics, and Economics (PPE) at the University of Oxford, upon leaving the hugely expensive Eton College. Their white, wealthy families set them up, from conception, for that straight pathway to success. Boris Johnson, for example, took this pathway—with the exception that he chose to study Classics rather than PPE at Oxford—and has repeatedly been allowed to fail upward.

It does have to be noted that academia and the culture of overwork demanded from many faculty jobs can create a queerer temporality for a wider range of people than has thus far been considered, including academics from wealthy white families. Obtaining a PhD means the start of a career often happens much later than for others, while fixed-term posts requiring a significant number of long-distance moves are currently the norm for a number of years post-PhD. This means that "straight" milestones such as obtaining a mortgage, being in a long term-stable relationship in the same geographical location as one's partner, and having children are often delayed by several years, with some abandoned completely. The level of overwork demanded by the academy, especially when precarious, also means that evenings, weekends, and holidays often have to be used to play catch up with a workload that is too large to fit into the working week: teaching preparation, marking, and conducting the research that contracted hours do not allow for. Unfortunately, the people who suffer most are the ones already penalized by the way universities function: people who were raised working class with no parental handouts for mortgage deposits or to simply buy some time while waiting for an academic job; women who delay motherhood only to find how much academia ensures motherhood negatively impacts careers; people of color who do not progress from graduate student to faculty member because of racist hiring committees or the knowledge that the places they would have to move to for work are so blatantly racist they would be unbearable.

Widening Participation. Then What?

Some background to situate this work and my approach to the academy and sharing: I was raised in poverty by a single mother, a part-time cleaner on benefits, in a small town in Northeast England, where we lived in a council house and I attended the local state school. There were no networks of privileged professional friends and family, who create success for their own through private education, nepotistic sharing, and social capital, but I did learn how sharing life's essentials, rather than hoarding assets as the wealthy do, was necessary to survive. This has informed my life and my work since: sharing with those in need over embracing individualistic neoliberalism or trusting classist, racist institutions.[1] Half of my immediate family, with whom I lived, are Black and so I have been aware from a relatively young age that, despite financial and other hardships, my whiteness gives me a huge amount of privilege in everything I do because of the racism of the systems we live in and because of many individuals within those systems.

The first in my family to go to a university, my identity impacted my choice of institution, both because I was led to believe from messages all around me that Oxbridge was not for the likes of me, despite my flawless grades, and also because I was a lesbian living in a small town. I chose the University of Manchester, located in a city famous for its gay scene. The forms I completed to go there asked what my parents' occupations were and, both embarrassed to state these and fearful they would be used against me, I wrote "relevance?" in the box, unaware that these were perhaps to be used for positive discrimination rather than weeding out the likes of me through a straight sharing. My vast experience of classism in UK HE means I know I would have been discriminated against by some had they had access to such family information. Throughout my three degrees in Manchester, I specialized increasingly in queer studies (while we were taught feminist and queer theory, we never heard, for example, the name Bourdieu mentioned in class) and have since dedicated my academic career and much of my private life to the cultural representation and sociopolitical reality of disadvantaged groups, including LGBTQI+, working-class people, BIPOC, and people with disabilities.

When I became chair of the Scottish Queer International Film Festival, I expanded my research from looking at how identities were represented on page, stage, and screen, to also encompass how these people are welcomed and included in arts spaces. Dismayed to notice that universities' supposed successes around EDI in the arts (i.e., "world-leading" publications, "impact," external funding) was actively contributing to concealing institutions' own bad EDI practice, I have more recently turned my gaze inward to consider how EDI functions in UK academia. While I am eternally grateful that education changed my life beyond recognition, giving me access to types of cultural, social, and economic capital I never thought possible, being a senior lecturer (and before that a teaching fellow and a postdoctoral researcher) has made me recognize the extent to which I was an exception and how our universities are failing so many students and potential students from backgrounds like mine. It is painful to think how many underprivileged people should be here in place of the people who made it because of their intersections of privilege providing an easy pathway.

As social policy academic Teresa Crew makes clear in her book about working-class academics in the UK, which stands on the shoulders of work by other working-class scholars such as Bev Skeggs and Diane Reay, "social class is more than household income. It's the friends you have, the music you like and the school you go to. In other words, cultural and social capital play a considerable role in distributing people into class positions" (Crew 2020: 3). Her work demonstrates how class pervades academia and rubbishes the notion of a meritocracy, a flimsy logic delivered to us by powerful people, often connected to each other, for whom cultural, social, and economic forms of capital work very well. Academia was traditionally dominated by wealthy, white men and remains dominated by privilege: cis, white, middle-class+ people without disabilities. This is particularly in pre-1992 institutions, which are also disproportionately represented in metrics, funding, and REF.

Supposedly operating to change this familiar pattern of privilege, university Widening Participation initiatives aim to meet intake quotas for pupils from state schools in "deprived" areas. This may give the impression that entrance to the university is actually tipped in favor of the less privileged, and there are certainly many privileged students and academics who weaponize this against working-class students, but the reality is that the most privileged people continue to gain places in privileged spaces, even without stellar grades, and that this privilege perpetuates in terms of both academic success (degree obtained) and academic exclusion (privileged students and academics taking up the majority of space and even trying to oust underprivileged students and academics by bullying and making them believe they do not belong there). Instead of a focus on lowering grade boundaries to grant access to those less privileged, we need UK HE to recalibrate the grades of those educated in fee-paying schools and with the type of privilege that accompanies not being born into poverty. These include: having someone at home to help with reading and homework; not having to work alongside education, whether outside the home for money to support oneself (and family) and/or at home through significant caring duties or household chores; having access to a wide range of cultural pursuits and opportunities such as music lessons; having the money to access technology, private tuition and other resources needed for learning; and having heating and food and shelter so that learning is not hindered by hunger and other stressors. A refocusing on all of the advantages that students from white, wealthy backgrounds have, which create a straight and therefore easier pathway into elite institutions, is vital in ensuring that the most privileged students are not the only ones to receive a place to study. Moreover, such a refocusing on the mechanisms of advantage is one way to stop universities from giving the impression that the wealthy and privileged are kindly sharing *their* spaces and resources with poorer students.

No reliable protections exist for working-class students or academics if they do gain entry to university. Unfortunately, but unsurprisingly, class does not belong to the current protected characteristics in the UK's 2010 Equality Act, which are: age, disability, gender reassignment, marriage and civil partnership, pregnancy and maternity, race, religion and belief, sex, and sexual orientation. The ways that universities function mean that working-class people are not always safe when there. A "corridor talk" example: a group of working-class women undertaking a degree at an elite institution always sit together in seminars and do not speak up unprompted. This is fully understandable to the lone working-class academic in the department because seminars are dominated by Received Pronunciation and the loud, confident voices of students from public and private schools. Indeed even the working-class academic has had her regional accent repeatedly mocked, and therefore undermined when leading seminars, by an old Etonian student.[2] Some other academics teaching on the degree program, however, begin to talk unkindly about the group of working-class students, as if they are a nuisance to be tolerated and somehow less able than the posher students. They discuss how to deal with this "problem," including a suggestion that they could split the working-class women up. This consideration of removing the working-class women from their support network would, surely, make the situation even worse. What should be addressed in such a scenario is how learning environments, including the attitudes of privileged students and academics, negatively impact the working-class students' experience of university and their confidence to speak in class. *These* are the issues which are long overdue in being addressed. In this case, however, classism was perpetuated by treating working-class students less favorably than the more privileged cohort members. Some academics in the department also used this experience as part of a decision to end a particular degree combination, which had run for the first time with the working-class women students. The way this was handled serves a dual purpose of maintaining privilege at the student and staff level: closing off a degree pathway that was more likely to attract working-class people and letting the lone working-class academic know their place through the example of how working-class students were treated.

Policies such as "Dignity and Respect" or "Dignity at Work" claim to ensure that staff and students are treated well within their university and should mean that working-class students, including those who arrive via Widening Participation, are treated with respect. Unfortunately, such policies are only of use to those aware of them and are open to abuse by the most privileged, who come from backgrounds which give them the confidence and knowledge to play the system in their favor. Take an example, again "corridor talk": a privileged line manager is part of a powerful clique of "straight sharers" at an elite academic institution. She crosses professional boundaries with a working-class colleague she manages, which makes the junior colleague uncomfortable. Because of the power imbalance and the cliques in place, there is pressure on the junior colleague to be a sycophant, even though this crossing of professional boundaries includes the line manager gossiping with multiple colleagues and at evening social events about information she requests from the junior colleague in formal and confidential work meetings (think: maternity meetings or suchlike). The information sought by the line manager in meetings, and then shared socially afterward, relates to the junior colleague's relationship, family, and health. When the junior colleague asks her line manager about her breaches of confidentiality in order to make them stop, the line manager repeatedly refuses to apologize and, in addition, begins fabrications about the employee, seemingly to try and cover her own back and to punish the junior employee for daring to speak up about the manager's repeated lack of professionalism. When the line manager is asked by the junior employee to provide evidence to support her fabrications, the line manager does not (because she cannot) provide any evidence and instead Human Resources (HR) steps in to tell the junior employee that she is violating the "Dignity and Respect" policy because of her "tone" when asking the manager why she is both breaching employee confidentiality and fabricating stories. The employee lets HR know how classist, racist, and ableist the policing of tone is, citing the work of queer scholar of color Sara Ahmed (2017). She also asks why HR is allowing the manager's breaches of confidentiality and fabrications to remain unchallenged, even though they also surely go against the "Dignity and Respect" policy, and why this policy is instead being used to silence the victim. HR, in turn, chooses not to respond to this question.

Just as loud voices can be used to dominate a space and to silence (working-class, BIPOC) others and make them believe that they do not belong, the opposite of this privileged loud domination is also used to maintain privilege. With a strategic silence, powerful people and places opt not to respond when challenged. This strategic silence is an active choice, unlike underprivileged people being silenced. In the "corridor talk" case earlier, HR chose to ignore someone calling out their unfair application of a policy because to respond would mean to engage in a conversation about institutional wrongdoing. Silencing and strategic silence are a significant part of straight sharing as they contribute to the inequitable status quo.

Widening Participation does not address the ways working-class students are treated or mistreated, once they are accepted into elite HE institutions. We need to implement a queer sharing with class and "race" at its center so that, among other things, children raised in poverty not only have access to third-level education but also are made safe and treated with respect when attending university. They should not expect working-class students to suddenly become more like the privileged academics and students within, but rather they need to make teaching and other spaces more welcoming of heterogeneity. There is also the problem of what happens when working-class students leave. It is well documented that, in the UK context, networks and economic privilege play a more significant role in the types of careers students walk into when graduating than their degree performance, which makes unfortunate sense when we consider which students have the social networks to open career doors and family money to support them while they undertake internships or low paid work in expensive cities to boost their CVs (Deuchar and Bhopal 2017). While universities are not responsible for this social dynamic, there are ways that they could help to counteract some of it. Institutions should not claim that a degree from them opens a pathway to careers in X, Y, and Z, therefore instilling false hope, without acknowledging the other privileges that students who walk into such jobs have. We also desperately need a financial fund and mentoring running alongside, and for some time after, the degree program for working-class students to support them in unpaid and other internships, which are usually only accessible to students whose parents' wealth passes down, via straight sharing. Advice by mentors who understand their situation could help students without connections to navigate education and work systems designed for the most privileged.

Recolonizing through "Decolonizing"

As I began writing this chapter, I received a mailing list email from a professor at a very elite UK institution, one of the most privileged in the world. The professor, a white, cishet woman who speaks with Received Pronunciation, advertised her project on equality and diversity in her subject area. While it is possible that there are hidden disabilities in cases where a principal investigator (PI) appears to have so many intersections of privilege, it is important that there is some vocal or visible difference in those leading such initiatives. I am not saying that representation alone is enough—the current UK Conservative government demonstrates this is not the case—but privileged people taking center stage on EDI matters demonstrates how wrong they are for the role, yet academia repeatedly allows this to happen. There has been a growing issue with performative allyship:

> An ally is someone from a nonmarginalized group who uses their privilege to advocate for a marginalized group. They transfer the benefits of their privilege to those who lack it. Performative allyship, on the other hand, is when someone from that same nonmarginalized group professes support and solidarity with a marginalized group in a way that either isn't helpful or that actively harms that group. Performative allyship usually involves the "ally" receiving some kind of reward—on social media, it's that virtual pat on the back for being a "good person" or "on the right side." (Phillips 2020)

While some straight sharers openly embrace the -isms and -phobias which allow them to maintain their privilege, others pretend to fight these, using their performative allyship to profit, personally and professionally. The earlier example is far from standalone. Academic projects about oppressed groups are too often led by cishet middle-class white women, with the fact they are women supposedly, and very problematically, ticking the diversity box (see Ahmed 2017). Privately educated, wealthy, white, cishet professors without disabilities should not be the leading voice or vision of diversity and decolonization projects, although they do have a duty to keep speaking up and working hard for diversity without centering themselves, by instead supporting, amplifying, and promoting the much harder work of less privileged and more precarious colleagues.

In 2019 I was sought out and invited by a different PI to be a member of a team of academics who wanted to create a project on global trans film. I questioned whether it was ok for me to be part of the project because I am white and cis, and suggested someone much better, an expert on the topic who is also Black and trans. We were both invited to join, only to find out the PI was a cishet white woman who, alongside me, a cis white lesbian, had also invited two cis white gay men academics to the project. Aside from the person I had suggested, nobody was trans and nobody was BIPOC. The PI had assembled an all-white, all-cis team for a trans BIPOC project. I raised my concerns once again, which were met with one of the cis white gay academics stating he was already part of a trans project comprising only cis researchers and by the white cishet PI attempting to make the situation better by inviting a white trans woman to join our team, though her research had nothing to do academically with any of the group's topics. I expressed my growing concerns and the project was paused. A goal of the global trans cultures project was to obtain a large sum of research funding, which made the make-up of the group even more problematic, and it has since increasingly been brought to public attention, thanks to social media, that research funding is not fairly distributed to BIPOC, with hashtags such as #FundBlackScientists used to draw attention to funding inequalities and change the straight pathway of funding between white academics.

Other hashtags, including #BlackLivesMatter and #DecoloniseTheCurriculum have led to more academics talking about racism and to more universities including works by Black academics on course reading lists, but when the majority of these courses are taught to white people by white people, we have to ask ourselves what, if anything, is being decolonized? Unfortunately, as I write this during Black History month, there are fears that academics, including a number of Black scholars, teaching an MA in Black British History at Goldsmiths University in London could be made redundant. The inclusion of work *about* BIPOC (as well as disability, working-class, and LGBTQI+ issues) on courses and in the REF return can work well for the institution (money, metrics, box ticking) but we need to consider how BIPOC academics and students are mis/treated within academia. Furthermore, many of the staff in the UK paid to research and teach about Black studies and postcolonial studies are white. When white people are employed to do work about, and therefore profit from, Black studies and postcolonial studies, while Black people are the objects of study and rarely the voice and vision of the work, there is a recolonization, an erasure, and the antithesis of a queer sharing. We need a significantly larger proportion of Black and working-class academics and students across all of HE, where fewer than 1 percent of UK professors are Black, in addition to the often tokenistic strategy of adding a few Black women to reading lists in the wake of Black Lives Matter.

Social media plays an ambiguous role in academic racism. While it has been used by BIPOC academics to draw attention to injustice relating to unjust hiring, firing, and funding practices, it is also used to promote the erasure, by white academics, of BIPOC scholars. Alongside some Black people, I spoke up when a university advertised on Twitter that a white woman professor was to speak on an all-white panel at an event about the enslavement of Black people. While the event was clearly going to be impactful for the academic and her institution, Black people were only to be the objects of study and those spoken at, without a voice on the panel. We received no response (again, the use of silence), then questioned it once more, before it was rectified by inviting some Black academics to the panel. That same institution, however, advertised only months later that a white male academic was to be on an all-white hosting team for POC arts events. I spoke up, once again, to let it be known that such practice is not considered acceptable. Corridor talk: in a case like this one, strategies of both silence and silencing were employed. Instead of responding to the social media comment (strategic silence) or getting people of color involved (silencing of POC), a white academic got his manager to speak to the manager of the academic who commented on the issue (silencing of an ally).

Academia desperately needs a different kind of fair, transparent, accountable sharing which stops the current racist, classist systems of privilege. Considering how HE allows people to gain further cultural, economic, and social capital, and how this influences their futures, there absolutely needs to be a rethinking of who has access to which academic institutions and why; of how much academic knowledge is kept behind paywalls and within expensive ivory towers *unless* the university will benefit from sharing to audiences beyond; and of the classist, racist, ableist systems that influence not only what is taught and who is allowed to teach and to learn but also who receives the funding, time, and status to research. While universities cannot be "decolonized" without starting afresh from the ground up and with BIPOC and working-class people as foundational rather than diverse tokens to be "included," white people can play a significant role at an individual level such as amplifying and supporting, rather than erasing at every step, those who are BIPOC.

Congruence and Case Studies

As we have seen thus far, "straight sharing" is what happens in the neoliberal university, where the academic and/or the institution controlling the sharing reaps most of the rewards from it. This approach, which is the antithesis of community-minded practices of sharing, is summed up in Knowledge Exchange leading to Impact when neatly packaged for REF as the impact case study, for which the primary aim is not to freely share knowledge from publicly funded research but to gain further (government, research council) funding and promotion. Indeed, a university cannot submit to REF and subsequently receive any government funding unless they have one impact case study per ten (or FTE) members of staff on a contract with a research element.

Working-class and BIPOC academics can be great at knowledge exchange because of how we often already have to code switch and operate between two spheres, from our home lives with friends and family to the posh, white ivory tower. Having learned to speak across registers of class and status, we can often connect easily with nonacademic audiences. My wish to connect with people beyond academia, coupled with my passion for social and economic justice, means I have done a lot of volunteering with people and organizations beyond academia. As a result, I was asked to produce an impact case study for REF2021. "Changing film cultures in Scotland, the UK and internationally," as my institution named it, drew exclusively on my own research about LGBTQI+ and working-class representation onscreen, on LGBTQI+ film festivals, and on my work with film festivals, cinemas, screening spaces, and audiences. This research generated, to use the language of REF, significant cultural, social, health/well-being, and economic impact.

My impact case study was to span the decade after submitting my PhD, from 2010 to 2020, meaning it incorporated, as is allowed by REF, the time when I was not employed in academia (the months immediately after submitting my PhD, when I was taking tentative steps onto the brutal academic job market); the time I was employed by academic institutions other than the one submitting my "impactful" work; and the time when I had temporary teaching fellow contracts (and was therefore paid only to undertake a huge teaching and administration load, with neither time nor pay for research). Even with a research contract, much of the "Impact" packaged in my REF case study happened when I volunteered (through choice) in my own time or when I worked (with less choice) in my own time to meet further REF targets.

An impactful sharing of work by academics can happen without a fair sharing of labor within the institution. KE is not always paid for or formally acknowledged in workload models, and there can be a lack of transparency about who receives internal KE time buyout and who does not, with this information shared, if at all, through "corridor talk" (Pereira 2017). Indeed, it was through "corridor talk" in the photocopying room that I found out from a colleague in another section that there was some teaching buyout available for Impact. While working in one's own time and sometimes at one's own expense to produce impactful KE can pay off in terms of promotion and pay rises, this is problematic not only for those undertaking the work instead of other activities in their personal time but even more so for those with caring responsibilities or disabilities who simply cannot give so much of themselves on evenings and weekends beyond their contracted hours (see Dawson 2020a; and Dawson 2021).

My impact case study included the testimony of filmmakers, artists, and curators who are under the LGBTQI+ umbrella, while several are also in poverty and/or BIPOC and/or with disabilities, because of the focus of my research and sharing beyond academia. One of the people providing testimony for my impact case study, also in his own time and unpaid, was a Black trans man working in the film industry, who graciously delivered glowing statements, at the request of the university, about the impact of my work. The case study documentation was finalized during my maternity leave in 2019. At this time, a small group of BIPOC students hosted the 2019 Resisting Whiteness conference, about which the right-wing *Daily Mail Online* ran the headline "University of Edinburgh is accused of 'blatant racism' for hosting an equality conference where white people are BANNED from asking questions." The article states:

> Edinburgh University has been slated for hosting an event where white people will be banned from asking questions—which has been described as "blatantly racist." A Q&A event—Resisting Whiteness 2019—will bar Caucasian guests from speaking from the floor. There will also be two "safe spaces"—one of which white people are banned from entering. . . . University bosses have "raised concerns" about aspects of the event. A spokesman for the University of Edinburgh said: "Tackling racism is an important topic for debate and the University is supportive of events addressing this issue. However, we are an organisation that places great value on issues around equality and voice. Consequently the University has met with the event organizers to ensure the event is compliant with our values. We have expressed our concerns to them about certain aspects of the format of the event and they are revising their 'safe space' policy for the conference as a result." (*Daily Mail Online* September 27, 2019)

Having attended the inaugural Resisting Whiteness event in 2018, it was made quite clear to the few white people in the audience (indeed white people, including academics whose work focuses on "race" and colonialism, were conspicuous in their absence) that the purpose was to amplify the voices of people of color and that we were welcome to pose questions to panels or individuals after the floor discussion. It is also fully understandable why one of the "safe spaces" might only be for people of color, considering the white supremacist structures in which the conference had to operate and the weight of the topics discussed.

The Black trans man providing testimony for my case study took part in the 2019 Resisting Whiteness event. Soon, concerns arose for me about institutional congruence when it appeared the university was using a trans person of color for my impact case study, on the one hand, while offering questionable quotes to right-wing media about the Resisting Whiteness event he was part of, on the other. Months before Resisting Whiteness, another event at my institution had made national headlines, with trans rights activists labeling it transphobic. I asked why we were submitting a case to REF about my research leading to a positive impact for BIPOC and LGBTQI+ people while, elsewhere, that work was being undone. We need to be cautious that impact case studies, while bringing in money, do not function in a tokenistic capacity just as institutions include people of color in their outward-facing promotional material to performatively demonstrate how inclusive and diverse they are when that is not congruent with the whiteness within.

In the wake of the press coverage of Resisting Whiteness, I asked to oversee that the testimony from the Black trans man working in the film used in my impact case study was fair and congruous. I had also asked that other "evidence" was removed: a piece of testimony intended for a totally different purpose than the impact case study had been passed, without my knowledge or consent, to a colleague working on impact. I expressed my growing concerns about confidentiality and GDPR and stated that information provided to a university for one purpose should not be made use of, including publicly, for another purpose without knowledge or consent. Because so many contributors to my work are LGBTQI+, BIPOC, disabled, and in poverty, this fear of institutional exploitation rose. Despite the earlier positive feedback, I was later told that there was insufficient evidence of the impact in my case study and it was not to be submitted. Concerned about the labor, including that of administrator colleagues, being wasted, I offered more pieces of research and evidence, which neither compromised nor exploited others. These included my article "Culture in Crisis: A Guide to Access, Equality, Diversity, and Inclusion in Festivals, Arts, and Culture" (Dawson 2020a). That article, written specifically for people with disabilities, people who are working class/in poverty, and parents/carers in mind, led me to write the Independent Cinema Office's most widely read blog manifesto, "Welcoming People Who Are Working Class and/or in Poverty" (Dawson 2020b) and to numerous policy changes. I was not allowed to add any further evidence of impact. While I imagine some of my colleagues created brilliant impact case studies, I wait to be convinced that all of the work submitted was more "Impactful" (impact case studies are published on www.ref.ac.uk in 2022), rather than better fitting a "straight sharing" narrative.

A paint-by-numbers approach offers a neatly packaged narrative with a straight progress from X (research) to Y (Knowledge Exchange event) to Z (Impact and its evidence). A past to present to future temporality is favored over the often sprawling and looping impact that happens when work is done organically and with a passion for social and economic justice. Running counter to the straight narrative, that work seeks benefits for people and places beyond the academy rather than gathers evidence with the primary purpose of winning funding. The huge amounts of money I brought in and the policies my research changed meant metrics were very easy to foreground in my case study, but I saw even greater value in individual lives transformed: a socially isolated trans woman coming to my events and building community through them, or a young gay man completing an eight hour round trip from his island home to an event I hosted on the Scottish mainland, even though he could have watched the film easily at home (it was available for free online) because he was isolated and wanted to be around LGBTQI+ people and find some community. Alongside issues with congruence, the impact case study offered no space for emotion, happier lives, or the twists and curves of queerness and an organic growth, alongside improved finances and policies.

Another of Halberstam's books can be brought in here: *The Queer Art of Failure* (2011), which positively frames failure as a form of queerness. Much like my earlier consideration that queer time versus straight time needs to be read alongside class and "race," Halberstam's queer failure needs to be thought of in terms of socioeconomic reality (Halberstam employs fantasy, a series of animated kids' movies, to evidence his points). Some of us are born to fail because of systemic racism, ableism, and/or classism. The bar is set so low and so little is expected of us that this can at times feel liberating. However, this freedom is within systems of oppression, meaning the freedom is not freedom at all, outside of the sensations from the aforementioned short bursts of pleasure. If people born into poverty then aspire beyond that low bar, aiming for lives and careers more typically expected of white middle-class+ people, there is no room for failure because we have no financial or social safety net to rescue us. The fall is significant, so we have to keep excelling to achieve a fraction of what privileged people have handed to them. In contrast, many privileged people, like the aforementioned Boris Johnson, fail upward. The straight sharing pathway means he will continue to succeed no matter how badly he performs and fails.

All of my volunteering to make culture more inclusive, which formed the impact case study, may be considered by some to be a failure because the case study was not eventually selected internally for REF2021 (while some of my four star publications, the hundreds of thousands of pounds of research funding I won, and the research network I founded were to be used), but I consider my volunteering work employed in the case study to be one of my great successes. Because I helped people. Queer and trans people. People with disabilities. People of color. People in poverty. Straight sharing, as we have seen, benefits the most privileged people and places, allowing them to invest even further in the future. While highly rated impact case studies mean universities will be given more money to perpetuate privilege, I will continue my queer, working-class sharing to benefit the least privileged rather than contribute to the straight sharing of an institution's Impact agenda. Much later I found out—although they never expected me to—that while I had been hospitalized at 22 weeks pregnant because of bleeding, with the fear that my baby would be born so prematurely that there was a high likelihood that he would not survive, colleagues working on Impact were expressing written concern that my hospitalization meant that my impact case study evidence would be delayed. It was not lost on me that Impact box ticking appeared to be worth more to some than the most impactful thing of all: life.

We Need a Better Academia

This chapter considered some current buzzwords in UK academia, which in theory promote "sharing" and EDI but can in practice be rather self-serving and help to conceal bad practice. I theorized a "straight sharing," which is the norm by which wealthy white privilege is perpetuated, and I instead proposed an anti-racist, anti-ableist, queer, working-class sharing. I used this to highlight issues in academia surrounding policies, as well as metrics and rankings, which are employed as smokescreens without a genuine commitment to equality for academics who are BIPOC, working class, and with disabilities. We need a reworking of Widening Participation to truly widen and therefore create a welcoming and comfortable space in the homogenous elite university environment for a broader range of students. We need systems in place to help them to thrive rather than to struggle with the pressure to be a pastiche of privilege or to attempt to silently go under the radar. We need to reconsider "Decolonizing the Curriculum" and keep asking how institutions founded on systemic racism can ever be decolonized. We need to ensure BIPOC and working-class scholars, students, and other "stakeholders" are foundational in recreating the present and the future of universities, rather than allowing a continuation of straight sharing based on institutions' problematic pasts.

This requires a reconsideration of rankings and hierarchies, such as the supposed tiers of universities. What can pre-92 UK institutions learn from their post-92 siblings, rather than the vice-versa norm? Post-92 institutions are much more likely to be attended by working-class students and academics. Just as there are many mediocre academics and students at supposedly elite institutions, there are numerous outstanding students and scholars at post-92 universities, where heavier teaching loads and reduced access to funding based on institutional snobbery can make it more difficult to find time to research. The latter also clearly impacts REF, with the "straight sharing" of the exercise and resulting academic funding perpetuating a racist, classist, sexist, ableist academia. This "straight sharing" of money means we need to rethink who and what is funded: a consideration of finances should include full remuneration and time allowance for all labor, an end to the exploitation of fixed-term contracts, and room for emotional labor, which should be recompensed.

We need an end to the colleagues who work by punching down while waving upward or outward, who leech rather than truly share, who approach the workplace just as wealthy white cishet men have approached their private lives, using women, minorities, and poorly paid and precarious staff to do the unwanted tasks while they reap the benefits and the glory. In order to get anywhere close to fairer academic structures, it is imperative that BIPOC and working-class leaders are hired (they are not a minority in the world, so why are they treated as such in the UK university system?), that traditional hierarchies are undone, and that universities commit to creating anti-racist, anti-classist, anti-ableist spaces. While UK academia currently only works for the most privileged people, strike action in recent years has shown that even a significant proportion of them are disillusioned, pointing us further toward the need for a kinder academia based on queer sharing.

References

Ahmed, S. (2017), *Living a Feminist Life*, Durham, NC: Duke University Press.
Binns, C. (2019), *Experiences of Academics from a Working-Class Heritage: Ghosts of Childhood Habitus*, Cambridge: Cambridge Scholars Publishing.
Bourdieu, P. (1984), *Distinction: A Social Critique of the Judgement of Taste*, Abingdon: Routledge and Kegan Paul.
Crew, T. (2020), *Higher Education and Working-Class Academics: Precarity and Diversity in Academia*, Palgrave Pivot.
Dawson, L. (2020a), "Culture in Crisis: A Guide to Access, Equality, Diversity, and Inclusion in Festivals, Arts, and Culture," *MAI Feminism*, October 5. Available online: https://maifeminism.com/culture-in-crisis-a-guide-to-inclusion/ (accessed March 24, 2022).
Dawson, L. (2020b), "Welcoming People Who Are Working Class and/or in Poverty," *Independent Cinema Office*, November 6. Available online: https://www.independentcinemaoffice.org.uk/blog-manifesto-05-welcoming-people-who-are-working-class-and-or-in-poverty/ (accessed March 24, 2022).
Dawson, L. (2021), "Investing in People Before Buildings: The Case of Filmhouse Edinburgh," *MAI Feminism*, February 17. Available online: https://maifeminism.com/investing-in-people-before-buildings-the-case-of-filmhouse-edinburgh/ (accessed March 24, 2022).
Deuchar, R. and K. Bhopal (2017), *Young People, Social Control and Inequality: Problems and Prospects from the Margins*, London: Palgrave Macmillan.
Gant, J. (2019), "University of Edinburgh Is Accused of 'blatant racism' for Hosting an Equality Conference Where White People are BANNED from Asking Questions," *Daily Mail Online*, September 27. Available online: https://www.dailymail.co.uk/news/article-7513201/Edinburgh-University-accused-racism-conference-white-people-ask-questions.html (accessed March 24, 2022).
Halberstam, J. (2005), *In a Queer Time and Place: Transgender Bodies, Subcultural Lives*, New York: New York University Press.
Halberstam, J. (2011), *The Queer Art of Failure*, Durham, NC: Duke University Press.

Pereira, M (2017), *Power, Knowledge and Feminist Scholarship: An Ethnography of Academia*, London: Routledge.

Phillips, H. (2020), "Performative Allyship Is Deadly (Here's What to Do Instead)," *Forge* (Medium.com), May 9. Available online: https://forge.medium.com/performative-allyship-is-deadly-c900645d9f1f (accessed March 24, 2022).

Quinn, J., A.K. Hollingworth, S. Hollingworth, U. Maylor, J. Osgood, and A. Rose (2014), "Dialogue or Duel? A Critical Reflection on the Gendered Politics of Engaging and Impacting," in Y. Taylor (ed.), *The Entrepreneurial University: Engaging Publics, Intersecting Impacts,* 202–222, London: Palgrave Macmillan.

Rooke, A. (2010), "Queer in the Field: On Emotions, Temporality and Performativity in Ethnography," in K. Browne and K.J. Nash (eds.), *Queer Methods and Methodologies: Intersecting Queer Theories and Social Science Research*, 25–41, Farnham: Ashgate.

Taylor, Y. and M. Addison (2011), "Placing Research: 'City Publics' and the 'Public Sociologist,'" *Sociological Research Online*, 16 (4): 6. Available online: http://www.socresonline.org.uk/16/4/6.html.

Williams, G. (2012), "The Disciplining Effects of Impact Evaluation Practices: Negotiating the Pressures of Impact within an ESRC-DFID Project," *Transactions of the Institute of British Geographers, Royal Geographical Society*, 37 (4): 489–95.

Chapter 7

THE PARADOX OF BEING SEEN: STORIES FROM TWO QUEER EDUCATORS AT A NEW YORK CITY HIGH SCHOOL

Tiffany Lenoi Jones and Elana Eisen-Markowitz

This chapter explores the possibilities and limitations of intersectional queer feminist pedagogies as nonhierarchical intellectual and creative engagements that can and do exist in secondary schools. We focus specifically on the paradox of being "seen" and "valued" for "embodying diversity" in a self-consciously progressive secondary school steeped in neoliberal individualism (Ahmed 2009). We (E.M. and Tiffany) are two very different queer educators who are proud of our pedagogical collaborations with one another, with our queer artist-activist networks outside of schools, and with our students and coworkers at a publicly funded secondary school in New York City, United States that we call Metro High School. We are proud of the work we've done to develop anti-oppressive, interdisciplinary, intergenerational, distributive models of sharing knowledge and resources to care for people and shift culture; and also we're left questioning the sustainability and depth of any culture-shifting models that depend entirely on the labor of individuals from marginalized identities. This chapter reflects on what we've been doing (practices) and why (theories) during our six years of queer intersectional collaboration at Metro High School. We emphasize the tensions of visibility; bringing ourselves, identities, and politics to our work in secondary schools prepares and requires us to imagine new and exciting ways of being together, but these ways of being can also run us into the ground if there aren't ongoing structural supports to protect and sustain them. Here we offer both the idealism and the skepticism, the joys and the precarity of this work, as we grapple with the paradox of *being seen* in the context of a school.

In writing about the burdens and precarity of intersectional queer visibility, we add our stories to the well-established field of educators and academics of historically marginalized identities both doing and critiquing diversity work and care work in the neoliberal educational institution. As Sara Ahmed argues, there is a particular visibility for people whose literal bodies are sought out to contribute to the "diversity" of an educational institution: "Our arrival is read as evidence of commitment, of change, of progress. Our arrival is noticeable" (Ahmed 2009:

41). In the Western institutional push for "Diversity, Equity, Inclusion" (DEI) over the last three decades, there is an undue focus on "happy diversity" that (1) prioritizes visibility and "image management" over challenging organizational culture (Ahmed 2009) and (2) leaves "noticeable" individuals vulnerable, overworked, and precarious, especially queer Black women (hooks 2000; Jones 2006). Moreover, "minoritised academics visibly marked as 'embodying diversity' are disproportionately responsible for doing care-full institutional diversity work" (Breeze and Taylor 2020: 67). This combination of hypervisibility operating alongside invisible, unrecognized labor often creates a precarious and personally painful dynamic.

Though much of the existing literature about diversity work and minoritized educators focuses on DEI in colleges and universities, our experiences at publicly funded secondary schools in NYC—and at Metro High School in particular—reveal a similar (and enticing) neoliberal ideology that the presence of marginalized individuals will somehow lead to structural change. As Rowena Passy wrote in 2013,[1] educators and Western educational institutions have been "socialised into a [neoliberal] tradition of isolation, individualism, self-reliance and a belief in personal autonomy," where there is outsize importance given to "teachers' personal qualities as distinct from their knowledge and skills" and this influences even how we think of our own work (Nias 1989). For us, this means we understand that being seen and noticed as individual educators for our personal qualities means being assigned value in a capitalist context. For us, this means that we understand that we have, to differing degrees and in different ways, been socialized both into mainstream cultures of neoliberal individualism *and* into collectivist, collaborative care-full cultures of Black queer feminism. We experience simultaneous impulses: "I want to be seen for *who I am*," *and*, "I do not want to be 'noticeable' and assigned value," *and*, "We want our collaborative work to be seen, valued, and supported." The neoliberal DEI model is predicated on invisible labor: we're visible but the work we're doing isn't! This exploits and exhausts. However, we write here not to dismiss caring and diversity work but to call for "the vital labour of care to be made 'visible, valued, and equitably distributed'" (Breeze and Taylor 2020: 134). We write here to share and document the joys, freedoms, and deep connection of bringing *who we are* to work, alongside the vulnerabilities and burdens of hypervigilance at school. It's precisely these simultaneous truths that, for us, define the precarious *paradox of being seen*.

In order to locate our reflections in the tangible realm of our work as teachers, we've written the rest of our chapter in sections based on common stories from our time together at Metro High School. Each of these vignettes is a snapshot of a moment, event, or experience we shared—starting in the plural first person because we wrote it together about our overlapping perspectives. Then, we each write to/about/in response to that story, bringing in our own unique perspectives and connections to theory and theme. Even in the structure of this chapter, we hope to communicate some of our ethics around sharing and the intentionality of intersectional queer politics: solidarity sometimes looks like a collective voice and sometimes requires making space for individual voices.

Arriving Together: We're Both Noticed at Metro High School

We still remember the feeling of walking together out of our day-long interview at Metro High School. As we ambled down Canal St, laughing and talking quickly, we felt a synergy and a relief—like we had found our place and our people. We had spent close to eight hours all told, interviewing, writing, sharing—and side-by-side, we felt our boldness and honesty grow. We felt we were being seen, maybe for the first time in our careers (and lives?) the way we wanted to be seen: politically radical, personally and politically queer, thoughtful intentional facilitators of learning, plus so many of the other layers, lineages, and experiences that make us each who we are. By the time we had both been offered the jobs and started as part of a pretty large cohort of new teachers at Metro High School (and joining a small number of Black folks and queer folks already on staff), we were already friends and collaborators.

Historically, the culture of Metro High School has been aspirational, humanizing and accessible, and self-consciously and self-congratulatory "progressive." Since the 1970s, Metro High School has prided itself on a unique approach to teaching and learning that includes internship and work experiences; here, the school transcends the boundaries of the classroom walls to position the city, community, and youth as essential collaborators. Here, we are encouraged to invest our energy in being ourselves instead of surviving School, which ideally makes space for confidence and creativity to flourish. This sense of belonging is a founding principle of Metro High School. The invitation for us and for our students to "be ourselves" is incredibly seductive and is offered in direct contrast to what many of us feel at more traditional schools and/or in our past schooling experiences.

During the period we were both being recruited and interviewed, we recognized in one another many of the reasons and experiences that pushed us to Metro High School and that set the aligned foundation for a friendship that transcended a work relationship. And, once we met our students, our connection was solidified. There was something precarious yet familiar about them. In hindsight, what we were able to see in our students is similar to what we were seeing in each other during our group interviews. All students at Metro have to choose to re-enroll in high school in order to attend. They are recovering from some interruption to or violence from their schooling. They have a certain self-awareness, wisdom, and drive, already having challenged the world in such a powerful way by saying, "I'm going to take control over my education, I don't have to do what's already available, I can choose a different pathway." Our young people have an urgency around being authentic, which guides us to be more true. And this urgency of being and being seen for the fullness of *who we are* seemed—at first and in contrast to our past schooling experiences—to allow all of us to be in our most powerful state to practice the queer feminist pedagogies and nonhierarchical intellectual and creative engagement we know are possible.

TIFFANY: Schools, like many institutions, perform as sites to maintain, sustain, and reproduce white dominance and anti-Blackness. Therefore, as a Black, femme, and neurodivergent, queer woman, I experience, more often than not, schools as a site of oppression and harm both as a student and educator. Throughout my education, I have experienced school, from childhood to adulthood, as an unloving and harmful space. As a student it was tiring trying to prove that Blackness, queerness, learning ability (I am dyslexic), and all other intersections were academically capable, worthy, and valuable. As a result I and many other Black students, especially in historically white institutions, learned and mastered how to survive and sometimes thrive within the confines of academia by, for example, utilizing class projects to fill in the gaps of white-dominated curricula, coalition building with peers and organizing to advocate for institutional change. Jarvis R. Givens describes this common and shared experience of Black folks in education as the "The Invisible Tax":

> The invisible tax that Black students pay manifests through the mental, physical, and emotional resources that they ... utilize to merely survive as students in a racially hostile campus environment. The constant coping deployed by Black students, and the fatigue it often causes, are both endemic to the invisible tax. In other words, the invisible tax is comprised of both Black students' strategies of resistance and the eventual exhaustion they experience from their labor. (Givens, 2016: 62)

The invisible tax I endured certainly primed and prepared me for my experience as an educator in historically white, yet ironically self-proclaimed "progressive" schools. I often wonder if progressive and alternative can actually mean challenging and dismantling structures of hierarchical and oppressive power. And if it does then this labor is outsourced to marginalized folks to identify, exemplify, and lead the charge in moving institutions forward. I am often in a recurring cycle within educational spaces where all too often meaningful institutional growth occurs after harm, neglect, and abuse have been both experienced and named by a marginalized body. As a Black, educational professional, I find myself paying the highest cost for institutional growth: my well-being, healing, safety, and sustainability are sacrificed for the awakening of privileged bodies. And, as a Black femme, neurodivergent, and queer cisgendered woman, race, sexuality, gender, and other intersections of my identities shape how I educate as well as how I am understood, educated, treated, respected, and supported. Through Black Feminism I am able to understand my own intersectionality and how it impacts my experiences in and out of schools. In their 1977 statement the Combahee River Collective, a groundbreaking collective of Black Feminists in the 1970s and 1980s, explains Black Feminism as a movement to combat the manifold and simultaneous oppressions that all women of color face. Black Feminism teaches me theory and strategy. Black Feminism acknowledges that anti-Blackness is a global pathogen that erodes all efforts toward freedom and is enacted by everyone including Black people. Black Feminism refuses anti-Blackness as the "normal state of being," thereby affirming that on every level my humanity as a Black, queer, and neurodivergent woman is enough and deserving of care, gentleness, and love as a practice of freedom.

After teaching at two different school communities where folks survived by making themselves small and invisible in different ways, I became clearer on what I could not tolerate. I learned how to be only parts of myself in each of these schools. I adapted by fragmenting and silencing parts of myself, and I worried that I was informally teaching youth how to hide in plain sight or affirm a culture of secrecy. When selecting a new school community, I considered my requirements for safety: unconditional acceptance, trust, care, and belonging. I refused to be burdened by withholding my queerness, my Blackness, or my neurodivergence. At Metro High School, I observed what appeared to be the signifiers and aesthetics of unconditional acceptance, belonging, and creative expression. The walls tell a long history of radical acceptance and progression like an AIDS/HIV mural from the 1990s, a daycare for teen parents, the absence of metal detectors, and the presence of youth laughter. It seemed I promised myself the next school community I joined would be one in which I and especially students were not required to omit or hide any parts of themselves. Finding Metro High School felt like a relief and an invitation to be my full self.

E.M.: As a white, gender nonconforming (gnc) person—a masculine-presenting woman—in this time and in most places, I am often read as gay or different before I "come out" or talk about my gender, sexuality, or politics. However, being perceived as gay certainly isn't the same thing as being respected or cared for. At the beginning of my teaching career, I was usually the only queer person on staff "out" to students and families, and even when I wasn't, the combination of my whiteness and gender expression often made me the most widely recognizable queer staff member. Though most of my individual relationships with colleagues, young people, and their families in these contexts were indeed full of love and learning, homophobia, heterosexism, and the gender binary was as baked into our school culture as it is in the rest of society: Why should our school uniforms be different for "boys" and "girls"? Why isn't my supervisor intervening when a parent is accusing me of making her trans kid "this way"? Why am I the only US history teacher that is teaching about queer cultures during the "Harlem Renaissance"? Why are all of the queer and questioning kids eating lunch in my classroom? The burden of educating on gender and sexuality through my own experiences (and especially as a new teacher in my twenties) was heavy and I didn't have mentors or peers to collaborate with in my school. So, what originally drew me to apply for a teaching position at Metro High School was its history of progressive and experimental education, the age diversity of its educators, and its racially and socioeconomically diverse student body. Metro High only serves students who started school elsewhere; they come to Metro because something happened to interrupt their schooling. I didn't initially know that about 50 percent of the students each year self-identify as LGBTQIA+, in large part because queer students—especially queer students of color—experience disproportionately high rates of school push-out. During the intensive teacher interviewing sessions where I first met Tiffany, it became clear that many of the same societal forces that pushed our students to Metro High School pushed and pulled me and Tiffany there too.

In my long career as a social studies teacher in secondary schools in NYC, I've had experiences of feeling both silenced and empowered and have likely cultivated conditions for my students that are both silencing and empowering. Reflecting on and navigating my responsibilities to education as liberation is fundamental to my pedagogy and my character. As a queer, white, Jewish, able-bodied, gender-queer woman who grew up with two graduate school-educated, upwardly mobile middle-class parents in big cities in the United States, I find myself navigating both power and marginalization in simultaneous and shifting ways. These experiences of my own identities, especially in the context of coming of age in diverse and divided neighborhoods in and around Washington, DC, in the 1980s and 1990s pushed me into social justice education and organizing as early as when I myself was in grade school. From even before I was a teacher, I was committed to "educational practice as social activism," which I learned about, experienced, and saw modeled for me by my own Black women teachers as a child and through college.

During the first eight years of my teaching career, I taught at two schools where being a queer gnc educator trying to engage educational practice as social activism made me lonely and sometimes targeted. And, I know that being queer—in terms of my political and personal identities—is a central part of why I connect to our students, to Tiffany, and of why I was hired at Metro High. After so many years in schools being told explicitly and implicitly to tone it down and shape myself to what is or isn't "professionally appropriate," arriving at Metro High School alongside Tiffany in 2014 was a revelation in being seen. This school (50%) full of queer-identifying kids helped shake loose some of the rigid normative expectations of us as teachers—and I'll never stop being grateful for that. Tiffany has said, "we learn how to be radical through our students." I've learned how to be the kind of queer adult I needed as a young person, the kind of queer adult I want to be, by observing our students be the queer teenagers they are right now. It's reciprocal affirmation and growth that must be cultivated through intentionally anti-oppressive, nonhierarchical, and intergenerational learning. And, especially in retrospect, I really struggle with the idea that being me is enough to shift culture; actually, it's the work we all do together that can shift culture.

Out and About Together: School Without Walls, Learning Across Time

We ended up all together at the New Museum, our students wandering from room to room solo, in pairs, in giggling triads. We took a now-infamous us-ie photo in the elevator and the kiddos squealed as they recognized model Grace Jones and then activist Marsha P. Johnson in the multimedia displays on the fourth floor. We'd spent the day already walking through the queer history and queer present of NYC's West Village and Lower East Side—and stopping for lunch all together at a restaurant by school that none of the students had ever wandered into by themselves and now acted like the place was theirs. We'd read and given feedback on each other's poetry, short stories and visual art. We'd walked by The Piers, Judson Memorial Church, Julius, the Keith Haring bathroom and the LGBTQ Archives at The Center, the memorials at the Stonewall Inn, and met with organizers from community organizations FIERCE and HOLLA—and many of our students knew these spaces intimately already because its where they live their young queer lives. We felt the walls of the school blur into the rest of the city and the rest of our lives. We were enlivened and exhausted.

We see our work as fundamentally both of the school and beyond it. We accept responsibility and hold ourselves accountable to the necessity of queering work inside of mandatory, publicly funded schools and always already connecting beyond the school. Mandatory public secondary school is where so many (queer, Black, poor, neurodivergent) young people are, so we feel we must be here. And, schools as institutions are limiting and limited; places where liberation is impossible and moving beyond its walls (and limitations) is just as necessary as working inside them. Much of what we did together and apart during our time at Metro High School was about the laborious and difficult work of creating anti-oppressive, interdisciplinary, intergenerational, distributive models of sharing knowledge and resources to care for people and shift culture. We did this work because it is what *we* need, what we want, and what we believe in—yes, in part because of *who we are*. However, our identities and our "embodied diversity" aren't what created meaningful, experiential, and even joyful curricula with and for our students. That happened because of a collaborative commitment to education for liberation.

E.M.: This day—the culmination of a three-day mini-course I coplanned and cotaught with Tiffany—is perhaps the clearest illustration of what's most important to me in my life and work. Focusing on local organizing for justice as a lens for learning everything else: communication, interdependence, creative expression, suppressed histories (especially of queer Black, indigenous, and people of color), critical literacy skills, future building, capacity for holding multiple truths, student leadership . . . . The process of planning for this expeditionary learning experience was collaborative and values-based, emergent, and flexible. We started with a central question: *How have queer people used art and activism to push for social change in NYC and the USA? How can we use the arts to reimagine our society to demand liberation for all?* And we called upon our own relationships and experiences with queer art and activism across the city. We of course had to do a lot of preparatory labor to create the outline of the project that students would engage with, make appointments at museums, archives, and community centers, get signed permission slips from parents and caregivers, and hustle to secure resources to make this mini-course entirely free to Metro High School students— but ultimately, the actual learnings from the three full days of this "intensive" course were shaped by the needs, creativity, and leadership of the seventeen students (of many genders, races, and sexualities) who participated. As Ahmed (2009: 45) explains, "'Diversity' is appealing as it does not necessarily challenge organizational culture, even if it allows a change in appearance." To me, it's how we intentionally shape these experiences and hold space for continuous learning and building, not just *who we are* or *what books we read*, that potentially challenges organizational culture and oppression.

TIFFANY: In these moments of collectively cultivated liberatory joy, fellowship, learning, and teaching I am hypersensitive and curious about how these sacred moments reveal the most essential shared values, practices, and relationships that feel like freedom. I remember vividly when we stood in front of a new luxury condominium that was built onto the historical site of St. Vincent's Hospital, one of the first hospitals to provide care to HIV/AIDS patients in NYC during the 1980s' AIDS epidemic. We all stared in silence for a lapsed amount of time at the structure and sighed as we witnessed yet again the physical manifestation of "revitalization," development, and gentrification. As I told the very important history of St. Vincent's hospital I noticed their attentive stillness, the sorrow in their sighs as they digested the information, and their confusion as they stared at the disappearance of an important place. Most importantly I was struck by their grief and gratitude for what happened there. I paused my storytelling so they could speak: *How could they just demolish such an important place for condos? Why is our history not preserved? How do we remember? I can't believe I didn't know this, how will our places be protected in this city?* They could relate to how important St. Vincent's was for queer folks in the 1980s. They understood how much it is a struggle to find care as a queer person and how beautiful it is to receive in our most crucial time of need. They mourned and celebrated on the corner of 7th Avenue. What emerged in this moment is a value for the interconnectivity of the past, present, and future, an awareness of how our actions today shape tomorrow, and the need to center the experiences of the most marginalized. Though I love learning and teaching and I've found ways to make school a space for me, it was and is tiring to prove that I am academically capable. Now, I work to reimagine learning spaces where all abilities and intelligences are seen and valued beyond the school walls. I join and amplify the movement of dismantling schools as we know them, and centering learning that happens in our lives and cities.

Learning and Loving Together: Meaningful Intergenerational Classrooms

We're preparing for an exhibition of our learning that's been eight weeks in the making and everyone is rehearsing their roles and setting up their stations. Along with us, the space is full of high school students ages sixteen to twenty-two, mentors and family members and even two-and-a-half-year-old Robin. In this corner, students Nicole and Masha are preparing lavender to offer to all those who visit the student-created Apothecary. Across the room, working artist-in-residence Meshell Ndegeocello is listening to the final version of Rosa & Mitri's original song recording, and down the hall Victor is arguing a court case about school uniforms in front of a LGBTQ rights lawyer from the American Civil Liberties Union.

We see our roles as queer educators working toward collective liberation to be *both learner and guide* in a Freirean sense: we become radicalized with and through our students, regardless of the realities of the education system. Friere says, "I do not believe that institutionalized education systems can be used as a lever for liberation. . . . Each has to work out what is appropriate in the particular setting and seek to put it into effect. In history, one does what is historically possible and not always what one would like to do" (Freire 1975). We know we're not going to find the freedom we want in schools, *and* we recognize and cherish the mutuality of intergenerational relationships with queer young people centered on making a change in the world. At 3:00 p.m. every day during our first year at Metro High School, the Day Care on the first floor of the school would close and two-and-a-half-year-old Robin would join her mom—a nineteen-year-old senior in high school—first in Tiffany's art class and then in E.M.'s *We the Students* American government class. Something about this humanizing experience of intergenerational learning was both spectacular and mundane. It was nothing we'd experienced before in a school and also it felt natural and familial. And, specifically as queer adults trying to make sense of our own lives, families, and futures, it made us both feel like *the future exists now.*

TIFFANY: The art room of Metro High School is a sacred space, like many art classrooms. As an art teacher, I am the conduit/cultivator of imagination and creativity. I am inspired by the brilliance of artists who invite us to value the essentialism of imagination and creativity. Without imagination and creativity, we find ourselves paralyzed by the limitations of our current realities. As an art teacher, I find it my essential work to re-engage and validate the imagination and creativity of youth. As adrienne maree brown says, right now we're sitting in the "realization of someone else's imagination. but we dream another world, and we make it come true."[2] *Uprising: The Legacy of Stonewall, SoulHouse Apothecary, Dear America, Searching for WildSeed, Afro-Futurism, A Journey Home* . . . . My classes are all about daring to dream and connecting to the past and the future. In one class, students chose to honor elders who gave birth to the modern queer liberation movement and led a teach-in to educate their communities. In another, students shared their community arts projects at a museum and work with mentors to gain the skills to make the projects come true. In another, students learned herbalism and how to support their peers in experiences of anxiety in school and when living in a city. These are all about using our classes as a practice ground for imagining and creating the worlds they want to live in. I want to affirm what they know and love who they are. There is a world now in which I'm honored. I don't have to wait until I'm older and I don't have to be the sole person fighting for it.

I often wonder who we would be if love were centered in education. I imagine we would be loved and therefore acknowledged, celebrated, energized, and humanized. The kind of love I imagine is rooted in the wise words of bell hooks who explains "the moment we choose to love, we begin to move against domination, against oppression. The moment we choose to love we begin to move towards freedom, to act in ways that liberate ourselves and others. That action is the testimony of love as the practice of freedom" (hooks 1994). When love is an embodied practice of freedom then the ways in which anti-Blackness and white dominance inform our interpersonal, professional, and institutional relationships in and out of school are named and challenged. My leadership, pedagogy, and entire life are rooted and grounded in love as a practice of freedom.

E.M.: Tiffany and I built our relationship through a commitment to our students' expressions of humanity—our love especially for our queer students and their contexts bonded us. But it was our commitment to the creation of experience-based, student-centered learning, and leadership that reaches beyond the school walls that cemented our trust and collaboration. The courses I taught and cotaught through my time at Metro High, classes like *We the Students*, *Stories of Migration*, *Queer Visions for Liberation*, and *Restorative Justice Leadership*, are project-based courses that center on the knowledge and experiences of the students in the class, engage different kinds of student collaboration, and cultivate connections to people and resources outside of the classroom and school building. For example, in *We the Students*, students work in teams to study and reimagine and reargue US Supreme Court cases that had to do with students in public schools. The culminating project of the course is to argue that case in front of practicing lawyers, who give feedback. In the Restorative Justice Leadership class, students work in pairs or small groups to learn about and train as leaders in the school: they may choose to become conflict mediators, design and host whole-school Town Hall meetings, and/or help plan and facilitate events for Queer New Year or Black Lives Matter Week of Action. It's not just the existence of both toddlers and teenagers in the same classroom that offers a model of nonhierarchical sharing but the insistence that our work and our learning are meaningful outside the school walls. There is no way I could have designed these classes without my queer community of friends, family, activists, and organizers. Our models are based on our values and our relationships. It's all so deeply personal, not institutional or structural. So, if I leave or take a break from Metro High School, my connections and community largely go with me—and these invaluable resources are hardly even recognized by my colleagues or supervisors. There is pressure and precarity to this. Whose responsibility is it to make this work long-term sustainable?

Celebrating Together: Whole-School Events

It's snowing outside in NYC in January, but it's very warm in the bustling art room where three of us queer teachers are dressed up as Chavela Vargas, Frida Kahlo, and Diego Rivera and ranchera music fills the space. Zeke, a student coplanner, makes the announcement over the intercom for all of Metro High School to hear: "Today is the kick-off for Queer New Year! Join us in the art room for a Frida Khalo lunch to learn about her politics, her work and her love life. We'll be creating flower crowns, taking Frida inspired portraits, and watching part of a new documentary about one of her lovers, Chavela Vargas. Hope to see you there!" We had to limit attendance at this lunch, but we've got eight other events planned through the rest of January to celebrate the history, literature, art, music, and complex lives of queer people in our school, city, and world. This was the third January in a row where we spent the whole month celebrating "Queer New Year," which culminated in a school-wide book club and a gathering with a living queer author.

When we think about Queer New Year now, we think about the irony of it, the paradox of being seen: the annual school-wide event was birthed exactly because we were and are visible and queer, and ended because the labor that went into its creation was unrecognized and unevenly distributed. Several years ago, a straight white cis woman colleague at Metro High School got a grant to invite an LGBTQ+ author to come speak at our school (good!). She came to us and said, "I don't know what I'm doing, can you help?" (good?). We excitedly imagined together something we wished we would have had as teenagers. We wanted to challenge the idea that we had to wait to talk about queer stuff in June. We wanted to create a series of school-wide activities that celebrated the expansiveness of gender and sexuality in ways that everyone would and could participate in. And we did it: for three years, we convened our colleagues and students to coplan a series of two to three events per week throughout January that spanned from a queer-focused sexual health seminar to a student-led Open Mic, to a straight Black colleague doing a teach-in about Bayard Rustin. It was fun. We felt special. Kids felt special. Joy and laughter abounded. We were out here in the middle of a school day celebrating the polyamorous relationships of a queer icon (Frida Kahlo)! For us, it started with a feeling of "it's radical to be seen." But on an institutional level, it was not sustainably shifting culture.

After we started Queer New Year, we were pulled into coplanning a variety of other school-wide activities to create community and inclusive, learning-focused, connected culture at the school: Black Lives Matter Week of Action, Experience the Experience Learning Exposition, Mental Health Awareness month, quarterly student-led Town Halls, a Haunted House in October . . .. It was wonderful and it was a lot. When a colleague came up to us and asked, "so, what are we doing for Women's History Month?," we knew we'd played into unfair and unsustainable expectations. But also, we felt stuck. As Tiffany says, "If I'm not involved in antiracist, queer-affirming, anti-oppressive work at the school, it might not happen. And if I am involved, it could kill me."

Reflecting on six years of queer intersectional collaboration at Metro High School, we feel about Queer New Year pretty much how we feel about "being seen" for "embodying diversity" more broadly: we're proud of what we've cocreated with one other, with our students, colleagues and queer artist and activist networks, *and* we recognize the precarity and the limitations of our work. These celebrations were always in some ways superficial and unsustainable, feeding the visibility monster, and running off the fumes of our invisible labor. We resent the oversimplified neoliberal "Diversity"/DEI narrative that asserts that the presence and celebration of marginalized individuals will lead to structural or cultural shifts and we demand that our labor—not just our bodies—be "noticeable," respected, and protected.

What are the ways out of this *paradox of being seen*? Administrators, colleagues, and policy-makers: stop contributing to a world where we're erased and/or disrespected while also expecting us to be the most visibly working to undo the policies, practices, and systems that oppress us. For example, planning for Queer New Year wouldn't be so tiring if we weren't planning Queer New Year with one arm and fighting off racism, transphobia, and heterosexism with the other. As Tiffany says, "I want my arms to be doing the same thing! Either get out of my way or move with the necessary confidence to actualize solidarity with me. What I actually want to happen: I want the gates to fall, the harm to stop, and the unconditional acceptance to flow." If you recognize and *see* our laboring toward queer intersectional liberation, show it. Take on the logistics of new schedules, courses, and school-wide initiatives. Protect our time and energy. Take other work off our plate if you value the "care-full diversity" work we're doing for and beyond the school.

References

Ahmed, S. (2009), "Embodying Diversity: Problems and Paradoxes for Black Feminists," *Race, Ethnicity and Education,* 12 (1): 41–52.

Breeze, M., and Y. Taylor (2020), *Feminist Repetitions in Higher Education*. London: Palgrave.

Brown, Adrienne Maree, *St. Louis Racial Equity Summit 2021 Keynote*, Available online: http://adriennemareebrown.net/tag/grace-lee-boggs/ (accessed March 9, 2022).

Combahee River Collective Statement, Library of Congress, Available online: www.loc.gov/item/lcwaN0028151/ (accessed March 9, 2022).

Freire, P. and M.B. Ramos (1975), *Pedagogy of the Oppressed*, New York: Continuum.

Givens, J.R. (2016), "The Invisible Tax: Exploring Black Student Engagement at Historically White Institutions," *ERIC*. Available online: https://eric.ed.gov/?id=EJ1169798 (accessed March 9, 2022).

hooks, b. (1994), "Love as the Practice of Freedom." Available online: https://uucsj.org/wp-content/uploads/2016/05/bell-hooks-Love-as-the-Practice-of-Freedom.pdf (accessed March 9, 2022).

hooks, b. (2000), *Feminist Theory: From Margin to Centre*, London: Pluto Press.

Jones, C. (2006), "Falling Between the Cracks: What Diversity Means for Black Women in the Academy," *Policy Futures in Education*, 4 (2): 145–59.

Nias, J. (1989), *Primary Teachers Talking: A Study of Teaching as Work*, London and New York: Routledge.

Passy, R. (2013), "Surviving and Flourishing in a Neoliberal World: Primary Trainees Talking," *British Educational Research Journal*, 39 (6): 1060–75.

Weeks, K. (2011), *The Problem with Work: Feminism, Marxism, Antiwork Politics, and Postwork Imaginaries*, Durham, NC: Duke University Press.

Part III

QUEER COMMUNITY PEDAGOGIES

Chapter 8

SHARING ACROSS GENERATIONS: THE LGBTQ+ INTERGENERATIONAL DIALOGUE PROJECT

Adam J. Greteman, Nic M. Weststrate, and Karen Morris

An Opening Example

During the second year of The LGBTQ+ Intergenerational Dialogue Project a small group discussion took place between students and elders as they planned a collaborative art project. Taylor, a master's student, brought up the concept of queer time as they described an idea about a possible direction for the project. Taylor noted:

> I was also thinking about . . . I read a recent paper [Farrier's "Playing with Time"] about a queer performance that was playing with queer time. And because it's a time-based performance, I was almost wondering if there is a way we can incorporate that. Umm, just in terms of queer time as challenging notions of heteronormative, straight time.[1]

Taylor was working to make sense of this article and the concept of queer time, bringing in a quote from the article to provide some clarity. "Time becomes so important to legibility," they read from the small group's working document, "that it sits at the root of humanness and citizenship to the extent that to be legible is to be correctly in time" (Farrier 2015: 1401). They started to explain . . . "It's just talking here about . . . " realizing, perhaps, that they didn't quite know what the author was talking about—an ever-present challenge in queer studies—turning again to a direct quote from Farrier who wrote:

> queer work on temporality, [on the one hand], is a queer articulation of time that seeks to expose the temporal power play in legibility. [On the other hand], the work is manifest as lived experiments with ways of life, forms of identity, cultural activities and modes of existence that upset the smooth flow of reproductive straight time. (2015: 1400)

Still sensing their own uncertainty with "queer time" and its meanings, Taylor shifted gears asking, "Is everyone following? I hope it's making sense . . ." Hope is a rather common thing one does in a pedagogical encounter with queer studies as one navigates complex and often opaque language. The work of making sense or making meaning of new concepts and ideas, often not within mainstream discourses and conversations, is no easy task, and a task that is often sadly limited to those with access, time, and interest in such queer ideas.

Danie, a seventy-year-old trans elder, spoke up in response to Taylor's question, saying "I'll admit to having some difficulty understanding the concept. However, that being said, I sense the direction and the details . . . and I would be in favor of that." Danie, a generous and often quiet presence in the dialogues, helped put Taylor at ease, continuing, "I'm not quite sure what is being proposed, but I understand the language that you are using . . . even though I don't understand some of the definitions. Whatever you are talking about sounds really good to me and you can let me know how I can be a part of it." While neither clarity nor meaning was immediately found, what was offered in this initial conversation was an opening to a shared educational encounter with queer studies. It was not a shared encounter between a professor and student, but rather two participants who ranged in age from twenty-eight to seventy years old with little to no formal education in queer studies, broadly conceived.

Of course, the shared encounter did not just happen out of nowhere. We, the authors and cofacilitators of *The LGBTQ+ Intergenerational Dialogue Project*, are each tenured or tenure-track faculty at universities, meaning the professor-student dynamic is always present. Furthermore, we are white, cisgender, lesbian or gay, able-bodied, and middle-aged, placing our bodies in complicated positions among the participants who are diverse in age, race, gender identity and expression, sexuality, economic class, and education. In recognizing the need for sustained intergenerational dialogues, we wrestle with the ways our own identities and positions are implicated in ways known and unknown as participants, but also those looked at as being "in charge."

We begin with this exchange and our own positionalities, both brief, to capture the potentials that emerge when cross-generational contact is cultivated and sustained, bringing "queer studies," we might say, out of the classroom and into the community. As Russell and Bohan remind us:

> In [LGBTQ+] communities/families, contacts between youths and elders are not an intrinsic element of social systems, as is true in most biological families and in most other communities that face oppression by virtue of their members' identity (racial, ethnic, or religious communities). Rather, LGBT[Q+] interactions tend to be age segregated. . . . Any contacts across generations must be arranged with the explicit intent of creating cross-generational interaction. (2005: 2)

The exchange between Taylor and Danie was not happenstance but emerged through an intentional and sustained project creating intergenerational dialogues that provide space and time to share stories and more.

The LGBTQ+ Intergenerational Dialogue Project not only seeks to intentionally and explicitly create space and time for cross-generational contact but also provides a glimpse into an embodied queer pedagogy (Greteman, Morris, and Weststrate, 2021; Morris, Greteman, and Weststrate, 2022). This embodied queer pedagogy provides a concrete way to counter forms of epistemic injustice, particularly hermeneutical injustice described by Miranda Fricker (2007). This form of epistemic injustice exists where there is a lack of interpretive (hermeneutic) resources or tools that can be used to make sense of shared collective experiences rooted in difference. Hermeneutical injustice, as it impacts LGBTQ+ populations in the United States, exists as resources and language are rarely shared within and across generations to help make sense of LGBTQ+ experiences. This lack of resources and tools cross-generationally emerges, in part, because of the almost complete lack of any attention to LGBTQ+ histories and lives in US schooling (K–12 and beyond or ages five and up). Additionally, there are histories of controversy surrounding such attention seen in continued bans on books addressing LGBTQ+ issues in school libraries as well as parental advocates seeking permission to remove their children from lessons containing LGBTQ+ content. There is, however, a growing movement to seek LGBTQ+ inclusion in the curriculum of US public schools. Six states, as of this writing in December 2021, have such requirements, including California, Illinois, New Jersey, Colorado, Oregon, and Nevada. While this points toward a possible future, it does not address the historic ways LGBTQ+ exclusion perpetuates a widespread gap in the interpretive resources for making sense of one's LGBTQ+ individual experience and seeing those experiences within a broader historical narrative.

In exposing this form of epistemic injustice and the need for resources to counter it, Elzinga (2018), building on Fricker, asks, "how do we develop these resources and make them widely available to members of society" (Elzinga 2018: 60). How indeed is the question? A key part of *The LGBTQ+ Intergenerational Dialogue Project* is to develop such resources through intergenerational dialogue rooted in shared experiences and sharing a range of resources. As we have witnessed within the first three years of the project, the sharing of experiences and resources has helped younger and older populations see first-hand the material realities of LGBTQ+ life and the multifaceted and precarious ways those realities persist across time.

Participants in the project—across generations—are by and large among the poor, working and middle classes that have had less access to and involvement with queer studies as an intellectual pursuit and the resources it provides for making sense of "queerness." Yet, while they may lack the language of elite queer discourses, they carry with them the material and historical experiences that can help expand and educate others about LGBTQ+ historical and present circumstances. Our elder and younger LGBTQ+ folks have had little to no formal education in LGBTQ+ histories or issues, given, as just noted, that LGBTQ+ inclusive curriculum is in its early stages of implementation in only six states in the United States. Many of the participants are, through this project, experiencing their first foray into queer studies through a hybrid experience that vacillates between the "academy" and the "community." This allows, we have found, participants to help create a different form of queer studies informed by embodied histories, pedagogies, and the act of sharing with one another. This time together helps highlight and develop resilience and in small ways buffer against precarity that is felt differently due to age, class, race, gender identity, and more. Participants in *The LGBTQ+ Intergenerational Dialogue Project* share not only stories, but also time, resources, and space in ways that allow them, and the authors, to feel and think our ways into not only queer studies as a form of intellectual work but broader understandings of LGBTQ+ lives and realities.

From Coming Out to Coming Into

We use the language "coming into" quite intentionally. Coming out is, of course, the more commonly engaged action associated with LGBTQ+ lives. At its core, it is a moment that is repeated and remixed over one's life where one shares a part of one's self, which one has had to, for various reasons, keep hidden from family, friends, coworkers, and one's broader communities. Less engaged in discussions about coming out is that alongside them, one builds the momentum of coming into one's sense of self and LGBTQ+ communities. In recent decades, social scientific research has shown that LGBTQ+ individuals in the United States are coming out at younger ages than in previous generations (Grov, Rendina, and Parson 2018). Amid a political and cultural climate in the United States with increased political attention, media representation, and everyday interactions, LGBTQ+ visibility has increased as more LGBTQ+ individuals share this part of their identity with others. In the United States, a 2021 Gallup Poll on LGBT identification found a 1 percent increase in such identification since 2017, with 5.6 percent of respondents identifying as LGBT. This was attributed, in part, to the sense that it is more likely for younger generations to identify as something other than heterosexual (Jones 2021). More and more people coming out illustrates that queer adage "we are everywhere," but also raises questions about how and if coming out puts one into contact with others that are part of LGBTQ+ communities. As we share a sense of self through coming out, how does such an act assist us in coming into LGBTQ+ histories, politics, and communities?

Our interest in this chapter steps to the side of coming out to explore the work of coming *into* LGBTQ+ selves, histories, politics, knowledges, practices, and cultures through the work of sharing: sharing space, sharing resources, sharing stories. Put differently, it is often the case that when we come out, we come out into a still "straight" world that at best seeks to tolerate us, at worst seeks to extinguish us (Sedgwick 1991). We rarely have, in coming out, access to LGBTQ+ histories, politics, and cultures because we often lack access to other generations of LGBTQ+ people that have, in various ways, worked to sustain LGBTQ+ cultures in all their messy, complex, and contradictory ways. While the internet has broadened one's ability to access "queer" ideas and people, such access often lands within one's generational cohort and is complicated by material realities of access tied to geography and economic class. This siloing of experiences and ideas perpetuate the lack of contact across generations and related forms of difference. This lack of intergenerational contact perpetuates already elevated feelings of isolation and loneliness experienced by LGBTQ+ youth and elders (Emlet 2016; Garcia et al. 2020), while also creating divisions between generations that, on the surface, may appear quite different but upon closer examination may have more similarities than differences. Given these divisions, possibilities, and conditions, our work, like that of Brim, seeks "to look for queer theory elsewhere" (2020: 11) so as to challenge and expand the projects and possibilities of queer studies alongside the classroom.

The LGBTQ+ Intergenerational Dialogue Project

There is a need, we think, to not merely theorize the potential in intergenerational contact, but to experiment with ways that might allow a sustained queer educational encounter. Following Patti Lather, "Let's be a queer family with a different relation to generations" (2010: 75). These different relations to generations we hope, following Halberstam (2003), break the deadlock of intergenerational conflict (Lather 2010: 69). Instead, as becomes visible with *The LGBTQ+ Intergenerational Dialogue Project*, we create and sustain intergenerational relations that are rooted in sharing within and across generations. Such sharing as we explore in the following is neither simple nor without conflict. There are reasons why upon coming out, we face challenges of coming into LGBTQ+ culture. While institutions—most notably schools, but also affordable housing residences and nursing homes—have historically advocated against or ignored LGBTQ+ existence, there exist within LGBTQ+ communities and institutions challenges and conflicts (Lugg 2016; Ramirez-Valles 2016). The simple premise of the project is to counteract the legacies of homo-bi-trans-phobia perpetrated by "straight" society that has kept LGBTQ+ people separate from one another.

The project emerged out of a conversation in the summer of 2019 between two School of the Art Institute of Chicago (SAIC) faculty members and the manager of senior services at the Center on Halsted. The conversation was initiated to discuss possible collaborations that would be mutually beneficial to our work with both LGBTQ+ elders and college students. There was, we found, interest from both LGBTQ+ elders and young adults in having conversations with members of different generations.

The LGBTQ+ Intergenerational Dialogue Project responds to these interests and brings together diverse groups of LGBTQ+ young adults (18–28 years of age) and LGBTQ+ elders (60+ years of age) to engage in sustained dialogue about a range of topics (e.g., LGBTQ+ intersections with race, gender, activism, history, aging, and the HIV/AIDS epidemic) that flow from the participants themselves. Each year, the project welcomes a new cohort of fifteen students from SAIC and fifteen older adults recruited through a variety of networks including the Center on Halsted, the largest LGBTQ+ community center in the Midwest. Participants commit to a nine-month series of biweekly dialogues followed by shared meals. As part of their dialogue work, they collaborate in small intergenerational groups on creative art-making projects for the project's public-facing website (generationliberation .com). In its third year, the project expanded to include a faculty cofacilitator from the University of Illinois Chicago (UIC) with plans to bring UIC students into the project in subsequent years. The three cofacilitators who participate in the dialogues work behind the scenes to secure funding, address any questions that participants have about the project, make connections with other local groups organizing around related issues (e.g., housing, school curriculum), and strategize ways to make sure participant voices are visible (e.g., through the website, participation in conferences). This constellation of work pulls the cofacilitators in different directions while also helping us develop practices that get the work of the project out in diverse contexts.

Our interest in and sense for the need for more intergenerational contact emerges from the cofacilitators' own experiences teaching and working with different LGBTQ+ generations alongside research that has illustrated a lack of sustained intergenerational contact among LGBTQ+ folks in the United States (Brown 2009). This lack of sustained intergenerational contact between LGBTQ+ folks in the United States limits the sharing of intellectual, affective, and historical resources across social and economic divides within queer communities (Russell and Bohan 2005). Ageism and classism within both queer studies and LGBTQ+ social spaces render older LGBTQ+ people, the majority of whom experience heightened levels of financial, social, and health precarities (Choi and Meyer 2016), invisible. The "generation gap" between the youngest and oldest generations of LGBTQ+ people who are usually not actively involved in, or subjects of, queer scholarship, is further reinforced by the persistence of societal homo-bi-trans-phobic fears around the "recruitment" of youth (Graves 2009; Rosky 2017) and the scarcity of education and social services institutions where the existence of "gay people is treated as . . . a needed condition of life" (Sedgwick 1991: 23).

As Kristen Renn argued "although higher education is the location of much development of queer theory, it is not an especially queer system of organizations or a system of especially queer organizations" (2010: 138). Queer theory, as an elite discourse, aligns with the work of higher education, and in such alignment has not impacted the structures or organization of higher education itself that might engage the possibilities and conditions of queer existence. For Renn, thinking specifically about queer theory, "queering theory was acceptable, but queering the organization was not" (2010: 138). The work of theory, in such a normative positioning, can be disciplined and housed in ways that provide a certain badge of honor for universities while forgoing the work of disrupting the structure and organization of higher education to be more equitable or accessible.

The LGBTQ+ Intergenerational Dialogue Project expands the possibilities of queer studies beyond the classroom often inhabited by young people to interact with and connect to LGBTQ+ elders, many for whom studying "LGBTQ+" histories in school was simply unheard of during their school days. Following Matt Brim, we recognize that "Queer studies makes us gay (or queer) because it opens a door to rooms, in this case classrooms, in which we do queer stuff together" (2020: 119). And we recognize our work as well connects with similar projects concerned with intergenerational LGBTQ+ possibilities, for instance, The Age Project out of Europe (Paulick 2008), the Generations Project based in New York City, and the Stay Gold Project at the Museum of Contemporary Art, Tucson (Burke, Orr, and DiCindio 2021). The classroom doors opened here in our work are not only to rooms on a university campus but also include the doors of an LGBTQ+ community center's senior services program housed within one of only eight residential facilities in the United States for low-income LGBT seniors (ages fifty-five and up). Queer studies, in this sense, come out of the academy and come into conversation with communities, in our case, elder communities, who are on the vanguard again, helping LGBTQ+ elders retire out-and-proud.

Queer Sharing

While there is much to learn from the project, we turn to unpacking the lessons and importance of sharing across generations as a queer form of coming into LGBTQ+ sensibilities. Our focus on sharing across generations is multifaceted as we address not only the practical importance of sharing resources across institutions to fund and feed such educative opportunities but also the importance of sharing stories as a form of queer becoming and knowledge building. Taken together, our need to work through and address space and financing the project, namely meals, was done with the recognition that participants would join the project from a range of positions. And while some participants would be (and are) financially secure, we did not want economics to bar anyone from participating, much less cause undue friction. What we did want was the ability to talk and think through LGBTQ+ lives as always already implicated in economic realities and, in particular, economic precarity, which itself implicates gender, race, and ability. Or, put differently, economic diversity alongside other forms of diversity could not be ignored at any stage of the process from imagining, planning, and implementing to revising and learning what we could do differently.

Sharing Space

A key component of thinking through and developing *The LGBTQ+ Intergenerational Dialogue Project* involved thinking about space. As Samuel Delany (1999) illustrates in *Times Square Red, Times Square Blue*, space is central to thinking about what makes us gay for the ways spaces, particularly queer spaces in public, created opportunities for contact with others, including cross-class contact. The loss of such spaces—seen with the gentrification of Times Square for Delany—closed down opportunities for contact central to making us gay. Drawing on Delany, Brim notes:

> What makes us gay is not the fact of our being but the fact of there being places where being gay can have social meaning, spaces where people can be gay together. To be gay is to be able to live among others within the social constraints that produce (rather than merely oppose) opportunities for gay sociality. (2020: 119)

Space for LGBTQ+ sociality is not ever merely social but tied to spaces and their educational potential. In sharing spaces where "being gay can have social meaning" or where social meaning can be created about "being gay," opportunities arise to do something different with the knowledge and histories that have been documented for some time now.

Yet, thinking about space is not merely conceptual. Rather, it also involves practical concerns about inclusion. Since a few of the elders that had expressed interest as the project was in development had various mobility limitations, we needed to be sure that wherever the dialogues were held that such a space was accessible. LGBTQ+ sociality cannot, we understood, assume able-bodiedness, particularly as aging is factored in. Fortunately, since the project was a school-community partnership with the Center on Halsted, they were very early on able to commit to allowing us to use their "living room space." This living room space is connected to Town Hall Apartments, Chicago Housing Authority's (CHA) senior living facility for LGBTQ+ older adults. What's more, the space is located in a former police station, which provided participants young and old, including us as cofacilitators, a historical glimpse at a space with connections to LGBTQ+ life. This glimpse came by way of a few elders who are long-term Chicagoans sharing stories about their experiences with the space including being brought in and booked for being gay (e.g., for not wearing gender "appropriate" clothes). Such stories helped all of us connect current struggles against police violence with these legacies that came alive through the stories of some of the elders.

Being able to host the dialogues in this space provided a convenient option for elder participants who lived there and made the search for a space, which can be difficult, rather easy. The space was also easily accessible via the city's public transportation system. Of course, the location of the building was within the city's historic LGBTQ+ neighborhood which suffers from its own legacies of exclusion while encountering the impact of gentrification (see, for instance, Orne 2017; Sampson 2013). These legacies and histories can, as with any snapshot, tell a particular story of a moment in time that can miss other snapshots of a dynamic neighborhood that has given sustenance and inflicted violence on its communities, often simultaneously.

In sharing space, the Center on Halsted was able to provide the project a home base that was not only accessible, at least more so than the school's campus located in the city's business city center, but also provided younger participants the opportunity to think about and through queer aging in a space committed to LGBTQ+ elders. This was made visible in the first few months of the project when several of the residents of the adjoining apartments offered a tour of the building, including its outdoor terrace and other community-based features. Such a tour helped participants develop a certain intimacy with one another, as well as made manifest the reality that this generation of elders, one of the first "out-and-proud" generations to retire, must now navigate new questions about being out-and-proud while aging. This includes not only economic challenges but also questions of dignity in growing old as an out LGBTQ+ person. Sharing the physical space of an old, converted police station connected to a housing facility materializes what research illustrates about economic precarity within LGBTQ+ communities. As Hollibaugh and Weiss (2015) illustrated, affluence in LGBTQ+ communities is more a myth than a reality. This "living room" space also allows for such a space to tell stories of its past as sexualities, genders, races, and classes interact. The walls of these buildings may not be able to talk, but the people sitting surrounded by those walls are able to tell stories that bring to life what haunts those very spaces. Some elders have expressed that their sense of being as an LGBTQ+ person is so inextricably connected to physical spaces that they fear what, for example, the disappearance of gay and lesbian bars might mean for their selfhood and even existence. For them, sharing such space across generations is tantamount to being seen, understood, and, eventually, remembered.

Sharing Resources

Early in the development of *The LGBTQ+ Intergenerational Dialogue Project*, the cofounders decided that an essential component of each dialogue should be a shared meal. We thought eating together would allow us to create a space for continued sharing. We could, we envisioned, help build community and relations by breaking bread, so to speak. There was a recognition, as well, that within histories of LGBTQ+ lives, the family dinner table has been a fraught site (Schulman 2009). The biological family table has, for some, been a site of violence and exclusion (Ahmed 2006). Yet, for others, it has been a site of acceptance and inclusion. Furthermore, dinner with one's "logical" or "chosen" family has similar histories, fraught with angst and love. We assumed, as we planned, that our own attempt at bringing together LGBTQ+ people across generations for a meal would lead to similar dynamics since no dinner table is ever simple.

To envision such shared meals and their potential importance is, of course, one thing. Funding such meals is another thing. The role of the project's three host institutions (SAIC, Center on Halsted, and UIC) is complicated by their dependence on state and federal aid alongside, for the colleges, tuition dollars. SAIC is, for instance, completely tuition-dependent, charging an exorbitant tuition that puts most of its students (many of whom receive federal aid) into a huge amount of debt. Additionally, 77 percent of its teaching faculty are part-time and underpaid (AICAD 2020; Carsel 2018). The Center on Halsted depends on fluctuating external public and private grants and donations to function. UIC, a public research university, depends on revenue from a lower tuition rate and state funding that has recently decreased.

These underlying realities have a direct impact on the project, requiring constant efforts by the authors to secure funding to support the project's meals, website, and collaborative artistic production. While Center on Halsted was able to share their space with the project, including a kitchen for any meal preparation, it was the work of the faculty facilitators to try to find money to pay for the meals and any other related costs that would emerge. Early on, in a conversation with the Dean of Community Engagement at SAIC, some seed money was secured that allowed the project to get off the ground. This money was secured, in part, we think, because of the administrator's recent reading of Rebecca Makkai's *The Great Believers* that provided a fictionalized history of the AIDS epidemic in the neighborhood where the project would take place. It took the administrator back to their own youth during the 1980s and being a student themselves of the school navigating those neighborhood streets and bars.

Initial seed money to get the project started, however, would not sustain meals for the entire year. So we applied and received a small grant through our college known as a "Compassion and Belonging" grant that was focused on developing programs that could cultivate diversity and equity initiatives. With this award, we realized we had to take a different approach to meals since catering them, while efficient and able to cater to different nutritional needs, was not economical. One of the cofacilitators, who has volunteered with the senior services programs for over a decade, drew on his own networks to see if another volunteer, Harold, a retired nutritionist, would be willing to develop and cook healthy meals to feed 30–35 people with additional help. Fortunately, he was happy to share his expertise and in doing so allowed us to stretch our budget dollars while we worked to secure additional funding for future years of the dialogue.

Unfortunately, the COVID-19 public health pandemic began seven months into the first year of the dialogue project, leaving us with grant money that would no longer be needed to fund in-person dinners. With the city, community center, and the school shut down along with emerging concerns about the food insecurity of many elders now homebound and at high risk for COVID-19 infection, we used the leftover funds to donate food and other essential items to the community center, which was starting a food pantry for residents and other elder patrons. This was, in part, because the funds needed to be used by the fiscal year since university budgets, themselves in crisis, still needed to be used up within the awarded fiscal year. It was also a way in the early weeks of the pandemic when so much uncertainty prevailed that we were able to ensure the funds secured for meals were still used for meals for a vulnerable community population amid the uncertainty.

COVID-19, of course, upended more than just our meals. In the early days, we assumed the project would need to go on hiatus because of the shelter-in-place orders and the reality that many students were leaving Chicago to go to their respective families' homes. However, as Dunn, Chisholm, Spaulding, and Love (2021) argued, "COVID-19 has provided conditions which ruptured the norm in a way that may enable the growth of hope and trust" (2021: 216). "Ample time to reflect, (re)focusing priorities, evaluating what we can do to support one another in the face of adversity, and sharing resources," they continued, "are the type of actions made possible by the pause in normal daily life that COVID-19 has demanded of us". Such was the case for the project, as almost immediately younger and older participants reached out asking if the dialogues could continue virtually. Having not planned or expected this, we went to work communicating with the participants about our rapid transition online, which initially involved twice-weekly Zoom calls, made possible through the faculty facilitators' university Zoom accounts, that allowed all of us to have much-needed social contact. This was made possible by the fortunate reality that all participants had access to some form of technology that connected to Zoom (e.g., phone, tablet, or computer). This rapid transition to Zoom, however, further illustrated the importance of sharing space together, albeit now a virtual space that allowed us to enter one another's private spaces. Project participants became involved in subsequent (mostly unsuccessful) efforts to secure funding to support our newly forming website and artistic production by submitting grant applications, writing letters of support, and mining their own networks for funding ideas. Zoom allowed us to share space and resources in new, sometimes more intimate ways. It also allowed, quite significantly, for the continued sharing of stories.

Sharing Stories

A key component, often overlooked in coming into one's LGBTQ+-ness, is the work of sharing stories. Digital technologies allow us access to infinite amounts of information as we simply ask Alexa, Siri, or Google questions. These technologies and their predecessors have been, in some regards, central to connecting LGBTQ+ people across spaces within the anonymity of cyberspace. As demands for anonymity have changed as LGBTQ+ people become more mainstream, such digital resources now provide access to information that continues to expand. This allows emerging generations access to stories of yesterday's queer past in rather unprecedented ways, be it through something like the ACT UP Oral History Project coordinated by Jim Hubbard and Sarah Schulman, OUTspoken LGBTQ+ Storytelling at Sidetrack (and through podcast) in Chicago, or Eric Marcus's book and podcast *Making Gay History*, to name just a few. Gone, so to speak, is the need for searching out content in the library stacks, hoping to find something that allows one to make sense of and reach toward understanding one's feelings and desires. However, there remains a need to connect such content to our lived realities and the ways our "now" must respond to challenges not only to our queer pasts but also to possibilities for queer futures, which include LGBTQ+ individuals who have and continue to age. We continue to need opportunities to meet others that allow us to talk about and through the ideas and practices we encounter; this is done, we believe, through stories that join conversations across space and time.

Stories are, we believe, central to the conversations that emerge during intergenerational dialogues. Simple as conversations might appear at the outset, they entail more than meets the eye, particularly as such conversations touch on topics, ideas, and issues like activism, healthcare, pronouns, and queer spaces that have changed for LGBTQ+ folks across time while simultaneously often remaining the same. This is true for LGBTQ+ people who have experienced an extensive array of changes throughout the twentieth century and into the twenty-first, but the stories of such changes are often not shared, in conversation, with others from different historical moments. By this, we mean quite literally, conversations in the presence of others in what we conceptualize as an embodied queer pedagogy (Morris, Greteman, and Weststrate 2022).

It is within the work of storytelling or sharing stories that we most visibly see ways to counter hermeneutical injustice. Hermeneutical justice, as a reminder, points toward the gaps that exist in interpretive resources used to make sense of and meaning of social experiences. The lack of hearing and sharing stories of LGBTQ+ lived experiences, on a certain level, limits the knowledge that exists within and across generations and curbs its potential to help us interpret the world. Stories, we have seen, help open deeper dialogues and reveal resources often already present within LGBTQ+ communities. As participants develop certain levels of trust with one another, they can share their stories that invoke a range of realities—joyful, traumatic, and more. Such sharing illustrates that LGBTQ+ individuals do not so much lack interpretative resources on a small scale, but rather there is a wide gap in such resources being shared collectively on a larger scale (e.g., through schools or other institutions). Stories and the tensions that arise in their telling make apparent in action the process by which hermeneutical injustice is countered with participants learning new ways to understand the complexities that exist within LGBTQ+ lives and communities.

An ongoing tension that became visible in the first year of the project and extended into the second year was around the expanding understanding of gender identity. This tension became most visible as participants took the reins of the project and proposed topics to focus on, notably one topic that an elder lesbian called the "disappearing lesbian." Believing, as facilitators, that the tensions and complexities of LGBTQ+ life cannot be stepped around or glossed over but need to be worked through slowly and patiently, a set of dialogues was planned and developed by participants. One would focus on stories of expanding experiences of gender and another on stories of lesbian history.

Needless to say, many stories and conversations happened, so we want to focus on a particular moment where a breakthrough emerged. A number of elder lesbians shared their stories about growing up lesbian and their diverse experiences in lesbian spaces. As they told these stories, a certain theme emerged around the ways lesbian spaces have disappeared. As the stories ended and conversation started, student participants started to express a realization that they had never really thought about lesbian spaces, nor did they share the elders' sense of loss, as they have never had access to them. However, numerous students expressed a certain concern about the "disappearing lesbian" framework because they had only ever encountered it through stories of "Trans Exclusionary Radical Feminism" (or TERFs), which told a story of lesbians being "forced" to transition. Yet, as they listened to the elder lesbians, they realized that the elders were wanting to articulate and express their grief and mourning about lost spaces, spaces that had given them sustenance and helped them come out and live their lives. Disappearing lesbians was not coded for TERF views, but a need, perhaps even a desire, to mourn and grieve the disappearance of lesbian spaces. This breakthrough moment also allowed students to teach the elders about TERFs, which the elders were completely unfamiliar with—at least conceptually—since they were familiar with historical tensions around the inclusion of trans women (e.g., Michigan Womyn's Music Festival). Such a moment where stories help unpack and connect differently did not change things immediately, but it did open up a space that allowed participants to see, quite literally, the different assumptions that were being made about the descriptions or language being used. Disappearing lesbians, to elders, touched on their concerns about loss of lesbian spaces and culture, while to younger folks, disappearing lesbians was a coded way of erasing trans existence through fears of "lesbians going extinct." Both viewpoints, of course, exist and are important. Yet, when the issues are collapsed without opportunities to unpack them, the resources that exist to both mourn losses and counter transphobia are lost.

This describes, in part, the role of time in engaging in conversation across generations. Concerns around gender were ever present and embodied differently due to histories of gendered oppression. Such conversations around gender across generations are not commonplace in everyday life, happening, if at all, often within the space of bars or one-off programming. And a lot can be lost or missed within such ephemeral encounters as assumptions and stereotypes are made along with a general reality that collective understandings of different LGBTQ+ realities are lacking. If the dialogues had not been sustained, the suspicion and misunderstanding around gender across generations would have persisted. Yet, the participants in the project entered the project with a range of experiences, ideas, resources, and more that were shared and unpacked over time. We each entered intergenerational spaces at different points in the process and have had to work to make sense of where the conversations are, how we might contribute or fit in, and how and when we might leave the conversations, which continue without us present. Sharing one's story to be in conversation with members of other generations in any sustained manner is rather difficult because of the layers of issues that are in play and often unspoken. However, sustaining such conversations even amid tension or complications allows for resources to be developed and understandings to emerge that are rooted in experiences shared and unpacked together—in one another's presence (physical or virtual)—and not through the disembodied realm of social media and sensationalist reporting that, as we learned, was a key component in some ways participants had come into contact with stories of LGBTQ+ lives.

On Being Implicated: A Conclusion

Imagining, planning, and engaging an embodied queer education is no easy task as it requires not thinking about the historical and conceptual issues in play but also everyday material, economic, and structural concerns. Such questions, we learned, became even more important and the consequences even more visible as the COVID-19 pandemic unfolded. *The LGBTQ+ Intergenerational Dialogue Project* is an embodied queer education that refuses to keep queer studies in the classroom focused on texts (written or filmic), but to implicate the issues and insights of queer studies in the everyday lives of LGBTQ+ people both within and outside the academy. Queer studies scholars, as Allan Bérubé (1995) argued, "can't enjoy the luxury of standing on the sidelines as innocent bystanders" to the "racialized class inequality and confusion that structure the larger society." For Bérubé, "we have been implicated" (1995). Decades later, queer studies scholars continue to be implicated in these complex and intertwining inequalities as we have become even more ensconced in higher education with all its complications (e.g., budget cuts, enrollment issues, tuition costs) and legacies (e.g., white supremacy, Eurocentrism). It is not lost on us, nor is it coincidental, that we, the project's cofounders and facilitators, are white, cisgender, and tenured or tenure-track faculty members at institutions of higher education. We believe our implication is important as it means that rather than being on the sidelines as a bystander, we now have skin—including practices, methodologies, and histories—in the game to expand and build on the work of generations of LGBTQ+ people. We can, to draw again on Lather, "have different relations to queer generations" (2010: 69). Such generations are slippery, of course, as they are themselves implicated in politics of race, gender, class, and more that impact access to not only institutions of higher education, but also communities. However, it is necessary we believe to think with and across the slipperiness of generations to grapple with the different cultural, social, political, and material realities that formed and informed each generation's work within communities and institutions of higher education.

We began this chapter with a story where Taylor, a student participant, and Danie, an elder participant, showed a glimmer of what happens when queer studies concepts move outside of the classroom and into dialogue with those outside the academy who bring different histories and experiences. The moment could have gone any number of directions. Danie could have scoffed at the language—convoluted and obtuse as it might be seen. She could have remained silent in protest to the language or out of embarrassment that she didn't understand it. Instead, Danie joined the conversation, expressed her lack of understanding, but concluded, "Let's keep going and I'll get there." There, in that comment to keep going, to make sense, we saw the potential of sharing across generations and the ways such sharing assists both younger and elder participants to come into LGBTQ+ historical and contemporary discourses, politics, and yes, "lingo." The space—digital due to COVID-19—provided an opportunity to engage in queer intellectual and creative engagement that refused a hierarchy but embraced a process of sharing.

As we conclude writing this chapter, a year after Taylor and Danie's first dialogue around queer time, the two are preparing for a national academic conference in which they will discuss the final product of their small group's collaborative work on queer time. A collection of collages using participants' personal photographs overlaid with transparencies bearing hand-drawn images and hand-written stories, the artwork reflects members' journeys to locate and celebrate moments of "queer joy" in their own lives. Their sharing of an art piece realized through community-based, intergenerational exchange among LGBTQ+ folks with academic and professional conference attendees offers a glimpse of the ways that new forms of "queer studies" that travel out of the academy can enter back into, and contribute to, the field.

References

Ahmed, S. (2006), *Queer Phenomenology: Orientations, Objects, Others*. Durham, NC: Duke University Press.

Association of Independent Colleges of Art and Design (2020), *School of the Art Institute of Chicago*. Available online: https://www.aicad.org/schools/school-of-the-art-institute-of-chicago/.

Bérubé, A. (1995, February), "Class Dismissed: Queer Storytelling Across the Economic Divide," Keynote address at Constructing Queer Cultures: Lesbian, Bisexual, Gay Studies Graduate Student Conference, Cornell University.

Brim, M. (2020), *Poor Queer Studies: Confronting Elitism in the University*, Durham, NC: Duke University Press.

Brown, M.T. (2009), "LGBT Aging and Rhetorical Silence," *Sexuality Research and Social Policy*, 6 (4): 65–78.

Burke, E., H. Orr, and C. DiCindio (2021), "Stay Gold: An Intergenerational LGBTQIA+ Arts Program," in B. Bobick and C. DiCindio (eds.), *Engaging Communities Through Civic Engagement in Art Museum Education*, 269–89, Hershey, PA: IGI Global.

Carsel, C. (2018), "Precariat Professors: Where SAIC's Part-Time Faculty Stand," *F Newsmagazine*, March 8. Available online: https://fnewsmagazine.com/2018/03/precariat-professors-where-saics-part-time-faculty-stands/.

Choi, S.K. and I.H. Meyer (2016), *LGBT Aging: A Review of Research Findings, Needs, and Policy Implications*, Los Angeles, CA: The Williams Institute.

Delany, S. (1999), *Times Square Red, Times Square Blue*, New York: New York University Press.

Dunn, D.C., A. Chisholm, E. Spaulding, and B. Love (2021), "A Radical Doctrine: Abolitionist Education in Hard Times," *Educational Studies*, 57 (3): 211–23.

Elzinga, B. (2018), "Hermeneutical Injustice and Liberatory Education," *The Southern Journal of Philosophy*, 56 (1): 59–82.

Emlet, C.A. (2016), "Social, Economic, and Health Disparities Among LGBT Older Adults," *Generations*, 40 (2): 16–22.

Farrier, S. (2015), "Playing with Time: Gay Intergenerational Performance Work and the Productive Possibilities of Queer Temporalities," *Journal of Homosexuality*, 62: 1398–418.

Fricker, M. (2007), *Epistemic Injustice: Power and the Ethics of Knowing*, Oxford: Oxford University Press.

Garcia, J., N. Vargas, J.L. Clark, M. Magaña Álvarez, D.A. Nelons, and R.G. Parker, (2020), "Social Isolation and Connectedness as Determinants of Well-Being: Global Evidence Mapping Focused on LGBTQ Youth," *Global Public Health*, 15 (4): 497–519.

Graves, K. (2009), *And They Were Wonderful Teachers: Florida's Purge of Gay and Lesbian Teachers*, Champaign: University of Illinois Press.

Greteman, A.J., K. Morris, and N.M. Weststrate (2021), "Countering Epistemic Injustice: The Work of Intergenerational LGBTQ Dialogues," *Studies in Art Education*, 62 (4): 408–13.

Grov, C., H.J. Rendina, and J.T. Parsons (2018), "Birth Cohort Differences in Sexual Identity Development Milestones among HIV-Negative Gay and Bisexual Men in the United States," *Journal of Sex Research*, 55 (8): 984–94.

Halberstam, J. (2003), "Reflections on Queer Studies and Queer Pedagogy," *Journal of Homosexuality*, 45 (2–4): 361–4.

Hollibaugh, A. and M. Weiss (2015), "Queer Precarity and the Myth of Gay Affluence," *New Labor Forum*, 24 (3): 18–27.

Jones, J.M. (2021), "LGBT Identification Rises to 5.6% in Latest U.S. Estimate," *Gallup*, February 24. Available online: https://news.gallup.com/poll/329708/lgbt-identification-rises-latest-estimate.aspx.

Lather, P. (2010), "Response to Jennifer Gilbert: The Double Trouble of Passing on Curriculum Studies," in E. Malewski (ed.), *Curriculum Studies Handbook: The Next Moment*, 73–7, London: Routledge.

Lugg, C. (2016), *US Public Schools and the Politics of Queer Erasure*, London: Palgrave Macmillan.

Morris, K., A.J. Greteman, and N.W. Weststrate (2022), "Embracing Queer Heartache: Lessons from LGBTQ+ Intergenerational Dialogues," *International Journal of Qualitative Studies in Education*, 35 (9): 928–42.

Orne, J. (2017), *Boystown: Sex and Community in Chicago*, Chicago, IL: University of Chicago Press.

Paulick, S. (2008), "Age Project: Intergenerational Dialogue with(in) the LGBT Community," *ILGA-Europe/IGLYO*. Available online: ILGA Europe. https://www.ilga-europe.org/sites/default/files/Attachments/age_report_ilga-europe_iglyo_2008.pdf.

Ramirez-Valles, J. (2016), *Queer Aging: The Gayby Boomers and a New Frontier for Gerontology*, Oxford: Oxford University Press.

Renn, K. A. (2010), "LGBT and Queer Research in Higher Education: The State and Status of the Field," *Educational Researcher*, 39 (2): 132–41.

Rosky, C. (2017), "Anti-Gay Curriculum Laws," *Columbia Law Review*, 117 (6): 1461–542.

Russell, G.M. and J.S. Bohan (2005), "The Gay Generation Gap: Communicating Across the LGBT Generatonal Divide," *The Policy Journal of the Institute for Gay and Lesbian Strategic Studies*, 1: 1–8.

Russell, S.T. and J.N. Fish (2019), "Sexual Minority Youth, Social Change, and Health: A Developmental Collision," *Research in Human Development*, 16 (1): 5–20.

Sampson, R.J. (2013), *Great American City: Chicago and the Enduring Neighborhood Effect*, Chicago, IL: University of Chicago Press.

Schulman, S. (2009), *Ties That Bind: Familial Homophobia and its Consequences*, New York: New Press.

Sedgwick, E.K. (1991), "How to Bring Your Kids Up Gay," *Social Text*, 29: 18–27.

Chapter 9

PERMEABLE SPACES: CREATING STRUCTURED YET FLUID CULTURAL EXPERIENCES FOR LGBTI+ ELDERS

Lou Brodie and Lewis Hetherington

In May 2019 the National Theatre of Scotland (NTS) launched its new production *The Coming Back Out Ball*. Originating in Australia, *The Coming Back Out Ball* (TCBOB) was created by the independent arts organization All The Queens Men (ATQM). The Scottish premiere of the project was delivered by NTS in partnership with Luminate; Scotland's Creative Aging Organization, Eden Court; Scotland's largest multi-arts center base in Inverness and ATQM. In this chapter we use our own and others' experience of being a part of TCBOB to explore the devising of queer "permeable" spaces situated in participatory art practices in the context of queer precarity. Through the writing of the chapter, we have been struck not only by the complexity of the experience created but also by the layers of implicit learning that took place for the various actors involved in the project. TCBOB Scotland was originally designed to be a yearlong project, culminating in a June 2020 Ball. The arrival of COVID-19 meant the project was extended for an extra year, during which almost all of the activity was delivered online including *The Coming Back Out Ball* itself which eventually took place in June of 2021, bringing the project to a close. Throughout this chapter we draw on testimony from individual interviews with the four other members of the team who delivered the project's central community building: LGBTI+ Elders Social Dance Club and a small focus group of LGBTI+ Elders who attended both offline and online activities. Through these materials we uncover the learning from the project's delivery pre-COVID-19 and during the COVID-19 health crisis. We discuss the precarity within and highlighted by the project, both for the LGBTI+ team and Elder participants, arguing that their intersectional locations often put them in situations of social and institutional precarity.

The majority of the frontline team who delivered the core aims of the project are all precarious freelance cultural workers. We (Lou and Lewis) are both freelance creative practitioners who were contracted by NTS to be part of the team that delivered The Coming Back Out Ball event itself and the preceding longer-term community-building phase of the LGBTI+ Elders Social Dance Clubs, which are the central element of the project. Lewis was the project lead and Lou was one of four freelance facilitators brought on to deliver LGBTI+ Elders Social Dance Clubs. The freelance team was supported by a member of staff from Eden Court and two members of NTS staff throughout the duration of the project. Other staff members from the project partners were drafted to work on the project at certain points when needed.

Elders are the participants who voluntarily took part over the course of May 2019 until the project's culmination in June 2021. The use of the word Elder comes from the project's roots in Australia and its cultural relationship of Indigenous Elders as those who have gained knowledge. We use the abbreviation LGBTI+ throughout the chapter to refer to all members of the queer community who sit under the longer LGBTQIA+ abbreviation. In this chapter we adopt LGBTI+ as modeled by the founding artists, ATQM, and as this abbreviation was used throughout delivery. We note that the project abbreviation's lack of the Q is an omission of the word "queer." While in many respects this was done as a shorthand and assumed an inclusion of the full spectrum of the community, it is also the case that identifying with queerness is not commonly part of this generation's vernacular and can be a word or identity that they actively reject. We as a team did not avoid a conversation on queerness but this idea of "queer" was generally more implied than made explicit.

NTS is Scotland's national theater, a self-declared "theatre without walls" defined on their website as a desire to "break down the walls that prevent people from engaging with our work, whether economic, cultural or physical" (National Theatre of Scotland 2021a, b). This project was borne out of the current artistic director's (AD) knowledge and admiration of the work of ATQM in addition to her observation that LGBTI+ Elders were an underserved audience group. Indeed, NTS's most up-to-date strategic plan for 2018–23 notes "gender and sexually diverse people" as a priority group, although it does not mention age (National Theatre of Scotland 2021a, b). This individual knowledge combined with organizational strategy led to the programming of *The Coming Back Out Ball* in NTS's 2020 season—but it also points to our innate connection to and precarity within the project. The project could have easily fallen through without the choices, actions, and connections of the AD, including a commitment to and made with ATQM.

Further Scottish partners were brought in: Luminate, Scotland's creative aging organization, and Eden Court, Scotland's largest multi-arts center based in Inverness in the Highlands. Luminate state one of their key aims as working "to ensure all older people in Scotland can enjoy high quality arts and creative activities, whatever their background and circumstances and wherever they live" (Luminate 2021). Luminate's goal is, in our opinion, a much-needed aspiration particularly when combined with an approach to intersectional experiences of aging and the agenda this can serve in making lived experience visible. Both organizations are arts charities working to provide different sections of Scottish society with quality arts provision. In 2020 Eden Court employed around 200 people while Luminate is a small organization with five members of staff, only one of whom is full-time.

Eden Court is Scotland's largest combined arts organization. They "present and make work with, by and for the people of the Highlands and Islands and those who visit them" (Eden Court 2021). They supported Proud Ness and the first pride march in Inverness in 2018, through in-kind donation of space and staff, and also a financial contribution. From its base in Inverness, Eden Court serves the Highlands and Islands which has a land mass of 26,484 square kilometers and holds a population of 469,365. This compares to the 265 square kilometer land mass of Greater Glasgow, which has a population of around 1.2 million people. These numerical comparisons show a stark difference and begin to paint a picture of what the nuances of rural isolation might be for the queer community both young and old, as a patchwork of little to no provision in an area where you must travel significant distances to reach even partial and temporary provisions. Eden Court's support of Pride laid the foundations for supporting projects such as TCBOB. However, much like NTS, continued support relies on organizational priorities coinciding with staff knowledge, taste levels, and interest.

It is worth noting that Scotland's TCBOB project is made up entirely of arts organizations. LGBTI+ organizations were engaged throughout, through recruitment, consultation, or guest contributors at social dance clubs; however, there are no specifically LGBTI+ organizations as part of the project partners. Whether an oversight or a conscious choice, we posit that the lack of LGBTI+ project partners speaks to the minimal amount of visible conversations taking place in Scotland around LGBTI+ Elders' needs and points to their precarity as a specialist group within the LGBTI+ community and our aging population. For the project partners "participation has been framed in terms of positive measures and outcomes ... as a necessary and desirable component of arts-based initiatives" (Robinson 2014: 149) not as a potential opportunity for arts and activism/as/by/for LGBTI+ to collide.

Based in Melbourne, in the Australian state of Victoria, ATQM built on the significantly more developed political and social conversation taking place in Victoria around aged care services for LGBTI+ Elders. ATQM describes themselves as "a radical organization where everyone is welcome and space is created for voices less heard to be amplified" (Meecham and Reid 2021). The company website further describes ATQM as a leading creative voice within the LGBTI+ community nationally and internationally, most specifically for championing the rights of LGBTI+ Elders. The company's practice, expressed through projects such as *The Coming Back Out Ball*, *LGBTI+ Elders Dance Club*, and *Rainbow Reviews*, aims to enable LGBTI+ communities improved access, not only to arts experiences but to broader community health and social services (Meecham and Reid 2021). The Council of the Ageing website for the state of Victoria lists a number of charity and third sector organizations that focus on the needs of LGBTI Elders including Val's LGBTI Ageing and Aged Care, which produces an annual LGBTI+ Ageing and Aged Care Conference (LGBTIQ+ Elders and Ageing 2021). The first Australian Coming Back Out Ball, and all subsequent events, took place in conjunction with one of these conferences, placing the project in a national conversation and offering a wider context for visibility and connectivity of an art project with this focus. TCBOB emerged from an existing conversation across arts, charities, health, and policy organizations. Interestingly none of the organizations listed are academic or educational in nature but they are all doing education and advocacy work. Most are working at a grassroots or frontline level while also contributing to a body of knowledge on the experiences of LGBTI+ people at the intersection of aging. The conversation around LGBTI+ Elders and aged care is a very new agenda in Scotland and the UK, growing, albeit slowly and in small pockets. Luminate in collaboration with LGBT Age had recently commissioned the film *Return to the Closet?* made by film artist Glenda Rome. Working with volunteer participants Rome's short film explores the current challenges and anxieties faced by LGBTI+ people who are in or will soon be entering aged care, and shared evidence of older people concealing their sexuality or gender identity in their final years for fear of prejudicial treatment by caregiving staff or fellow residents in supported accommodation. The work of these organizations and projects can therefore be seen as contributing to education through a process of platforming lived experience and building a body of evidence and understanding in this area.

These partnerships, knowledge, organizational agendas, and tentative social and political conversations are the background from which the project emerged in Scotland. Following the Australian model, the LGBTI+ Elders Social Dance Clubs were the core community-building creative initiative at the center of *The Coming Back Out Ball* project. The Ball itself is one night of spectacular queer culture, celebrating and highlighting the stories of LGBTI+ older people and bringing visibility to the generation who faced criminalization. It is significant to note that we were directed by the NTS to use the ATQM model, though as we mentioned their work emerged from a context in Victoria where issues around LGBTI+ Ageing have much more traction and resources. It is not an uncommon experience for us as freelance practitioners to be given a model which we must try and wrangle onto a different context from which it emerged organically.

Prior to the pandemic, social dance clubs were held in person from May 2019 to March 2020 with monthly hubs taking place in Inverness at Eden Court and in Glasgow at the Tron Theatre. One-off, pop-up social dance clubs were facilitated across the country in Perth, Edinburgh, Ayr, and Wick[1]. In-person social dance clubs lasted around two hours and consisted of conversation, dancing, creative activities or exercises, and free refreshments. Dancing was an artistic vehicle used to create a dynamic and welcoming social space aimed at those aged above fifty-five from the LGBTI+ community.

In response to the lack of strategic conversations around LGBTI+ aged care, the team, and in particular Lewis, developed *The Coming Back Out Conversation*. It was to be a day-long symposium taking place the day before the Ball. Much like the annual conference produced by Val's LGBTI Ageing and Aged Care, its ambition was to find opportunities to have a more direct political conversation around what this community wants or needs as they are getting older. Without explicitly naming it the project and its team were consciously trying to find ways to address the precarity facing our Elder participants. Supported by the project's producer in NTS we brought together a consortium of charities and professional bodies including Age Scotland, Equality Network, LGBT Youth Scotland, Scottish Care, and our community of Elders, and planned a day of discussions and workshops. Our ambition was to bring our Elders to consult directly with these groups, elected officials, and health and social care services on what their hopes and fears for aged care were, and to directly inform how these bodies either set policy, lobbied, or addressed service provision. The office of the Member of Scottish Parliament for Ageing and Equalities was also part of this discourse. This process also points to precarity; these larger organizational bodies are not yet leading the way for this dialogue and so it fell to Lewis, as an artist, to do this extra unpaid labor which unfortunately then dissipated due to the public health crisis.

Creating Permeable Queer Space

From the beginning of this project we were trying to create a space, which was fluid in its nature. Taking a cue from the Australian version of the project, we were keen to create a space where the focus was on celebrating older LGBTI+ people but was open to anyone supportive of that aim. We aimed to create a space that offered people the opportunity to share their stories on their own terms, without expectation or judgment. This approach is connected to a growing movement in community arts practice discussed by Catrin Evans in *The Arts of Integration*; "Whereby the focus is less on developing art for effect and more to do with understanding processes and celebrating—advocating for—a greater push for the creation of beautiful experiences" (Evans 2020: 62).

The notion of a permeable space is one we have applied in hindsight, exploring the boundaries and structures we created, and if and how ideas and people flowed in and out of them. The term permeable also calls to mind an organic movement, which echoes much of the language used to describe the elements of the project people found successful. We were always asking ourselves what barriers we could remove to allow people access. There is a complicated intersection of barriers which might prevent LGBTI+ Elders from attending our sessions, from financial, to physical and mental well-being, to people who are in different ways still closeted. Research has shown that LGBTI+ Elders are statistically more likely to experience isolation, poor mental and physical health, and financial precarity (Kneale et al. 2019). We attempted to remove barriers by making all the activity free, with delivery in LGBTI+ friendly spaces, and publicizing across a broad range of media. We asked existing groups to spread the word, designing "age-appropriate" activity, and with a high ratio of paid staff to participant and financial support available for expenses, etc. The reality is of course there are always barriers, which are hard to define because the people who are experiencing them are not in attendance to raise awareness of them. It is also the case that there were barriers we put in place to safeguard those who were attending. So perhaps being permeable is also useful as it reflects that the space was not totally open and fluid, but there were boundaries in place to act as support and structure, which we hoped were permeable enough for people to flow in and out as they needed it.

Framing the project as an organic entity was something which emerged in our focus group interview with the Elders. One of the interviewees described the project as, "A whole garden of flowers blossoming. It's been a wonderful experience" (Pat, Elder focus group interview, Tuesday, September 7, 2021). We were struck by this image of organic natural life, this notion of a "whole" garden of individual flowers blossoming. There is perhaps something inherently queer about the notion of being more than one thing at the same time, resisting easy definition. It's about community while also about individuals. Each flower has its own needs, presents its own colors, and craves shade or full sun.

The intergenerational nature of the project also spoke to this notion of queerness as resisting definitions. While we prioritized the foregrounding of the stories and visibility of Elders and designing physical activity with older bodies in mind, participants ranged from those in their twenties to their mid- to late seventies. In addition to this, the creative team who facilitated the social dance clubs are all in their thirties and forties giving the project an implicit intergenerational experience. This ethos is linked to the fluidity of the word Elder which connotes wisdom and the gaining of knowledge rather than a hard and fast rule about age.

> I was particularly struck when you said that it had come from Australia and their vision of working with Elders. And I really admire the fact that they esteem their Elders, you know they value them. And that's something that's not part of our culture. We don't do that in this country, we just don't. And so that was my first, first thing that drew me to it. (Pat, Elder focus group interview, Tue 7 Sep 2021)

All of those interviewed highlight the fluidity and complexity of the project being for older people, but not exclusively for older people.

> One of the big things [about the club being for older people] is that it encourages other people to take part, knowing that it's something specifically for older people, however something I did enjoy was that we had younger folk that joined us. I loved that, but I also really appreciated having a space that was predominantly for Elders. (Carrie, Elder focus group interview, Tue 7 Sep 2021)

> I think it's nice to have something that the people you have more in common with, more familiarity with the people, not that I have anything against young people! (Stewart, Elder focus group interview, Tue 7 Sep 2021)

> It was lovely that we had the young community coming in and joining us. But they don't always understand the needs of the community. (Tracy, Elder focus group interview, Tue 7 Sep 2021)

Despite the national ambition of the project, demonstrated by the two main hubs in Glasgow and Inverness, as well as the pop-up events in other parts of the country, the time and resources available still meant most people would have no event in their immediate locality. There were some examples of Glasgow members traveling to Inverness and vice versa, but these were a few exceptions rather than the norm. All of this shifted substantially when we moved online and geographical distance dissolved. People who had previously not attended physical events, due to barriers including physical disability, travel logistics, and the fear of being "outed" by attending an event, were now able to join with ease. The period of pandemic lockdown, with its restrictions, was very challenging, but, as we will go on to discuss, offered unexpected opportunities for deeper engagement across this community we were building.

COVID-19: Our Unexpected Collaborator

In response to COVID-19 and the March 2020 lockdown all partners agreed to extend the project, initially to autumn 2020 and social dance clubs were reimagined for the video calling platform Zoom. The project, in its current form, came to an end in June 2021 with an online, live streamed, and interactive reimagining of The Coming Back Out Ball, which also incorporated elements of the conversations, lived experience, and intention that would have been a central feature of the Coming Back Out Conversation.

Both the facilitators and the Elders that we interviewed were in no doubt of the positive and profound impact this extension had on the relationships that were formed. The COVID-19 crisis in fact revealed more of the vulnerabilities of some of those partaking in the project. The realities of the isolation disproportionately experienced by LGBTI+ Elders were exacerbated by the pressures of lockdown. The facilitators and participants became more acutely aware of the significance of the project through this second year. The digital sessions created a space where people from across the country were brought together, and this has translated into new friendships and relationships across Scotland and beyond between those who attended. The increased duration of the project deepened trust and relationships. As participatory artists it is very rare to experience the chance of working with a community for two years. It presented a profound shift in what we were able to achieve in addition to bringing about new challenges and opportunities. We have found ourselves asking the question, what would have happened with five years together?

Delivering online changed the nature, tone, and frequency of our interactions. In year one we had monthly social dance clubs in both Inverness and Glasgow, with some email and social media communication largely to encourage attendance at the live events. Year two saw one monthly social dance club online, still designed with LGBTI+ Elders in mind, but open to all, removing several barriers to attend while adding a new barrier for those unable to or uninterested in participating in digital socializing. We also held monthly forums for members to share their feedback on our events. As time passed we witnessed a substantial branching off of events from the dance club and the forum, organic offshoots borne out of desire and need. One Elder commented on how abrupt the end of a digital event can be, to go from dancing digitally with 30/40 others to being alone; and so the Elders began to host their own online "After Party" offering a softer, more informal transition out of the events. Other online activities popped up; including cookery classes, origami workshops, and an embroidery project which has now become a regular community-led social space taking place on Wednesday evenings. In addition to this, community members attended and became involved in other projects or activities that the creative facilitators were delivering as part of their portfolio of freelance work. Each of these interactions reinforced the web of mutual understanding and support between practitioners and participants. This web again speaks to the implicit learning process that flowed through the project that, in many ways, we are only able to fully appreciate through this process of writing. Through taking time to ask questions and consider the component parts of these two years of labor, we are able to draw out these layers of learning.

Our mode of communication also shifted. Email and WhatsApp messages were more regularly sent, there was an awareness of the importance of "checking in" and we used the NTS monthly dance club newsletter to disseminate information and project updates. Our Facebook page became more than just marketing, evolving into a space for social exchanges. Elders who were digitally fluent enjoyed this more regular, ad hoc, informal communication. For those less confident we created cheat sheets for accessing Zoom, set up Facebook profiles, and in one instance provided hardware. None of the team have specialist skills or training in digital access but we pivoted to providing this support in response to the needs of the group. A number of people who had attended regularly in person did not make the transition to digital gatherings. Some Elders were clear that the format did not appeal to them at all. Many others we lost, but we don't know why. The Centre for Ageing Better's report "COVID-19 and the digital divide" draws attention to the "significant digital divide" which is often most acute in older people; of the 3 million in the UK who are offline, 32 percent are aged between 50 and 69 and 67 percent are over seventy (Centre for Ageing Better 2021). There are other factors outlined in the report, such as financial hardship, but given that LGBTI+ Elders are more likely to be financially precarious than their heterosexual counterparts, they are at a particularly acute intersection of the digital divide.

As facilitators we became more emotionally and intimately aware of the isolation and lack of provision experienced by LGBTI+ Elders, but we were also acutely aware that we were not trained or resourced to support any specific mental health struggles. While the arts and arts practitioners play a vital role in maintaining and developing good mental health, it is a significant but indirect benefit of what we offer. For a number of our participants, we were one of the only points of contact, community, and care that they had. When we discussed this with our focus group of Elders, the need for connections was felt very deeply: "Sorry I'm getting quite emotional. I can't begin to think what lock down would have been without this social connection. I don't know how I would have survived it" (Pat, Elder focus group interview, Tuesday, September 7, 2021).

This also meant that for us as facilitators there was a shift in the type of emotional labor we were undertaking. This emotional labor also gave more depth to our experience, and it is something we lent into willingly, but it is something beyond what our other work might entail. We have reflected on the fact that often our role as freelance arts practitioners is to use our practical skills, our professional experiences, or our expertise, to manage and deliver projects. In this instance we were drawing on all of those things but also our lived experience as queer people, to give substance to the project: "I didn't expect to meet a sixty year old version of me and how hugely impactful that has been on me" (Amy, facilitator, individual Interview September 6, 2021).

Working on a video calling platform radically diminished the opportunity for spontaneous socializing and informal storytelling. At an in-person dance club, as facilitators, we would be having informal conversations at tables throughout the session. People could drift toward activity (dance, food, conversation) as well as certain people as they chose. On Zoom, the platform we used, everyone has the same-sized box. Pat noted that there was a democratizing aspect to that: "Everyone had their own box, it was the same size, you could see everyone at once, much easier than in person, it felt more like we were together" (Pat, Elder focus group interview, Tuesday, September 7, 2021).

That being said the facilitators were in control of the microphone, as it were, and it was often our boxes which were highlighted as the program is designed to give visual dominance to the speakers. We wanted to find ways to get the stories of the Elders to the foreground. We had a feature, inspired by the BBC's Desert Island Discs format, which we called Desert Island Disco, where each week an Elder would choose three songs and talk us through why they chose them. In preparation, one of the facilitation team would have a number of phone calls in the preceding week to make the Elder feel relaxed, to tease out the stories. Part of the success was that Elders were encouraged to determine the tone and content, some chose to celebrate LGBTI+ artists or their coming out experience, for others, it was about travel, work, or friendship. This convention, devised due to the limitations of Zoom, was their chance to tell their stories as an LGBTI+ Elder but without any expectation to speak directly or literally about sexuality or gender identity. Through these interviews, we connected further with each other and created space to introduce new members or for those who attended but seemed reserved. It gave us a reason to call someone and chat, which often felt like an important moment of connection even if they sometimes chose not to actually do the Desert Island Disco feature. Each month we invited an Elder to offer a "welcome toast" and "closing thoughts," and again they could take this in any direction. One person presented us with a queered Mary Poppins, one person spoke about losing people to the AIDS crisis, and another spoke about the holidays they had booked for once lockdown was over. These gave real moments of surprise, intimacy, and playfulness among the sometimes sterile and formal atmosphere of such platforms.

The introduction of these new conventions in turn had an impact on the ownership and authorship of the project. Throughout the project, the creative team endeavored to mold and shape their decisions based on formal and informal feedback from the community participants. The regular online monthly community forum gave weight to participant feedback due to its consistency and also the ease of access due to it being digital. Whereas feedback had previously been handled in small group discussions, now there was an open accessible forum. We supported dance club members to chair the meetings, and as much as possible it was a space for them to discuss and debate with their fellow Elders. Those who wished to and had capacity to attend the forum were able to very directly influence the direction of the project. It also added a layer of leadership to the community members engagement allowing them to act as an informal project steering group and it was in this forum that we as facilitators could support community members in the organization and delivery of their own peer-led sessions. It was a site for knowledge exchange in addition to a formal process of ongoing and real-time project feedback.

> I see the professional facilitators rather like a tree, the trunk of the tree, and the (Elder) hosts who are doing the smaller groups rather like the branches and you are linked in to the facilitation to make it possible, trees are beautiful and this has been beautiful. . . .. I hope this is the beginning of the branches growing more and more with the facilitators as the trunk, helping the branches grow. (Mairi, Elders focus group interview, Tuesday September 7, 2021)

The Personal in Participatory Practice

There was broad consensus from Elders and facilitators alike that moving online shifted the project in many positive ways. The Elders in our focus group notably talked about the events feeling more accessible, and the positive benefits of being connected to people nationally and internationally. We had attendees join us from the other UK nations, Australia, Germany, and South Africa. Our Elders were always aware of the project's origins in Melbourne, but now they got to meet their Australian counterpoints, dance together in a digital space, and celebrate this international network. It also meant those Scottish Members with LGBTI+ friends elsewhere in the world could invite them to be part of this new community they had helped build. This was a process though, it's important to say that it took a while for the online events to take shape.

> In the early days [of the digital dance clubs] I didn't feel welcome as much because there was more structured dances and we were told, let's all get out of our seats and copy me to dance to this dance . . .
>
> Later on, the ableism had gone. It's like "get out of your seats, if you want to, or you're able to," the language had evolved. It didn't matter, we could dance how we wanted. So having that go from structured, let's have four or five dances where we're told what to do, to join if you can or want to, it's that language, it's that evolution that made such a difference on that part. (Tracy Elders focus group interview, Tuesday September 7, 2021)

As facilitators we felt a sense of generosity and patience from Elders, as we evolved the program of activity to suit online delivery. It was very difficult for the creative team, especially in the early months of digital working to fully understand what kind of experience participants were having. The creative team worked on laptops to deliver sessions but participants accessed events through a variety of devices which offered very different digital experiences. There was kindness extended toward us as facilitators, which perhaps contributed to the project increasingly feeling reciprocal and intimate between participants and facilitators. There was a sense of shared experience across this intergenerational community at a historic moment.

For those who did join us, our events became for some of our participants, one of their primary sources of social interaction, something which they self-identify as of vital importance during the lockdown. COVID-19 seems to have in many ways drawn attention to existing fault lines in our societies and culture, and now we were feeling and observing, together, and with some emotional intensity, the realities faced by some older LGBTI+ people. Steward commented, "It gave something to look forward to, you know, the days that you feel diminished. I'm sure all our mental health would have suffered a lot more without having something to look forward to" (Stewart, Elder focus group interview, Tuesday, September 7, 2021). For Tracy:

> I think it was exactly what we needed, especially when this worldwide pandemic came in. We needed something. We needed something, nobody knew what we needed, the LGBT community themselves didn't know what they needed. But this was it. (Tracy, Elders focus group interview, Tuesday, September 7, 2021)

These moments in our interviews were very moving and emotional for us all. Issues about isolation and exclusion which had been the background of the origins of the project, and had been part of the intellectualized rationale for the project, were now very present in all of our lived experience, both physically and emotionally. The participants' emotional connection to the project was mirrored in the high-energy performance and spectacles we put together for our monthly digital dance clubs; we all went (willingly) above and beyond our job specifications with costume changes and props and backdrops. All of the facilitators reflected that online working exacted a larger toll on energy and the wave of emotions that would hit afterward. On more than one occasion Lou remembers weeping after a monthly dance club. It is perhaps then no surprise that the team would take time to talk through their experiences and observations after each monthly dance club and forums. Awareness continues to dawn on us about the intensity of the emotional landscape we were working in. As younger queer people we were all aware of the lack of older queer people in our life, and yet it could be overwhelming to connect to and create space for those people who have come before us, been part of paving the way for our rights. It brought us joy, but we have been reflecting on both how that extra labor was a chance for us to demonstrate our gratitude to these Elders and our commitment to intergenerational queer community.

Layers of Precarity: A Conclusion

The project could be seen as discrete and limited to including an underrepresented group (LGBTI+ Elders). However, the last two years have shown us that this group is chronically underserved; this is due to continued discrimination and diminishing social, community, and mental health services over ten years of austerity (contexts which persist despite improved legislation for LGBTI+ people). A recent article by Kolbe (September 2021) explores this pressure and the ongoing impact of austerity on their practice:

> Austerity politics and public funding cuts were reported by all respondents to negatively affect the scope of their work to fulfil a social function, however defined, while being symptomatic of current economic conditions (i.e. decreasing public services, higher poverty and escalating inequality) in which the necessity for the arts to take on such a function is amplified. (Kolbe 2021: 1)

There is arguably a precarity to any arts practice, as the cultural sector has suffered severe austerity measures while feeling increasing pressure to patch over the gaps in provision left by other sectors. This pressure is even more acute for community arts practitioners due to long-term government policy, producing inequality which predates contemporary austerity and crisis contexts, as Kolbe identifies:

> Thatcher era drastically opened the path for privatisation and commercialisation, increasing the financial incentives for private and corporate arts sponsorship via tax breaks or Public-Private Partnerships. . . . This process continued during the New Labour years which not only incentivised corporate arts sponsorship further but also pushed for the adoption of economic rationales within the cultural sector more widely, turning the latter into an increasingly entrepreneurial (creative) industry: financialised logics, ranging from a "value for money" rhetoric to the implementation of commercial attitudes more broadly, pushed arts organisations and cultural workers "to be entrepreneurial, embrace risk, look after their own self-interest." (Kolbe 2021: 1)

This notion of an artist generating profit, exploiting the project and participants for personal gain would run counter to everything our venture was attempting to achieve. It is also the nature of almost all arts programming that is defined by its ephemerality. There is an awkward tension between claiming commitment to supporting an oppressed group and only having a short window of time to do so. There can be a perception and concern that an arts project is "parachuting in," from both participants and artists alike. Through a reflection on our experiences and those of our fellow facilitators and Elder participants of The Coming Back Out Ball project, we have discovered the layers of precarity surrounding the project, its facilitators and participants and how this has intersected with our lived experiences as queer individuals and in queer community with each other.

The project was at times emotionally and physically exhausting for the freelance creative practitioners who were the public face of the project, representing a series of decisions which we did not make, and bearing the weight of a political and cultural context which undermines the kind of work we want to make. An uncomfortable truth is that our entire professional careers have existed within the era of austerity, so this kind of pressure and precarity is normalized, and through the writing of this chapter we are reminded of the conditions we labor within. It is important to note that the scale of resources committed to the project from the NTS would only be possible from a handful of other arts organizations in Scotland, and so this project is comparatively extremely well resourced. And while it is the case that NTS has no obligation to serve the LGBTI+ audience and community, and that this project did come about through a fortunate chain of events, the desire to create a positive cultural experience for this group felt, on the whole, a sincere offer from the organization.

This Scottish iteration of The Coming Back Out Ball was defined by its precarity, and in that context worked hard to identify what we were and were not able to address. We were not qualified to support mental health, we were not able to directly and immediately influence policy, and we were not looking for stories to shock and surprise a wider audience; arguably we engaged critically and often positively with all of these things over the course of the two years, in an organic way. Primarily we recognized that we could create spaces which said to our Elders, you deserve to be celebrated, you deserve to have cultural experiences which are beautiful, playful, and enriching, and you deserve to be able to create your own journey of engagement on your own terms.

References

Centre for Ageing Better (2021), *COVID-19 and the Digital Divide*. Centre For Ageing Better. Available online: https://ageing-better.org.uk/publications/covid-19-and-digital-divide-supporting-digital-inclusion-and-skills (accessed December 2, 2021).

Cotavic (2021), *LGBTIQ+ Elders and Ageing*. Available online: https://www.cotavic.org.au/information/looking-for-information/lgbtiq-elders-and-ageing (accessed December 2, 2021).

Eden Court (2021), *What We Do*. Available online: https://eden-court.co.uk/about/our-mission (accessed December 2, 2021).

Evans, C (2020), *The Arts of Integration* (Unpublished doctoral dissertation), University of Glasgow.

Kneale, D., J. Henley, J. Thomas, and R. French (2019), "Inequalities in Older LGBT People's Health and Care Needs in the United Kingdom: A Systematic Scoping Review," *Ageing and Society*, 41 (3): 493–515.

Kolbe, K. (2021), "Unequal Entanglements: How Arts Practitioners Reflect on the Impact of Intensifying Economic Inequality," *Cultural Trends*, 31: 1–16.

Luminate Scotland (2021), *What We Do*. Available online: https://luminatescotland.org/about/what-we-do/ (accessed December 2, 2021).

Meecham, T. and B. Reid (2021), *Company Biography AllTheQueensMen*. Available online: https://allthequeensmen.net/about/services/ (accessed December 2, 2021).

National Theatre of Scotland (2021a), *A Theatre Without Walls Strategic Plan*. Available online: https://www.nationaltheatrescotland.com/about/who-we-are/reports-and-documents (accessed December 2, 2021).

National Theatre of Scotland (2021b), Available online: https://www.nationaltheatrescotland.com/about (accessed December 2, 2021).

Robinson, Y. (2014), "Researching Theatre Doing Participation Creative Publics and Public Sociology," in Y. Taylor (ed.), *The Entrepreneurial University*, 146–60, London: Palgrave.

Rome, G. (2018), *Return to the Closet* (video). Available online: https://vimeo.com/465945483 (accessed December 2, 2021).

Chapter 10

QUEER KINSHIP AND THE PRACTICE OF FAITH DURING COVID-19

Sadie Counts

Introduction

In the autumn of 2019, I began fieldwork at the Metropolitan Community Church of Knoxville, Tennessee (MCCK) to support my master's thesis which this chapter is drawn from (Counts 2021). When I first attended a service, I found myself shocked at the demographics of the congregation, mainly in the sense that I was twenty or thirty years younger than all in attendance. While I was concerned initially that I would not be welcomed in the space, I experienced quite the opposite as my work and myself were embraced with open arms by the congregation and its staff. It soon became clear to me that the church is not only a religious space but also a space for communion outside of religion, one where queer people feel they can congregate and socialize, often without a religious agenda to attend to. This space of gay culture is one that is designated by its sense of family, where legal families in the form of married couples create kinship ties with friends, where gay couples who actively eschew marriage for the sake of queerness are just as much family as those who are siblings, parents, aunts, and uncles.

The Metropolitan Community Church (MCC) was founded in 1968 with the goal of promoting civil and human rights by addressing issues of race, gender, sexual orientation, and global human rights worldwide, with an emphasis on advancing those especially queer rights. According to their main denominational website (mccchurch.org), they were the first church to perform same-gender marriages and have been at the forefront of the fight for equality among gender, sexual, and racial minorities within the larger geopolitical context of the United States. The Knoxville branch of the MCC advertises itself as serving the LGBT+ (lesbian, gay, bisexual, transgender, and more) and straight communities of Knoxville and East Tennessee. As an LGBT+ serving church, MCCK functions both as a haven and a refuge for marginalized groups, and while serving these purposes, takes religious meaning as secondary to fulfilling those needs.

MCCK functions as a special place of queer culture, one that is welcoming to all but caters particularly to an aging population, ones whose days of going out to bars to socialize and meeting friends or cruising at clubs are, for the most part, long gone. The church is made up almost exclusively of white, cisgender, gay, lesbian, and bisexual men and women who are in their fifties or older. The patrons tend to be middle class as many of them are retired or, those who do continue to work, have the luxury of working from home. While there are occasionally visitors who fall out of this demographic, those regular members and most attendees tend to follow these patterns as I observed over the course of my sixteen months of fieldwork there.

MCCK is a family, distinct from birth or nuclear families. Yet like (hetero) normative nuclear families, queer MCCK families share in ways that can be (homo)normative and based in material relations (Duggan 2002; Phelan 1997). MCCK families share meals, space, time, and touch. There is an inherent intimacy in sharing, one that is maintained through the kinship ties that have been created at MCCK. This became apparent to me on my very first visit to MCCK, where I, a stranger, was met and welcomed with kindness and enthusiasm, with no need to defend my religious ascriptions or my sexual orientation. A family became evident to me through the people I met, many of them couples. Within this sense of family, I argue that MCCK presents a site of queer kinship via a shared sense of otherness and a negotiation of heteronormativity. Queer kinship refers to the ways in which queer groups, individuals, and communities create kinship networks differently than the biological ones that we are more familiar with in a heteronormative society (Donovan, Heaphy, and Weeks 2001). Through studying relationships and care networks in San Francisco throughout the 1980s and 1990s, Kath Weston argued that by leaving their biological families, queer individuals were not revoking the idea of "family" but rather redefining it through different types of relationships (1991). That is, rather than reject the idea of a "family" in the heteronormative or nuclear sense, queer people often form communities and families of their own that manifest in both similar and different ways to the heteronormative families of white suburbia that exist as the default of many definitions. Taking Weston's theorization into account along with larger studies of kinship in anthropology that view sharing, economic exchange, and the sharing of food—or sharing among a hearth—as forms of kin relation, it becomes possible to infer the ways in which "family" is a practice of particular kinds of sharing. These theoretical intersections can aid in understanding the ways in which queer groups form bonds and communities which can become family structures through material forms of sharing. While Weston's study is now canonical within queer anthropology, I argue along the same lines as Weston that the family established at MCCK is established not only on choice—"families we choose"—but also in a shared sense of community that is tied together via exclusion, isolation, and trauma in relation to gender and sexuality. However, I also posit that these families, especially in the case of a community such as MCCK, are rooted in a particular sense of shared trauma, where the sense of family is built on traumatic memories and experiences associated both with queerness and AIDS.

Current anthropological theory has moved away from understanding kinship based solely on consanguinity, substantivism, and marriage (Schneider 1968, 1984) and now views kinship as a fluid, evolving relationship that is based more so on sociality and relationality through mutuality (Sahlins 2013), which may occur through choice (Franklin and McKinnon 2001; Weston 1991, 2001) or via sites of power, relation, negotiation, and reciprocity (Mauss 1925; McKinnon 1991). This is based more prominently on the idea of a family being one that we actively choose during our lifetime over one that is preassigned to us before birth or dictated to us through social relationships (Weston 1991, 2001). Within the queer "community," which is situated as a group through not only sexual and gender minority identities but also through a shared marginalization, families by choice are often the main, or at times only, families that exist between and among queer persons.

The AIDS epidemic of the 1980s and onward provides an example of how shared marginalization and trauma can lead to specific forms of intimacy, kinship, and relationality through the materialization of trauma via memory (Crimp 1989, 2004; Cvetkovich 2003). Even after the "end" of the AIDS epidemic, memory continues to inform queer politics and relationships in the present and in the future (Crimp 1989, 2004). The trauma—and aftermath of care—created through the shared loss and survival of the AIDS epidemic becomes a part of the everyday for queer individuals and groups and is archived via a shared memory, such as lesbian public culture (Cvetkovich 2003). I argue that the COVID-19 pandemic has similar political and social consequences of memory, trauma, and shared public culture, especially among queer groups who have already suffered through one epidemic. I argue that the queer biosociality fostered through COVID-19 is a reconfiguration of the queer kinship and intimacy at MCCK. Much like AIDS, COVID-19 presents risk in the form of a virus that spreads through fluids, both exiting and entering the body via various orifices. COVID-19's presence within the everyday aspects of many people's lives has led to groupings based on risk factors or shared genetic identities (Rabinow 1996), shared biologies such as underlying conditions or compromised immune systems (Petryna 2003), and disease susceptibility or predisposition (Rose 2007). Within the scope of this project, I argue that the current COVID-19 pandemic can be understood as a continuation of the HIV/AIDS pandemic for those who maintain both a shared memory and shared traumas of the latter. Just as risk was vital to the materialization of their relationality in the 1980s and beyond, it is again vital to the maintenance of relationships of many of those within MCCK today. I argue that the stresses of AIDS created sophisticated networks of care which created the foundations of kinship and prepared the MCCK community to handle the emotional and physical toll of a pandemic rooted in necessary isolation and the denial of physical intimacy.

In historical and modern notions, churches have existed as spaces for specific communities, not simply religious communities but those religious communities deemed acceptable to use the space of the church. Within this project, the queer church exists as a space for queer community building and family "creating" through various forms of intimacy and kinship (Seitz 2017; Shirinian 2018). However, I argue that this space is one where religion is often included, but not deemed a necessity, for the space to be used by the community. This is often found in the distinction of church members between spiritual and religious, with those adhering to a more spiritual ideology seeking out the church as a primary site of socialization rather than religious fulfillment. I argue that both space and place play an important role in both the expressions of intimacy and kinship within MCC, and that the lack of a physical space has led to a reconfiguration of both kinship and intimacy which must be maintained by means other than physical touch. The existence of a queer space such as a queer church implies a level of queer performance as noted within and around the church setting. Queerness and queer performance do not exist independently but rather have spatial dimensions in which they occupy and are occupied as queer sociality within the context of a specific place and space (Gray 2009; Muñoz 2009). I argue that spaces such as these function toward multiple purposes for the queer community. As the church exists as a setting for queer communion via a religious backdrop, it is also a place for communion of LGBTQ+ persons within Knoxville, at times devoid of religion as the shared identity of "gay" often overrides a presumed identity of "Christian."

Examining queer "community" in its material forms of sharing and relating as a necessity for queer life contributes to queer theory's and queer anthropology's interest in understanding how intimacy and kinship are changed or altered by their relationship to biosociality and risk. Queer intimacies may disrupt traditional conceptualizations of risk through the importance of maintaining bonds during times of great risk in order to preserve the senses of kinship and community. Queerness is expressed in new ways within religious settings and its theoretical implications can be challenged when religion is added as an analytical tool (Seitz 2017). Within the scope of this project, I argue that the coexistence of both queer and religious spaces—particularly in the Southeastern United States—provides a refuge for a multiplicity of marginalized communities (queer, religious, and other). Churches have always been spaces of communion between members of a specific community, where bonds are made through material communion— the sharing of bread—among one another as a form of sociality (Polanyi 1944). I posit that within MCCK, these bonds are made not only through material communion but also through a social and psychic communion as well via shared memories and trauma. Within the setting of a queer church, specifically MCCK, bonds are formed not only through typical types of communion but also through intimacy and touch as well. Physical intimacy has been a kin-forming act for queer people through various means, whether through sexual touch, friendly touch, familial touch, or even nonfamiliar touches (Dean 2009; Sahlins 2013; Shirinian 2018).

The effects the COVID-19 crisis has had on many have led to changes in the ways that intimacy is shared and experienced, as intimacy can manifest contradictions, fear of loss, and forms of "nonsovereignty" and relationality that produce a loss of control and an internal confrontation of one's own limits (Berlant and Edelman 2014). This project seeks to understand how particular queer forms of sociality and relation may have been disrupted by the pandemic through an exploration of biosociality. Individuals must ask themselves who they are willing to risk touching and how much they are willing to risk to touch. For some this risk may cost nothing, while for others, it may cost them their lives. While biosociality has been explored through the lens of the Human Genome Initiative via the construction of genetic identities that produce sociality (Rabinow 1996), the aftermath of the Chernobyl disaster via the creation of biological citizens that create biosociality through a shared suffering that makes demands of the state (Petryna 2003), and the sharing of HIV as an affirmation of queer kinship (Dean 2009), this project aims to discover an alternative materialization of biosociality. By exploring questions of intimacy and kinship within the context of pandemics and the effects of these elements on the MCCK community (informed by queer studies' attention to these questions), this project aims to contribute to the anthropological inquiry of how biosociality is a site of both relation-making and risk-taking. With the closure of the physical space of the church due to COVID-19, I argue that while parishioners have moved to more normative—nuclear family or domestic partnership—forms of kin and intimacy creation, they have continued to maintain the intimacy and kinship established at and through MCC, just in different ways.

Choosing to understand various forms of intimacy as kinship leads to recognizing the importance that biosociality plays within these relations and the materialization of this relationality. While Dean sees biosociality as a sharing of fluids—and therefore the potential of sharing a virus—as an affirmation of life, identity, masculinity, and a formation of kinship (2009), others such as Petryna see biosociality as the sharing of a common biology on which political claims are made (2003). This project works through these analytic frameworks of risk and biosociality to think about queer spaces as sites of sharing risk as well as the consequences to those spaces when risk is actively limited. I argue that COVID-19 has demanded a reconfiguration of both kinship and intimacy, which has therefore impacted the biosocial nature of these forms of relation. The biosocial components of these types of bonds present a risk that is too great for the given community and therefore require a new understanding of forms of queerness. Beyond a shared biology that activates political claims (Petryna 2003), or as the production of social identities via biomedical knowledge and identities (Rabinow 1996), biosociality might also be understood as a form of relation made through risk, a risk that is shared between and among persons to create intimacy to overcome feelings of marginalization. While the pandemic is a time of increased risk, it is also a time of limiting this risk, posing real challenges to the maintenance of intimacy within a queer community.

Kinship Through Faith

While many church congregations may refer to themselves as a family—a family within and through Christ—MCC's conception of family is highly complex. Not only do parishioners have original or "birth" families to contend with, which are often associated with guilt and negativity. They also have their chosen, queer (nuclear) families. This chosen family may somewhat overlap with the church congregation, although this is not always true. These nuclear, queer families are mostly based in couples and occasionally children, although the members of MCCK who have children tend to have adult children who no longer live with them and therefore do not attend services with them. As Christians, they may also see themselves as a family with a global Christian community, which is larger but still encompasses the global MCC "community." Then there is the real community of MCCK which functions as a family through various material forms of sharing, networks of care, and reciprocity. While the congregation may see themselves as a family through and within Christ, they also exist as a queer family, a family that is chosen rather than assigned, one that represents many of the struggles faced by queer individuals globally. Many members of MCCK attend services or small group discussions with their primary chosen family, their partner, whom, as I mentioned earlier, may or may not be legally married to them. However, once indoctrinated into this very specific community, an additional level of queer family is developed, one based on social bonds, solidarity, and shared trauma. Many patrons of MCCs globally actually discover their primary partners at MCCs, such as the church's current pastor and intern, who both met their partners at their home MCCs before coming to work at MCCK, making this sense of family one that is even deeper. MCC is a global network with churches worldwide, and the denomination is based on an idea of a global community of individuals being tied to and connected with one another, even though many will never meet those outside of their home congregation. This idea of a family as preached by MCC's denominational ideology differs from the family that exists within MCCK, as it is small enough that all regular members do know each other, and many know each other intimately. This very real community is not only rooted in a distinct ideology or adherence to Christian values while living as a sexual or gender minority but also within a material reality of knowing each other and sharing time, space, and emotional intimacies with each other.

Until March 2020, when the COVID-19 pandemic began, this sense of queer family was exemplified through the social and physical interactions of MCC, especially within the context of sharing: sharing meals on the third Sunday of every month, or every single Sunday in my own experience, sharing stories, feelings, and thoughts within the context of small group discussions with personal anecdotes, and sharing touches, both with partners and with friends, whether friendly or sexual. As I've observed within the context of church functions, touch manifests in many ways, from hand holding during prayers to hand holding for no other reason than to be touching, to quick side hugs and long embraces, to kisses on cheeks, foreheads, and mouths with both intimate, sexual partners and close friends. For me, this intimacy truly culminates within the moment of individual communion, as a friend places a hand on your shoulder in prayer while another friend places a wafer and juice in your mouth, as I was brought into the intimate fold of the space during my first visit. The intimacy of allowing another individual to feed you is based on a sense of trust and care, potentially even love. While communion is rooted in the idea of Jesus's love for his disciples and the world, it manifests through the love of the congregation for one another, and in the context of this queer family space, communion becomes less abstract and more physically substantial.

COVID-19 and AIDS

COVID-19 and AIDS are vastly different pandemics—different death rates, different symptoms, and different demographics affected. However, for an aging LGBTQ+ population, COVID-19 feels far too familiar as senses of isolation and loss are prevalent characteristics of both pandemics. The collective trauma of AIDS has made the members of MCCK more sensitive to the implications of COVID-19, including its strain on physical and emotional intimacy and its limitations on social relationships. The history of AIDS in Knoxville is one that affected not only queer populations but also IV drug users, homeless populations, and eventually women, children, and straight men as well.

For an aging population of gay and lesbian Americans, a global pandemic such as COVID-19 may bring up painful and traumatic memories of the HIV/AIDS crisis of their younger years. As the pandemic continues to go on, with little being known about its symptoms, long-term effects, and longevity during its initial onset, significant similarities, and stark differences emerge when compared to HIV/AIDS. These comparisons became evident near the beginning of the pandemic, and as it has gone on there have been more similarities and differences that arise with time. Those who survived the HIV/AIDS epidemic have a unique perspective in understanding what it means to live through an epidemic, especially one that is viral and arguably mismanaged by the federal government. The irony of having already survived one pandemic is that those who were the most vulnerable population then due to sexual activity and stigma have now arrived at a point in life where they are again most vulnerable due to age and underlying health conditions.

The response of MCCK to the COVID-19 crisis is based on a necessary resilience that was developed during the AIDS crisis "because we weren't getting help anywhere else," as noted by the pastor during our formal interview. This led to the sophisticated and vital networks of care that continue to define MCCK as they see themselves as a family that must take care of one another, especially in times of need such as this one. MCCK's intern highlighted this resilience during our formal interview when they said, "We are such a social community because that's how we found a way to survive" in reference to the AIDS crisis and the emphasis on the ongoing activism of the church today. This demonstrates the continued effects of AIDS on the community that has been developed at MCCK, where familial ties not only sustain relationships and social needs but also help to sustain and maintain life in the most serious sense. It is the trauma of AIDS that led MCCK to be prepared to face another crisis, although this preparation does not lessen the pain, fear, and loss that is associated with the 1980s and beyond. The networks of care that were created out of necessity during a time when many might have died on the streets had it not been for queer family are the ones that continue today to strengthen the kinship ties and relationships of MCCK parishioners. They may in fact see each other as family because for many of them, it was the MCCK community who assumed the role of family when it was needed most during the first health crises they faced via HIV/AIDS. Now because of COVID-19, that sense of family is being challenged as many of these "family" members do not cohabitate, thus forcing the MCC community to be creative in the ways that they maintain their familial relationships with one another in a time of required nuclear isolation.

Adapting to COVID-19

Perhaps the most challenging facet of COVID-19 on the MCCK community has been its restriction on closeness, touch, and intimacy. As I observed when I first began attending MCCK in October of 2019, the sheer quantity of touch among church members was notable. I witnessed not only romantic touch (like partners holding hands or kissing) but also familial and friendly touches, mostly through hugs. MCC's aptitude for touch was noted by both the pastor and intern during interviews with MCC's intern remarking "there's nothing like physical fellowship, especially in our denomination, we're a huggy group, maybe because we were excluded for so long." For MCC's intern, "physical touch is part of the atmosphere in MCC[1], telling you you're welcome here and many of us need that, people get you here." This sentiment is not only something that they felt when they first attended an MCCK many years ago, as they shared with me during our interview, but also something I noticed as well during my first visit to MCC. The importance of touch comes from a site of exclusion as facilitated by AIDS, where touch between queer groups and non-queer groups was wrongfully linked to disease, dirtiness, and transmission. This led many of the members of MCCK to rely on their queer family for instances of touch, and why touch became a kin-forming act, both via and despite possibilities of transmission (Dean 2009). The importance of touch and intimacy has dramatically been uprooted by COVID-19, as the virus is highly transmissible, and therefore touch is prohibited. Touching each other is a risk, and it is a risk to touch. Church members must often weigh the importance of touch and how much they are willing to risk touching or to be touched. For those church members who cohabitate with their partners, touch is less of a risk as they are interacting every day. However, for those who live alone and who have lost one of their most important forms of intimacy, they may be willing to risk more to touch. This includes going out to bars or clubs or defying city-mandated curfews and safer-at-home orders, as some local businesses and their patrons have done. While talking about this issue during our interview, MCC's pastor noted that many church members are "hungry for hugs, especially those single and older or isolated members." Those who live alone are "hungry for physical touch [because] church is the one time a week you know you'll be touched" they pointed out, highlighting why intimacy is such an important part of the community and how touch helps the kinship within MCCK manifest. The exclusion from larger senses of community in relation to touch separates these notions of kinship from those of other small churches. Everyone I interviewed said that they "miss the hugs" in one way or another, as emphasis continues to be placed on the lack of physical affection that members are able to share online and how much of an impact that physical affection and intimacy has on their relationships with others and the importance of MCCK in their lives.

Perhaps COVID-19's larger effect on queer intimacy, kinship, and relationality has been the necessary transition to and reliance on digital technologies to maintain relationships. Prior to March of 2020, few average Americans were familiar with the communications software Zoom (I had used it once in 2018 for a long-distance interview). However, Zoom would quickly become part of everyday life for many (privileged) people who found themselves suddenly working from or attending school from home. In the context of MCC, Zoom quickly became the go-to for church services and other social events. The first mention of COVID-19 at MCCK came during the sermon on March 1, 2020, and the last in-person service would take place on March 15, 2020, with sermons immediately being moved to Zoom following that Sunday.

There was a multitude of concerns surrounding the virtual church as soon as it began. One of the biggest concerns continued throughout the pandemic has been a fiscal concern. If people are not attending services in person, will they still feel compelled to donate/tithe? Luckily for MCC, the congregation has remained loyal in their giving patterns, and MCCK has yet to have any monetary issues related to the pandemic. Another concern has been member interaction and retention, both during and in a post-pandemic scenario. The initial transition to a completely virtual church was a challenge for all, but more so for those members who either did not have reliable computers and/or Wi-Fi and those members who were fairly tech illiterate. While many of the older members of the congregation were well versed in using computers for everyday tasks such as writing emails and creating word documents or even using social media like Facebook, for those who did not use computers often the challenge of becoming acquainted with a completely new type of software such as Zoom was not one that was easily overcome. However, the increase in digital presence did create some positive outcomes, such as an increase in engagement from disabled or already home-bound patrons and an increase in engagement from out-of-town or out-of-state parishioners. The transition to a completely virtual format has made MCCK a more accessible space for some who were already (prior to COVID-19) unable to attend in-person services.

Conclusion

The members of MCCK have shown incredible strength and resilience in the face of multiple and complex forms of adversity. Queer kinship is largely intertwined with the current formation of MCCK, with members viewing other parishioners often more as family than friends. This is defined by their reliance on one another and the ways in which they see themselves not only as a community but also as a family that is formed through sharing, in substance and in trauma. Many of the members at MCCK discussed feelings of guilt or resentment toward their birth families that were tied to their sexual or gender identity. MCCK represents a place they can let go of all of that and share those feelings with others who have similar experiences. MCC is a site of both queer communion and family as queer people have defined family for themselves and made family for themselves when they had none.

This sense of family was largely developed through the shared trauma of the AIDS epidemic. This shared trauma (ironically) prepared the members of MCCK to live through yet another pandemic at a time when they were most vulnerable. The church's role during the AIDS epidemic, as a place of sanctuary and communion for many gay people who had nowhere else to go and no other sense of family, helped to establish the grounds on which the queer family discussed in chapter one would be built. The resilience shown by the community of MCCK in the late eighties and early nineties would again become helpful beginning in the spring of 2020 and onward, as they were prepared to deal with a unique circumstance of hardships. What they were not prepared to deal with, however, was the transition to an online world where the physical kinship and intimacy established within the walls of MCCK would be challenged.

The transition to life during COVID-19 has been challenging for some; however, the resilience of surviving AIDS has been carried through to allow for creative and flexible adaptations to new iterations of intimacy. This has been shown mainly through the maintenance of relationships via digital technologies such as Zoom, phone calls, and text messages. While intimacy within the confines of the church building has been halted, a social intimacy has been maintained and physical intimacy has evolved to reflect more heteronormative notions of nuclear households.

The community of MCCK has been experiencing COVID-19 in a multitude of ways. Due to the demographics of the congregation (age, underlying/preexisting health conditions, and sexuality), COVID-19 can be understood as a continuation of the AIDS epidemic—via the affected populations' responses—through its unique effects on the community as a vulnerable population during both pandemics. The shared and collective memories and trauma of AIDS make COVID-19 more impactful due to the emphasis placed on risk, isolation, and socialization. The relationships that the community of MCCK has built and maintained, through AIDS and beyond, have led them to understand themselves more as a family (both a queer and a faith family) than a church congregation or a group of close friends. The limitation on physical intimacy that COVID-19 has caused has not disrupted these feelings or these perceptions of relationships but simply required the MCCK community to reimagine and redefine them through digital means for the time being. While maintaining these ties in a digital world has proved difficult and less fulfilling, the congregation of MCCK has found ways to express these notions and bonds, even though physical touch and shared substance have been halted. While some have risked their lives in order to be close to others, many have chosen to manage these aspects of risk through the use of digital technologies and socially distanced and limited interactions. The effects have been damaging to some, causing feelings of depression and anxiety, but many remain optimistic and look forward to time together again. While COVID-19 has presented many unique challenges for an aging queer population, the resilience and kinship ties based in networks of care that were established during AIDS due to their exclusion and isolation from heteronormative circles have allowed the MCCK community to show great optimism and creativity in overcoming these challenges to maintain their chosen/queer/faith family, which for many of them may be their only family. The sense of family at MCCK is tangible, both in person and online, and a crisis such as COVID-19 is not substantial enough to break the bonds established during the AIDS epidemic that they survived and still continue to grieve.

References

Anderson, B. (2006), *Imagined Communities: Reflections on the Origin and Spread of Nationalism*, London: Verso.
Berlant, L. and L. Edelman (2014), *Sex, or the Unbearable*, Durham, NC: Duke University Press.
Counts, S. (2021), "Queer Spaces, Religious Places: Sharing Risk and Making in Within a Queer Church Amidst a Pandemic," Master's Thesis, University of Tennessee. Available online: https://trace.tennessee.edu/utk_gradthes/6190.
Crimp, D. (1989), "Mourning and Militancy," *October*, 51: 3–18.
Crimp, D. (2004), *Melancholia and Moralism: Essays on AIDS and Queer Politics*, Cambridge, MA: The MIT Press.
Cvetkovich, A. (2003), *An Archive of Feelings: Trauma, Sexuality, and Lesbian Public Cultures*, Durham, NC: Duke University Press.
Dean, T. (2009), *Ultimate Intimacy: Reflections on the Subculture of Barebacking*, Chicago, IL: University of Chicago Press.
Donovan, C., B. Heaphy, and J. Weeks (2001), *Same Sex Intimacies: Families of Choice and Other Life Experiments*, London: Routledge.
Duggan, L. (2002), "The New Homonormativity: The Sexual Politics of Neoliberalism," in R. Castronova and D.D. Nelson (eds.), *Materializing Democracy: Toward a Revitalized Cultural Politics*, 175–94, Durham, NC: Duke University Press.
Franklin, S. and S. McKinnon (eds.) (2001), *Relative Values: Reconfiguring Kinship Studies*, Durham, NC: Duke University Press.
Gray, M. (2009), *Out in the Country: Youth, Media, and Queer Visibility in Rural America*, New York: New York University Press.
Mauss, M. (1925), *The Gift: Forms and Functions of Exchange in Archaic Societies, Trans by Ian Cunnison*, London: Cohen & West.
McKinnon, S. (1991), *From a Shattered Sun: Hierarchy, Gender, and Alliance in the Tanimbar Islands*, Madison, WI: The University of Wisconsin Press.
Muñoz, J. (2009), *Cruising Utopia: The Then and There of Queer Futurity*, New York: New York University Press.

Petryna, A. (2003), *Life Exposed: Biological Citizens after Chernobyl*, Princeton, NJ: Princeton University Press.
Phelan, S. (1997), "The Shape of Queer: Assimilation and Articulation," *Women & Politics*, 18 (2): 55–73.
Polanyi, K. (1944), *The Great Transformation: The Political and Economic Origins of our Time*, New York: Farrar and Rinehart.
Rabinow, P. (1996), *Essays on the Anthropology of Reason*, Princeton, NJ: Princeton University Press.
Rose, N. (2007), *The Politics of Life Itself: Biomedicine, Power, and Subjectivity in the Twenty-First Century*, Princeton, NJ: Princeton University Press.
Sahlins, M. (2013), *What Kinship Is . . . and Is Not*, Chicago, IL: University of Chicago Press.
Schneider, D. (1968), *American Kinship: A Cultural Account*, Chicago, IL: University of Chicago Press.
Schneider, D. (1984), *A Critique on the Study of Kinship*, Ann Arbor: University of Michigan Press.
Seitz, D. (2017), *A House of Prayer for All People: Contesting Citizenship in a Queer Church*, Minneapolis: The University of Minnesota Press.
Shirinian, T. (2018), "The Nation-Family: Intimate Encounters and Genealogical Perversion in Armenia," *American Ethnologist*, 45 (1): 48–59.
Weston, K. (1991), *Families We Choose: Lesbians, Gays, Kinship*, New York: Columbia University Press.
Weston, K. (2001), "Kinship, Controversy, and the Sharing of Substance: The Race/Class Politics of Blood Transfusion," in S. Franklin and S. McKinnon (eds.), *Relative Values: Reconfiguring Kinship Studies*, 147–74, Durham, NC: Duke University Press.

EPILOGUE: QUEER FAILURE AND THE FIGHT FOR PUBLIC COLLEGE FOR ALL

Jennifer Gaboury

Vartan Gregorian recently passed away. Born to Armenian parents, he was raised in Iran and then Lebanon before immigrating to the United States as a young adult. He entered Stanford University and went on to graduate from the institution with a doctoral degree in history in 1964. For a number of years, he was a professor of history before going on to serve as the president of the Carnegie Corporation, the president of the New York Public Library, and the president of Brown University. Gregorian had ties to many institutions—including the public City University of New York (CUNY) system, where he served on the "Board of Visitors" that supported the Colin L. Powell School for Civic and Global Leadership. At Brown, Gregorian liked to sometimes ask an audience of affluent parents how many of them had connections, perhaps in their family, to CUNY. He'd always see hands raised. This is the immigrant story that he was proud to tell: that families from any socioeconomic background can lift themselves up by attending one of CUNY's community or baccalaureate colleges and one day have kids or grandkids that go to a place like Brown University. In this trajectory we see one version of a still-powerful broader narrative that links the American dream to participation in (elite) college.

What does it mean when we think of public institutions as serving the poor or being for everyone? Ninety percent of families in the United States send their children to public elementary and secondary education. Though many are proud to send their children to their local public school and are invested in its success, this is not always the way in which we think about public college (Education Data Initiative 2021).

Elitism in higher education is ubiquitous and for far too long has gone unchallenged, masked in meritocratic achievement and the re-production of class status. While in many communities there exist strong commitments to P/K–12 public education (pre-kindergarten through high school), many of those same people would never imagine public higher ed for their kid/s outside of its possible cost-saving value. Excellent students are urged to "do better."

Using CUNY as a case study, I argue that we need to build a movement for an anti-elitist commitment to public higher education, rooted in justice and an unruly mixing of people. In the spirit of unruly mixing, my argument has ties to queer, anti-racist, feminist conceptions of sharing of public space, and to the material conditions of liberation. We must see that the narrative of "doing better" is sustained through enormous acts of resource hoarding that preserve advantage for the few. The refusal of the false notion of meritocracy—that some are more deserving by talent and hard work rather than being the beneficiaries of advantage manufactured through the inequitable distribution of resources—opens the door to investing in strong, beautiful public colleges (and other institutions).

Who Is Public College For? A Brief History of Two University Systems

In her run for US president, Senator Elizabeth Warren (and former professor of law at Harvard University) pointed to her ability to start her career because she had an aunt who was able to move in and help raise her kids and that she was able to "take 50 dollars" and "go down the road" to University of Houston and pay tuition for a semester (Nolley 2019). In this way, we often rightly think about the decades in which public college was a critical engine that reshaped opportunity and access. We are also reminded of the intricate ways economic reproduction (affordable tuition becomes a lucrative legal and political career) depends on the "in-house" resources (an aunt turned caregiver) that drive social reproduction. Yet the educational landscape since the early 1970s has been fundamentally altered, and the question in part is whether or not it is possible to do what people like Senators Elizabeth Warren and Bernie Sanders have called for: to reverse course and reinvest in public institutions, making them tuition-free once again.

In their book *Austerity Blues Fighting for the Soul of Public Higher Education*, Michael Fabricant and Stephen Brier (2016) tell the story of the rise and fall of financial support for public higher education in the United States over the last century. Their work is part of the larger inquiry that Jeffrey Williams and Heather Steffan have termed "critical university studies" (Williams 2012). Part of their analysis contrasts the ways in which the states of California and New York built two of the largest public university systems in different ways. California took advantage of the Land-Grant College Act of 1862, in which land often obtained/seized from Indigenous people by the federal government was granted to states for educational purposes, to build the University of California Berkeley in 1868. The California system would grow into a mighty network of colleges in three tiers: the University of California campuses, the California State Universities, and the California Community Colleges. Its expansion was driven by a desire for "growing citizen and bipartisan political demands for the establishment of more tax-supported, public higher education institutions across the state" (Fabricant and Brier 2016: 50).

Critical to the Community and State systems in California are not only their value and open access but also the *comingled* prestige of the University of California research institutions. Part of that mixing is literal in that throughout the history of the California system, students have had the ability to transfer from one tier of the system to another. What's currently called the "Transfer Admission Guarantee" was recently overhauled to make the process easier, and it could benefit from expansion (UC Transfer Admission 2021). Nevertheless, what makes the California system different from some is its *in-system* linking of open-access community colleges with the more selective UCs.

There's more work to be done around selectivity and exclusion in admissions to the UC system, but as an entity it is a system where high-quality, prestigious degrees are conferred by public institutions. They are not thought of as a great value and a stepping stone to better things, that is, elite, largely private institutions of higher education. I say this as a third-generation graduate of the California system, but also as someone who experienced first-hand an extraordinary, if random, opportunity for educational comingling. I was in my first quarter of college at the University of California, Santa Cruz, when, on October 17, 1989, a 6.9-magnitude earthquake in nearby Loma Prieta shook our campus. For years, the City of Santa Cruz would rebuild, and we felt aftershocks for months. Understandably, students left the area. First-year students in particular withdrew, and this made room for others. By graduation we were a class of 75 percent of students who had transferred into the university. As a student in these "aftershock" classrooms, I experienced what it means for students with different perspectives to alter an educational space. Classroom seats were filled by transfer students from places like nearby Capitola Community College, where children of farmworkers were the first in their generation to go to college.

Across the country in New York State, another story of higher education emerged. New York State directed its public Morrill Act funding to help found a private institution, now part of the Ivy League, Cornell University. While today the public State University of New York (SUNY) system is among the largest in the country with more than 400,000 students, it wasn't founded until the post-war surge and thus was built late compared to its peers. Prior to the Second World War, when the huge influx of veterans with benefits from the GI bill would change the shape of higher education, New York State was content to satisfy the demand for college by relying largely on private institutions governed by a state board of regents (Fabricant and Brier 2016).

SUNY's story is also in contrast to the system that would become CUNY. In New York City, the demand for access to education came earlier in the movement for free, compulsory primary education. Townsend Harris writes in the *New York Enquirer* in 1847:

> No, Sirs, the system now pursued by that excellent society and by our ward schools is the true one, and may be advantageously applied to higher seminaries of learning. Make them the property of the people—open the doors to all—let the children of the rich and the poor take their seats together and know of no distinction save that of industry, good conduct, and intellect. A large number of the children of the rich now attend our public schools, and the ratio is rapidly increasing. ("Origins and Formative Years," CUNY)

Demands for municipal colleges emerged: the all-male Free Academy established in 1847 became the City College of New York in 1870; the women's "normal school" for training teachers became Hunter College in 1870. These were followed by Brooklyn College in 1930 and Queens College in 1937, both built during the Great Depression. These four colleges, made up of the white working class in New York City, were tuition-free. The commitments were significant for New York City, but they could not meet the demand of New Yorkers across the state who increasingly went across state lines seeking more educational options. Facing a wave of veterans in the post-war period, New York finally acted by building the SUNY system, with colleges serving students outside the metropole. Today, SUNY is the second largest university system in the United States, behind the California system, while CUNY is the largest urban university in the nation. Unlike the California system, however, SUNY and CUNY were not structured in a way to facilitate the transfer of students between and among their colleges.

The core mission of the CUNY has always been to educate and transform the lives of poor, working-class New Yorkers. CUNY has been one of the critical engines of mobility that makes New York City function by helping families to live and support the next generation through the promise of higher education. At the same time, CUNY has always attracted a share of high-achieving students who, one sometimes hears, "might have gone anywhere," meaning a more selective institution. Unfortunately, as I explore in the following, CUNY has more recently adopted a strategy that many public institutions are employing to try and compete for students who might have gone elsewhere.

Social Justice and Unruly Mixing

Public things, like schools, at their best involve a commitment to physical proximity and an acceptance of differences that transcend tolerance and necessity. The work of the "public" involves finding the good in spaces where we all, literally, bump against each other, as on public transit. It then means addressing the difficulties that come with exposure and the vulnerabilities that come with sharing spaces. And sadly it remains a radical thing in higher education to decouple achievement and quality from exclusivity.

CUNY has employed a strategy that many public colleges have used to attract students who might have attended a highly selective institution by establishing (and raising private funding) for honors colleges. Sometimes these are wholly independent colleges that operate inside of other systems; other times they are blended. At CUNY, Macaulay Honors College was established in 2001 to attract middle-class, high-achieving (white) students who, based on their achievements/resources, have the capacity to "go elsewhere" but who might be coaxed into a public education if it carries a designer label. The goal of the Macaulay Honors College is to raise the profile of the institution by creating an exclusive top tier. In the New York City educational landscape, the honors college serves the same purpose as some magnet or specialized schools. It's an elite system inside of a public one, and it should be abolished.

Macaulay students attend school tuition-free, receive a laptop, have access to dorms (while most other CUNY students do not), have access to sets of dedicated classes with smaller class sizes, and have dedicated advisers. In recent years, there has been attention to the lack of diversity of the institution—"MacCaulaySoWhite"— but it has stopped short of this chapter's call for the honors colleges, and honors colleges more broadly, to be abolished.

Honors colleges and other exclusive educational formations drag us in the wrong direction: up. Private college is considered more valuable than ever, and this logic is used to hike tuition and other student expenses. Further, private education costs have skyrocketed in precisely the era that has witnessed a massive disinvestment in public higher education, even as there's a need for more colleges. As result, there's often not enough public college to go around, and many students pay more (Mitchell, Leachman, and Seanz 2021). Sociologist Tressie McMillan Cottom (2017) estimates that in 2008 there were more low-income Black and Hispanic women enrolled in for-profit than in four-year public and private nonprofit colleges combined. During the pandemic, for-profit colleges offering false promises of job placement and part-time, online course work have ramped up for surges in enrollment. Public education thus follows a scarcity model in which admitting and supporting wealthier students means taking support away from a student with fewer resources (Kurzweil and Wyner 2020). And it is in this context that the call for tuition-free public college—for anyone who wants it—has been renewed.

A New Deal for CUNY

The legislature of the State of New York has, historically, been a challenging place to advocate for funding. It has been, infamously, a place governed by "three men in a room": the governor, the speaker of the assembly, and the president of the senate, where legislators have not possessed much power. Inside that culture, advocating for oneself as a state agency has been challenging. While I, an alumnus of the University of California, might routinely get asked to tell California lawmakers to fund public higher education, that is not the culture in the state of New York. CUNY does a terrible job tracking alumni, and when it does it fundraises from the college and has rarely asked graduates to raise their voices on behalf of the university system. Similarly, CUNY's administration and its Board of Trustees have been far from vigorous advocates for additional funding for the university. For decades, they have failed to even ask for the funding that the university system has needed to run. They have presided over false austerity and implemented deep cuts in the system.

Into this void stepped a number of advocates who worked together in the past decade to launch CUNY Rising Alliance. Among the most vigorous voices for additional funding has been the Professional Staff Congress (PSC CUNY), the union representing the faculty and a portion of the staff in the university. From this work, a coalition was born that has brought together student representatives serving in the University Student Senate, the advocacy organization New York Public Interest Research Group (NYPIRG), which has long-established chapters within CUNY, and community organizations with overlapping commitments, including New York Communities for Change, the Young Invincibles, Hispanic Federation, and local labor unions such as DC-37 and 32BJ. This work has been bolstered by building a coalition of unions, student government groups, community organizations, and alumni to advocate for increased support for CUNY through an organization called CUNY Rising Alliance and for a coalition in New York State that would raise more than 50 billion, in the Invest in Our New York campaign.

Working together this coalition identified critical needs flowing from disinvestment: the cost of attending college; the growing rate of adjunctification as poorly paid part-time employees replaced full-time faculty on tenured lines; the lack of adequate student advisers to help students navigate a complicated, overcrowded system; a lack of mental health counselors to help fill a need that's not being addressed outside the institution; and the desperate need to fix our broken campuses, falling apart after decades of deferred maintenance and rising enrollment.

The state of affairs was summed up in a report by New York City Public Advocate (and two-time CUNY alumnus) Jumaane Williams this way:

> Pressure to do more with limited funding has restricted the ability of CUNY colleges to hire additional full-time faculty, counselors and advisors, or pay nationally competitive salaries. More than half of undergraduate CUNY courses are taught by part-time adjunct faculty members who earn an average of $3,500 per course and may need to work a second job to make a living, leaving them unable to provide the support that some students need to succeed in a course. CUNY has also been forced to cut academic support services and course sections—with more than one-third of students reporting in 2016 that they could not register for at least one course, largely because there were no more remaining seats. Meanwhile, some libraries cannot afford books or journal subscriptions, and student advisors and mental health counselors have hundreds of students they must attend to on a daily basis. And underinvestment in infrastructure has contributed to CUNY facilities falling into a state of disrepair—marked by exposed wiring, persistent flooding, swarms of pests, and moldy ceiling tiles. ("Addressing the Underfunding of CUNY" 2019)

CUNY Rising Alliance was critical in formulating demands that would become a piece of legislation, introduced in 2021 in the New York State legislature. The legislation known as a "New Deal for CUNY" would: (1) make in-state, undergraduate education tuition-free; (2) establish per-student ratios for academic advising and mental health counseling; (3) hire 5,000 new full-time faculty (including converting some adjunct positions into full-time ones) and professionalize adjunct pay with parity with a full-time lecturer line; (4) fund CUNY's existing unfunded capital requests to improve our crumbling buildings and campuses.

In recent decades at CUNY, more than half of CUNY students come from households that earn less than 40,000 dollars per year, many of them recent immigrants and/or the first in their families to attend college. Williams identified funding for CUNY as one of the ways to realize race and class justice in New York ("The Underfunding of CUNY" 2019). Meanwhile, Comptroller Scott Stringer produced a report demonstrating not only the ways CUNY is an economic engine for New York City but also the ways many CUNY alumni (and often their families) are lifted into the middle class because of the impact of their education and access to the institution. With politicians and many communities backing a New Deal for CUNY, the time seems right for a change. But change will require us to face some of our most vexing questions.

Who Is Worthy of Investment?

A few years back, I was teaching in a classroom and water started to drip through the ceiling. Moments later, a portion of the ceiling tile hit a student in the head and more plopped onto her notebook and reading material. I had a giant reaction. What has stayed with me over the years is that she did not. Instead, she looked up at the ceiling with a kind of weary acceptance. "Is this all I'm worth?" Her conditioning to accept these kinds of conditions in a public space haunts me.

The student newspaper at UC Santa Cruz, the "public ivy" where I went to school, is called a City on A Hill. I went to university in a redwood forest that could have been a state park. My experience as a young white woman was being handed the best of what public education had to offer, even if it cost more than my parents paid a generation before me. I want this for every prospective college student and feel obliged to fight to try to move us closer to that world, where our core public institutions are strong and well-funded and for everyone.

A beautiful public is possible. Let's go. #freehighqualitypubliced4all.

References

"Addressing the Underfunding of CUNY" (2019), *Public Advocate for the City of New York*, December 6. Available online: https://advocate.nyc.gov/static/assets/CUNY%20Report.pdf (accessed March 24, 2022).

Cottom, T. M. (2017), "The Coded Language of For-Profit Colleges," *The Atlantic*, February 22. Available online: https://www.theatlantic.com/education/archive/2017/02/the-coded-language-of-for-profit-colleges/516810/ (accessed March 24, 2022).

Education Data Initiative (2021), "K-12 School Enrollment & Student Population Statistics," September 12. Available online: https://educationdata.org/k12-enrollment-statistics (accessed March 24, 2022).

Fabricant, M. and S. Brier (2016), *Austerity Blues Fighting for the Soul of Public Higher Education*, Baltimore, MA: Johns Hopkins University Press.

Kurzweil, M. and J. Wyner (2020), "Rich Kids Are Eating Up the Financial Aid Pot," *New York Times*, June 16. Available online: https://www.nytimes.com/2020/06/16/opinion/coronavirus-college-rich-kids.html (accessed March 24, 2022).

Mitchell, M., M. Leachman, and M. Seanz (2021), "State Higher Education Funding Cuts Have Pushed Costs to Students, Worsened Inequality," *Centre on Budget and Policy Priorities*, October 24. Available online: https://www.cbpp.org/research/state-budget-and-tax/state-higher-education-funding-cuts-have-pushed-costs-to-students (accessed March 24, 2022).

Nolley, Trevor (2019), "Did UH Cost $50 a Semester when Elizabeth Warren Attended?," *The Cougar*, October 17. Available online: http://thedailycougar.com/2019/10/17/warren-uh-cost-50-semester/ (accessed March 24, 2022).

"Origins and Formative Years," *City University New York*. Available online: https://www.cuny.edu/about/history/origins-and-formative-years/ (accessed March 24, 2022).

"UC Transfer Admission Guarantee" (2021), *University of California*. Available online: https://admission.universityofcalifornia.edu/counselors/files/tag-matrix.pdf (accessed March 24, 2022).

Williams, J.J. (2012), "Deconstructing Academe: The Birth of Critical University Studies," *The Chronicle of Higher Education*, February 19. Available online: https://www.chronicle.com/article/deconstructing-academe/ (accessed March 24, 2022).

NOTES

Chapter 2

1. Charlotte Uprising is an abolitionist community organization named after the September 2016 mass protests in response to the police murder of Keith Lamont Scott, a Black, disabled man sitting in his parked car, who officers claimed was wielding a gun. In a video recorded on her cell phone, Scott's wife repeatedly responds to officers' commands to drop the weapon, stating that her husband is unarmed and has a traumatic brain injury. No gun is visible in either this video or the officers' bodycam footage. During the protests that erupted in the aftermath of Scott's slaying, Justin Carr, an unarmed Black protester, was shot and killed. Although another protester was convicted of the murder, witnesses maintain that Carr was killed by police.
2. Canva is a free graphic design app that DCF members use to create fundraising posts for social media.

Chapter 3

1. The full series can be found at: https://headtailconnection.wordpress.com/headtail-connections/. Speakers were aware that they were being recorded for future online publication and were happy to do so without anonymization (accessed March 4, 2022).
2. Participant quotes are from author interviews.
3. Searching around the university HR website, I finally found a single page pdf with instructions for how faculty should approach HR if they wish to request a "reasonable accommodation."
4. It is also common for full-time faculty to take over an adjunct class if their own class does not meet the enrollment minimum, resulting in a similar last-minute loss of work.
5. A famous postmodern dance artist and founder of Twyla Tharp Dance Foundation. See https://www.twylatharp.org/bio.

Chapter 6

1. Disclosure: my auntie trained at college to become a teacher later in life and one of my (dozens of) cousins attended what were known as a polytechnic as a mature student before becoming a painter and decorator. None of my family, aside from my nephew and I, attended university and none aside from the aforementioned cousin and auntie,

as well as my niece who trained at college to become a hairdresser, was in education beyond sixteen.
2. The "corridor talk" I speak of here and throughout are situations I know happened. I am, however, not stating that this happened at my own institution or any of those I have worked or studied at.

Chapter 7

1. Passy, R. (2013). Surviving and flourishing in a neoliberal world: primary trainees talking. *British Educational Research Journal*, 39(6), 1060–75. http://www.jstor.org/stable/24463922
2. brown, adrienne maree. "St. Louis Racial Equity Summit 2021 Keynote."

Chapter 8

1. All quotes are taken from author interviews.

Chapter 9

1. Edinburgh is Scotland's capital city and the second most populous after Glasgow, Perth is a small city in the center of Scotland, Ayr a town on Scotland's south west coast, and Wick is a small town in the very northeast of Scotland in the Caithness region.

Chapter 10

1. MCCK hosted an intern virtually. Their home church is MCC, Los Angeles, and the observations they shared with me during our interview, specifically about touch, seemed to be true for both locations.

FURTHER READING

Ahmed, S. (2012), *On Being Included: Racism and Diversity in Institutional Life*, Durham, NC: Duke University Press.
Berlant, L. (2011), *Cruel Optimism*, Durham, NC: Duke University Press.
Bérubé, A. (2011), *My Desire for History: Essays in Gay, Community, and Labor History*, ed. John d'Emilio and Estelle B. Freeman, Chapel Hill: University of North Carolina Press.
Breeze. M. and Y. Taylor (2020), *Feminist Repetitions in Higher Education: Interrupting Career Categories*, London: Palgrave Macmillan.
Brim, M. (2020), *Poor Queer Studies: Confronting Elitism in the University*, Durham, NC: Duke University Press.
Butler, J. (2006), *Precarious Life: The Powers of Morning and Violence*, London: Verso.
Duggan, L. and J.E. Muñoz (2009), "Hope and Hopelessness: A Dialogue," *Women & Performance: A Journal of Feminist Theory*, 19 (2): 275–83.
Edelman, L. (2004), *No Future: Queer Theory and the Death Drive*, Durham, NC: Duke University Press.
Gabriel, D. and S. Tate (2017), *Inside the Ivory Tower: Narratives of Women of Colour Surviving and Thriving in British Academia*, London: Trentham Books.
Halberstam, J. (2011), *The Queer Art of Failure*. Durham, NC: Duke University Press.
Haritaworn, J. (2011), "Perverse Reproductions: Notes from the Wrong Side of the Classroom," *Journal of Curriculum and Pedagogy*, 8 (1): 25–8.
Harney, S. and F. Moten (2013), *The Undercommons: Fugitive Planning and Black Study*, Wivenhoe: Minor Compositions.
hooks, B. (2003), *Teaching Community: A Pedagogy of Hope*, New York: Routledge.
Mahn, C., M. Brim, and Y. Taylor (2023), *Queer Sharing in the Marketized University*, London: Routledge.
Puar, J. (2012), "Precarity Talk: A Virtual Roundtable with Lauren Berlant, Judith Butler, Bojana Cvejić, Isabell Lorey, Jasbir Puar, and Ana Vujanović," *TDR*, 56 (4): 163–77.
Sobande, F. (2021), "By us, for us? The Narratives of Black Women in Past and Present British Feminist Publishing," *Women: A Cultural Review*, 3–4: 395–409.
Taylor, Y. and K. Lahad (eds.) (2018), *Feeling Academic in the Neoliberal University: Feminist Fights, Flights and Failures*, London: Palgrave Macmillan.

INDEX

Note: Page numbers in Bold refer to tables and followed by 'n' refer to notes

501c3 status   44–5
2008 financial crisis   1–2
2010 Equality Act   105
2019 Resisting Whiteness conference   111
2021 Gallup Poll on LGBT identification   134

abolition
   principles of   28
   of prison industrial complex   28
   talks about   37
abundance, paradigm of   79
academic currency, recognizable   78
academic language   87–8
academy   22–5
   access to journals   23
   epistemic exclusion   23
   erasure   23
   exclusions, multiple   24
   experiences during pandemic   50–63
   Great Recession   23
   limited funding   23–4
   marginalization   23
   oppression   23
   professional conferences, participation in   23
   progressive work in universities   22
   queerness, epistemology and praxis   24
   scholarship, mutually constitutive relationship   83
   site of violence and refuge   22–5
   social policies   23
   survival in academy   24–5
   tenure-track positions   23
access to journals   23
ACT UP Oral History Project   141
adjuncts
   class identification   15
   demographic fluctuations   16
   description   11
   experience   11–13
   and faculty, mutual support   61
   fear   15
   labor   60
   organized labor   16–17
   sharing stories   15–17
   union organizing   13–14
The Adjunct Trap   60
African American Studies   23
African American traditions   90
'aftershock' classrooms   175
age-appropriate activity   151
Ageing and Aged Care Conference   149
ageism   136
The Age Project out of Europe   137
Age Scotland   151
Ahmed, S.   106, 117
AIDS   99, 155, 163
   care networks   167–8
   collective trauma   167
   and COVID-19   167–8, 170
   kinship and intimacy, reconfiguration of   165
   MCCK, response of   168
   shared loss and survival   163
   shared trauma   170
   surviving, resilience of   170
All The Queens Men (ATQM)   147–50
Amin, K.   71
anti-Black
   anti-Blackness   120–1, 126
   sentiments   46, 86
anti-capitalist and anti-colonial strategies   29–30
anti-harassment announcement   50
Anzaldúa, G.   4
apartheid   87
assessment metrics   87

ATQM model   149–50
austerity
    measures in cultural sector   158
    policies   21
Austerity Blues: Fighting for the Soul of Public Higher Education (Fabricant and Brier)   174
aversive racism   84

Balay, A.   4
Ball, M.   22, 24–5
Beattie, G.   87
Berlant, L.   27
Bernal, D.D.   87
Bérubé, A.   144
bio-kinship   70
biosociality   163–5
BIPOC queer students   5
Black, Indigenous, and People of Color (BIPOC)   5–6, 46, 67–8, 73, 77, 79, 99, 104, 107–12, 115
Black Feminism and anti-Blackness   120–1
#BlackLivesMatter   109
Black Lives Matter movement   51, 62, 97, 109
    Week of Action   126–7
Black members, in professorships   84
Black radical traditions   3
Black Student Coalition, work during COVID-19   36
Black trans femmes   35, 38, 41
Bohan, J.S.   132
Bostock v. Clayton County   26
Bourdieu, P.   98, 100–1, 104
Breeze, M.   68–9
Brier, S.   174
Brim, M.   23, 27, 136, 137
Brodie, L.   7–8
Brooklyn College   176
Brunsma, D.L.   89
burden sharing, theory of   54, 56
Butler, J.   2

California system, expansion of   174–6
Canva   41, 48, 181 n.2
care networks   29, 162–3, 166–8, 171

care work
    abolitionist scholarly and organizing work   28
    academy (*see* academy)
    anti-capitalist and anti-colonial strategies   29–30
    austerity-based policies   21
    care webs, care work through   29–30
    contestation in practice   27–30
    disability justice   29
    education sites   21
    gendered and neoliberal perspectives   27
    gender and sexuality, binaries of   26
    homonormativity, concept of   26
    identity limitations   26
    institutional resources   30–1
    lesbian and gay political movements, white people in   25–6
    LGBTQ extracurricular clubs and centers   21
    LGBTQIA+   25
    mesearch   22
    mutual aid, description and elements   28
    neoliberal policies implementation   21
    personal resources   31–2
    praxis, sick and disabled queer, trans, Black, and brown people   22
    prison industrial complex abolition   28
    punitive penal management   21
    queerness   25–7 (*see also* queer)
    queer scholars inclusion   22
    slow death, conceptualization of   27
    transformation through queer work   26–7
    violence and suicide   29
Care Work: Dreaming of Disability Justice (Piepzna-Samarasinha)   29, 68
CashApp card   41
Center on Halsted   135, 138–40
Centre for Ageing Better   154
Cervero, R.M.   90
Charlotte Uprising   37, 181 n.1
Chernobyl disaster   165
Chisholm, A.   140
Christ-MCC's conception of family   165

City University of New York (CUNY) system 5, 66–8, 173, 175–6
　aftershock classrooms 175
　critical university studies 174
　CUNY Rising Alliance 177, 178
　DC-37 and 32BJ, local labor unions 178
　demands for municipal colleges 175–6
　elitism in higher education 173
　expansion of California system 174
　job tracking alumni 177
　lack of mental health counselors 178
　Land-Grant College Act of 1862 174
　mission of 176
　movement for anti-elitist commitment to public higher education 173–4
　New Deal for CUNY 177–9
　private college 177
　Professional Staff Congress (PSC CUNY) 177–8
　selectivity and exclusion in admissions 175
　social justice and unruly mixing 176–7
　State University of New York (SUNY) system 175
　Transfer Admission Guarantee 174–5
　tuition-free public college, call for 177
　university systems 174–6
　Young Invincibles 178
civil rights
　demonstrations 52
　violations 49
Civil Rights Movement 51
CLAGS: Center for LGBTQ Studies 66
Clark-Stilianos, L. 59, 62
class identification, confused 15
classifying regimes, hegemonic 90–1
classism 3, 104, 106, 113, 136
class privilege and racism structures 4
Cohen, D. 87
Colin L. Powell School for Civic and Global Leadership 173
collaborative art project 131, 140
collective liberation 12, 125
colonialist practices 83

Combahee River Collective, 1977 statement 120
The Coming Back Out Ball (TCBOB) 147–50, 153, 158–9
The Coming Back Out Conversation 150, 153
communal work 53–4
community building and care 29, 53, 55, 67, 147, 150, 164
community forum 155–6
community-led social space 154
Compassion and Belonging grant 140
complementary discrimination 88
composition and psychology 68–9
conflict resolution 31
congruence and case studies 110–14
　2019 Resisting Whiteness conference 111
　impact case study for REF2021 110–11
　paint-by-numbers approach 113
　working-class and BIPOC academics 110
consanguinity 162
Contact Improvisation 63
contingency, insecurity, and impermanence 2
conversation, productive 49
"corridor talk" 99, 105–7, 109, 111, 182 n.2
Cottom, T.M. 177
Council of the Ageing website 149
counterstory 73–4, 79–80
COVID-19 36, 140–1, 147
　additional risks 60
　and AIDS (*see* AIDS)
　and digital divide 154
　kinship and practice of faith 161–7
　political and social consequences 163
　queer space 153–6
　restriction on closeness, touch, and intimacy 168
　sermons through Zoom 169
　shared trauma 170
　virtual church 169
Creative Aging Organization 147–8
credentialing 84–5
Crew, T. 104

crisis of Black trans people   37
Critical Race Theory (CRT)   66, 73
critical university studies   174
cross-disciplinary intellectual work   66
cross-disciplinary queer kinship   77
cross-generational contact   133
cultural capital   31, 100–1
Culture in Crisis: A Guide to Access, Equality, Diversity, and Inclusion in Festivals, Arts, and Culture (Dawson)   112
CUNY Rising Alliance   177–8

Dad Rock   72–4
Dalton, D.   22
Dancy, T.E. II   87
Davidson Community Fund (DCF)   5, 7, 35, 42
   501c3 status   44
   abolition talks   37
   anti-Black sentiments   46
   Black Student Coalition, during COVID-19   36
   Black trans people, crisis of   37
   CashApp card   41
   COVID-19 crisis   36
   direct communications   40
   donation flyers and fundraisers   41–2
   emergency fundraising   37–8
   focus on care   47–8
   Fratergy, frat wealth extraction strategy group   40–2
   George Floyd protests   41
   intergenerational organizing   39–40
   mutual aid   45–6
   nonprofits, role of   45
   origin   35
   QTIBIPOC Survival Fund   39
   queer/BIPOC identities   46
   redistributing resources   35–48
   relationship building   38
   traction on Instagram   38
   Venmo/CashApp   38, 41, 44
   wealth redistribution to marginalized   35–6
Davidson Young Democratic Socialists of America Instagram   43
Davis, C.   50–1
Davis, J.E.   87

DC-37 and 32BJ, local labor unions   178
DCF's Venmo   37–8, 41, 44–5
de-blacking   92–3
#DecoloniseTheCurriculum   109
decolonizing
   the curriculum   98, 101, 114
   recolonizing through   107–10
   universities   101
Delany, S.   137
demographic fluctuations   16
departmental value systems   63
deprivation   79, 102
Desert Island Disco   155
dialogue format   69–78
DiAngelo, R.   84
digital access, training in   154
Digital Classrooms   62
digital divide   154
digital socializing   153–4
digital technologies   141, 169–71
dignity
   and respect policy   106–7
   at work policy   106
direct communications   40
disabilities
   accommodations   54
   BIPOC with   99–100, 104, 108, 111, 113–14
disability justice   29
disappearing lesbian   142–3
DisCrit   66
Diversity, Equity, Inclusion (DEI)   63, 118, 122, 128
Diversity/DEI narrative   128
Diversity Studies   23
donation flyers and fundraisers   41–2
Dovidio, A.F.   84
Duboisian double consciousness   93
Dunn, D.C.   140

Earle, M.   6
eccentric economic practices   100–1
Eden Court, Scotland's largest multi-arts center   148–9
Edwards, K.T.   87
Eisen-Markowitz, E.   6
elitism   7, 15
   in higher education   173
   racial   89

Elzinga, B. 133
Email and WhatsApp messages 154
embodied diversity 123
embodied queer pedagogy 6, 133, 142
Embrick, D.G. 89
emergency fundraising 37–8
emotional labor 154–5
epistemic exclusion 22–4, 85
equality, diversity, and inclusion (EDI) 2, 5–6, 97–8, 104, 108, 114
  instrumentalization of 5
  practice 103
  widening participation 98
Equality Network 151
erasure 23, 90–1, 109
exclusion 5, 26, 75, 83, 91, 101, 133, 138–9, 157, 162, 168–9, 171
  academic 105
  in admissions 175
  epistemic 22–4, 85
  hierarchies of 85
  practices 85, 89
  recruitment and retention 89
  stories of Trans Exclusionary Radical Feminism 142
  structural 3
  and violence 139
Experience the Experience Learning Exposition 127

Fabricant, M. 174
fabrication 69, 106–7
familial and intellectual connection, narration 67
"families we choose" 162
family
  chosen and biological 75
  and kin, terminology 71
  oppressive notions of 70
Farahani, F. 23
Faulkner, M. 54, 56
fears, "lesbians going extinct" 143
fellowships 88–9, 124, 168
Flowers, A.M. III 89
Four Fights, Colleges Union campaign 8
Fratergy, frat wealth extraction strategy group 40–2
Free Application for Federal Student Aid (FAFSA) 53

freelance creative practitioners 51, 147–8, 150, 154, 159
Fricker, M. 133
friendlove 5, 75
#FundBlackScientists 109

Gaboury, J. 7
Gaertner, S.L. 84
Gasman, M. 89
gay rights movement 99
Gender and Sexuality Studies 23
gender and sexually diverse people 148
gender binary 121
gendered and neoliberal perspectives 27
gender and sexuality, binaries of 13, 26
generation gap 136
Generations Project, New York City 137
gentrification 124, 137–8
George Floyd
  killing of 97
  protests 38, 41, 97
Giordano, T. 39
Givens, J.R. 120
Gleich, J. 56
González, C.G. 92
The Great Believers (Makkai) 140
Great Depression 176
Great Recession 23
Gregorian, V. 173
Greteman, A.J. 6

Ha, S. 58
Halberstam, J. 22, 98, 100, 135
Hannah-Jones, N. 53
happy diversity 118
Harney, S. 3, 24, 47
Harris, A.P. 92
Harris, T. 175
Hartman, S. 86
herbalism 125
hermeneutical justice 142
heterosexism 121, 128
Hetherington, L. 7
hierarchization
  classroom 3
  of inclusion and exclusion 85
  and power-based behaviors 50
  racial and epistemological 92

reconsideration of 114
stratification 102
structures of academe 30, 50
higher education
    adjunctification of 4
    contemporary educational spaces 3
    crisis after 9/11 2
    cross-generational conversations 6
    equality, diversity, and inclusion (EDI) 2
    government austerity programs 1
    impermanence 1
    increased marketization 99
    intersectional class-race-gender 4
    LGBTQ+ outreach program 1
    misrecognition 1
    mobilizing collectivized queer insight 3
    politicization and collectivization 2
    precarity, patterns 1
    Queer and Gender Studies degree 1
    queerphobic backlash 1
    queer(ed) practices of care, inclusion, and kinship 3
    queer pushback 3–4
    structural discrimination 3
    unemployment 1
Higher Education Statistics Agency (HESA) 84
hiring disparities 88
Hispanic Federation 178
Historically Black Colleges and Universities (HBCUs) 87, 89
historically white institutions (HWUs) 87
HIV and AIDS care 99, see also AIDS
Holland, S. 39
Hollibaugh, A. 139
Holt, K. 58
homonormativity 26, 93, 100, 102
homophobia 22, 29, 121
homosexuality 26, 76
Horne, W. 52
How Do We Go Forward? How Do We Go Back? series 5, 49, 54, 61–2, 64
How to Do Things with Words (Austin, J. L.) 90
Hubbard, J. 141
Human Genome Initiative 165

Hunter College 176

idealism 117
identity
    declarative identity statements 6
    gender 25, 50, 72, 134, 142, 150, 155, 170
    impact on institution 104
    intersections of multiple 54
    limitations 26
    marginalized 117
    professional 66
    queer/BIPOC 23, 31, 46, 54
    sexual and gender minority 163
    sociocultural 77, 165
    trans/nonbinary gender 25
image management 118
impact case study for REF2021 110–11
Inayatulla, S. 5, 66
inclusion 25–6, 28
    birth certificate inclusion, same-sex parents 100
    hierarchies 85
    LGBTQ+ inclusion, schools curriculum 133
    limitations 22
    religious 25
    of trans women 143
    of work about BIPOC 109
inclusive, learning-focused, connected culture 127
individual and authority, formalized relationship 89
individualism 67, 72, 117–18
in-person dance club 155
in-person teaching 49
Instagram, traction on 38
institutional resources 30–1
institutional vulnerability 58
intergenerational classrooms 124–6
intergenerational contact among LGBTQ+ folks, in US 136
interruption methods 68
intersectionality 66, 120
intersectional queer feminist pedagogies 117
intersections, multiple identities 54
interviews, emotional 157
intimacy, as kinship 165

invisible tax   120
isolation   17, 29, 49, 77, 118, 135, 149, 151, 153–4, 157, 162–3, 168, 170–1
Iverson, S.V.   92

job tracking alumni, CUNY   177
Johnson, B.   113
Johnson-Bailey, J.   90
Jones, T.L.   6

Kang, S.   93
Kennedy, Fen   5
King, S.   90
kinship
    academic currency   78
    aggressions and silencing   74
    AIDS   163, 168–70
    bio-kinship   70
    biosociality   165
    Chernobyl disaster   165
    chosen and biological family   75
    Christ-MCC's conception of family   165
    community building and care   67
    composition and psychology   68–9
    counterstory   73–4
    COVID-19   163, 168–70
    cross-disciplinary intellectual work   66
    "Dad"   72
    'Dad Rock'   72–3
    definition   66, 69–70
    dialogue format   69–78
    digital technologies   171
    fabrication   69
    familial and intellectual connection, narration   67
    family and kin   71
    formations   67
    forms of "nonsovereignty" and relationality   164
    friendlove   75
    homosexuality   76
    Human Genome Initiative   165
    interruption methods   68
    and intimacy   164–5
    LGBTQ+ and BIPOC   68
    marginalization   163
    MCC community   166–7

    MCCK   161–2
    networks of care   163
    oppression   76
    paradigm of abundance   79
    queer (*see* queer)
    reciprocal collaboration   67
    scholarly inquiry   79
    shared sense of community   162–4
    sociality and relationality   163
    storytelling   73, 79
    through faith   165–7
    throupling   71–2
    Weston's theorization   162
knowledge exchange (KE)   6, 98, 110, 156
knowledge reproduction   102–3
Kolbe, K.   158
Kovel, J.   84

Land-Grant College Act of 1862   174
Lather, P.   135
learning across time   122–4
legitimate scholarship   92
LGBTI+ Elders
    group interview with   152
    histories, politics, and cultures   134–5
    LGBTI+ Elders Social Dance Club   147–50
    stories and visibility of   152
    underrepresented group   158
LGBTQ extracurricular clubs and centers   21
LGBTQIA+   25, 121, 148
LGBTQ+ inclusion in curriculum of US public schools   133
LGBTQ+ Intergenerational Dialogue Project   6, 131–45,
LGBTQ+ sociality   138
LGBT Youth Scotland   151
living room space   138–9
logical/chosen family   139
Lorey, I.   2
Love, B.   140
low wages   15, 60

Macaulay Honors College   176–7
McGuire, L.   87
McNeill, Z.   52
Making Gay History (Marcus)   141

Makkai, R. 140
mandatory public secondary school 123
Marcus, E. 141
marginalization 6–7, 23, 91, 122, 163, 165
marriage
   and civil partnership 105
   rights to marriage equality 26
   same-sex marriage 25, 100, 161
Martinez, A.Y. 73–4
Mental Health Awareness 127
mental health counselors 178
mental health problems 58
mentoring/mentorships 60–1, 85–6, 89, 107
Metro High School 119–22
   Black Feminism and anti-Blackness 120–1
   Combahee River Collective, 1977 statement 120
   culture of 119
   educational practice as social activism 122
   invisible tax 120
   recovering from interruption/violence 119–20
   self-identify as LGBTQIA+ 121–2
   self-proclaimed "progressive" schools 120
Metropolitan Community Church (MCC)
   expressions of intimacy and kinship 164
   global community 166
   goal 161
   queer communion and family 170
   queer-religious space 7
   social and physical interactions 166
Metropolitan Community Church of Knoxville, Tennessee (MCCK) 7, 161–71, 182 n.1
Mickelson, R.A. 88
military enlistment 25
minority/cultural tax 84
mobility limitations 138
Morris, K. 6
Moten, F. 3, 24, 47
motherhood and career 103
Musser, A. J. 79
mutual aid 45–6
   collecting and distributing economic resources through 32
   community-oriented and operated care program 45
   definition 28
   elements of 28
   fund 32
   networks 36–7
   and queer care 4, 29, 31
   student-led project 5

Nam, S.E. 58
naming 89–92
   African American traditions 90
   degrees 91
   description 90
   hegemonic classifying regimes 90–1
   importance of 91
   interrogation of 91
   "other-named" 91
   privileges, table of **90**
   recruitment and retention, exclusionary practices 89
National Theatre of Scotland (NTS) 147–8
neoliberalism
   DEI model 118, 122
   individualism 67, 103, 117–18
   policies implementation 21
network/networking
   care 29, 162–3, 166–8, 171
   career-making 85, 107
   form of social capital 86
   kinship 162
   lack of access to formal 86
   professional 91
   queer artist-activist 117
   research 113
   as social capital 86
   and sponsorships 88–9
New York Communities for Change 178
New York Public Interest Research Group (NYPIRG) 178
nonbinary academic teaching 49
nonhierarchical intellectual and creative engagement 117, 120
nonhierarchical social structures 31
nonprofits, role of 45

nonsovereignty and relationality, forms of   164
NTS, Scotland's national theater   148
nuclear family, celebration of   7, 100, 165

obsolescence   85
Office of Disability Services   57
Office of Diversity and Inclusion Young Scholars Program   55
Oliver, M.L.   88
oppression   12, 23–5, 27, 32, 49, 58, 66, 70–1, 73–6, 79–80, 113, 120, 124, 126, 132, 143
oppressive tactics   93
organized labor   16–17
otherisms   86
othermothering   89
OUTspoken LGBTQ+ Storytelling at Sidetrack   141

pandemic impact on students   55
Paris, D.   90
participatory art practices   147
Pearson, A.R.   84
peer-led sessions   156
performative allyship   108
performative sharing   98
permeable space, notion of   151
personal autonomy   118
personal resources   31–2
Petryna, A.   165
Phillips, T.   54
physical intimacy   164
Piepzna-Samarasinha, L.L.   29, 68
Pierce, J.M.   70
P/K-12 public education   173
polytechnics   99
Poor Queer Studies (Brim)   23
post-92 universities   99, 114
postdoctoral positions
  in higher education   88
  hiring practices and faculty promotions, discrimination in   93
power-based behaviors   50
praxis   22, 24, 26, 29, 46–7
pre-92 UK institutions   114
precarities, in and out of higher education, *see* higher education

Presumed Incompetent: The Intersections of Race and Class for Women in Academia (Harris and González)   91–2
private college   177
privileges   **90**, 100–1
professional conferences, participation in   23
Professional Staff Congress (PSC CUNY)   177–8
"progressive" schools   120
progressive work, in universities   22
Puar, J.   2
public engagement   98
publishing contracts   52
"publish/perish" mindset, academic institutions   53
punitive penal management   21

Queens College   66, 176
queer
  academics, value of   4
  in academy (*see* sharing in academy)
  access and equity principles   49
  anthropology   162, 164
  BIPOC identities   23, 31, 46, 54
  care work (*see* care work)
  as a concept   25
  description   25–6
  educators   6, 117, 122, 125
  epistemology and praxis   24
  faith in pandemic   161–7
  feminist pedagogies   117, 120
  gender sexuality, binaries of   26
  homonormativity, concept of   26
  identity limitations   26
  intimacies   164
  joy   144
  kinship (*see* kinship)
  language   71
  LGBTQIA+   25
  life   25
  marginalization   6
  pedagogy   5, 6, 133, 142
  pragmatism   4
  precarity   27
  queerness   25–7
  and religious spaces, coexistence   164

resources (*see* resources, sharing)
space (*see* space, sharing)
structural violence   27
studies beyond the classroom
    136-7
temporality   100-2
theory   3, 6, 15, 25, 66, 70, 80,
    98-101, 104, 135-6, 164
time, concept of   2, 113, 131-2, 141,
    144
transformation through queer
    work   26-7
vulnerability and honesty sharing   49
Queer, Trans, Black, Indigenous, and
    People Of Color (QTIBIPOC)   99
QTIBIPOC Survival Fund   39
The Queer Art of Failure
    (Halberstam)   113
Queer New Year   126, 127
queer sharing   137-43
    building tour, benefits of   138-9
    Compassion and Belonging
        grant   140
    conversation following stories   141
    COVID-19 infection risk   140-1
    gentrification   138
    hermeneutical justice   142
    lesbians going extinct, fears of   143
    for LGBTQ+ sociality   138
    logical/chosen family   139
    mobility limitations   138
    moments of queer joy   144
    resources   139-41
    role of time   143
    shared meals   139
    space   137-9
    stories (*see* stories, sharing)
    Zoom   141
Quinn, J.   67

race-based hiring practices   87
racism   3-4, 15, 41, 52, 73, 83-4, 87-8,
    90, 97, 99, 104, 109, 111-14, 128
racist "anti-agenda"   83
radicalization, political   46
rankings and hierarchies   114
Ray, V.   80
Reay, D.   104
Received Pronunciation   105, 108

reciprocal collaboration   67
redistribution
    of resources beyond academy   35-48
    of wealth to marginalized
        community   35-6
relationship building   38, 45
religious inclusions   25
Renn, K.   136
Research Excellence Framework (REF)
    87, 98
resources, sharing   139-41, *see also* queer
    sharing
Restorative Justice Leadership class   125,
    126
risk sharing   7
Rivera, D.P.   5, 66
Rome, G.   150
Russell, G.M.   132

same-sex
    marriage   25, 100
    sexualities   25
Sanctuary Publishers   52
Sanders, B.   174
Schmidt, A.   54
scholarly inquiry   79
scholars of color
    academia and scholarship, mutually
        constitutive relationship
        between   83
    academic language   87-8
    apartheid   87
    assessment metrics   87
    Black members, in professorships   84
    colonialist practices   83
    complementary discrimination   88
    credentialing   84-5
    de-blacking   92-3
    description   86
    Duboisian double consciousness   93
    epistemic exclusion   85
    faculty promotions   93
    hiring disparities   88
    inclusion and exclusion, hierarchies of
        85
    individual and authority, formalized
        relationship   89
    "legitimate" scholarship   92
    marginalization of   91

mentoring 89
minority/cultural tax 84
naming, coveted (*see* naming)
networking as social capital 86
networks and sponsorships 88–9
obsolescence 85
oppressive tactics 93
otherisms 86
othermothering 89
postdoctoral hiring practices 93
postdoctoral positions, in higher education 88
race-based hiring practices 87
racism, aversive 84
racist "anti-agenda" 83
unaffiliated 85–9
School of the Art Institute of Chicago (SAIC) 135
Schulman, S. 141
Scottish Care 151
Scottish Queer International Film Festival 104
self-censorship, in classroom 52
self-identify, as LGBTQIA+ 121–2
selfishness, idea of 50–1
self-reliance 118
Sensoy, O. 84
sexism 15
shame-based barriers 52
shared meals 136, 139
shared trauma 162–3, 170
sharing in academy 99–103, *see also* academy
  AIDS crisis of the 1980s 99
  capital 100
  deprivation 102
  eccentric economic practices 101
  gay rights movement 99
  HIV and AIDS care 99
  homonormativity 100
  increased marketization of HE 99
  knowledge reproduction 102–3
  motherhood and career 103
  nuclear family, celebration of 100
  privilege 100–1
  QTIBOPOC 99
  queer temporality and socioeconomic reality 102
  same-sex marriage legalization 100
  straight economic practices 101
  straight sharing 102
  temporality 100
Shin, J.H. 89
silencing and strategic silence 107
silencing factors 50
Skeggs, B. 104
skepticism 117
slow death, conceptualization of 27
social capital 86, 97, 100, 103–4, 110
social dance clubs 143, 150
sociality and relationality through mutuality 163
social justice 50–1, 69, 122, 176–7
social media 39, 41, 97, 108–9, 143, 153, 169
social policies 23
social solidarity 28, 31–2
"Sour Grapes" (Balay, A.) 4
space, sharing 137–9, *see also* queer sharing
Spade, D. 28
Spaulding, E. 140
Spieldenner, A. 58
state-recognized parenthood statuses 25
State University of New York (SUNY) system 175–6
Stay Gold Project at the Museum of Contemporary Art, Tucson 137
Steffan, H. 174
stories, sharing 141–3, *see also* queer sharing
storytelling 6, 11, 14, 73–4, 79, 124, 141–2, 155
straight economic practices 101
straight sharing 6, 98, 100, 102–4, 106–8, 110, 113–14
Stringer, S. 179
structural barriers 21–2, 64
structural inequalities 3–4
structural oppressions 49, 66, 70
structural violence 21, 27
structured breaks 59
Stuart, E. 50–1
substantivism 162
systemic oppression 24–5, 58, 91

Taylor, Y. 68–9, 131, 132
temporality 98, 100–3, 113

tenured/tenure-track faculty
members   132, 144
tenure-track jobs   23, 27
Thatcher, M.   99
"theatre without walls"   148
The Coming Back Out Ball (TCBOB)   149
theory of burden sharing   54, 56
throupling   71–2
time, role of   143
time off and independent workdays   59
Times Square Red, Times Square Blue (Delany)   137
Trans Exclusionary Radical Feminism stories   142–3
Transfer Admission Guarantee   174–5
transphobia   128, 143
Tuck, E.   66
tuition-free public college   177

UK academia
    2019 Resisting Whiteness conference   111
    case study for REF2021   110
    congruence and case studies   110–14
    #DecoloniseTheCurriculum   109
    decolonizing   107–10
    decolonizing the curriculum   98
    EDI: Widening Participation   98
    #FundBlackScientists   109
    impact case study for REF2021   110–11
    Knowledge Exchange (KE)/Impact   98
    paint-by-numbers approach   113
    participation   103–7
    performative allyship   108
    performative sharing   98
    post-92 universities   114
    pre-92 UK institutions   114
    public engagement   98
    rankings and hierarchies, reconsideration of   114
    Received Pronunciation   108
    Research Excellence Framework (REF)   98
    sharing (*see* sharing in academy)
    sharing and EDI   114

social media, role in academic racism   109–10
straight sharing   98, 106
working-class and BIPOC academics   110
underrepresented group (LGBTI+ Elders)   158
union organizing   13–14
University of Edinburgh   111
University of Illinois Chicago (UIC)   136, 139
university resources, sharing of   30

Venmo or CashApp   37–8, 41, 44–5
Villalpando, O.   87
violence
    academy, site of violence and refuge   22–5 (*see also* academy)
    of colonization   73
    and exclusion   139
    police   138
    state violence during national uprisings and pandemic   35
    structural   21, 27
    systemic   22, 29
virtual church   169
Vizenor, G.R.   70

Warren, E.   174
wealth redistribution   35–6
Weiss, M.   139
West, E. J.   90
Weston, K.   162
Weststrate, N.M.   6
whole-school events, celebrating together   126–8
Williams, J.   174, 178
working-class academics, in UK   104–5
Wyndham, L.   16

Yang, K.W.   66
Yes, M.   59, 62
Young Invincibles   178

Zoom
    rapid transition to   141
    sermons through   169
    video calling   153